Mobilizing Public Sociology

Studies in Critical Social Sciences Book Series

Haymarket Books is proud to be working with Brill Academic Publishers (www.brill.nl) to republish the *Studies in Critical Social Sciences* book series in paperback editions. This peer-reviewed book series offers insights into our current reality by exploring the content and consequences of power relationships under capitalism, and by considering the spaces of opposition and resistance to these changes that have been defining our new age. Our full catalog of *SCSS* volumes can be viewed at https://www.haymarketbooks .org/series_collections/4-studies-in-critical-social-sciences.

Mobilizing Public Sociology

Scholars, Activists, and Latin@ Migrants Converse on Common Ground

Edited by
Victoria Carty
Rafael Luévano

Haymarket Books
Chicago, IL

First published in 2017 by Brill Academic Publishers, The Netherlands.
© 2017 Koninklijke Brill NV, Leiden, The Netherlands

Published in paperback in 2018 by
Haymarket Books
P.O. Box 180165
Chicago, IL 60618
773-583-7884
www.haymarketbooks.org

ISBN: 978-1-60846-931-4

Trade distribution:
In the U.S. through Consortium Book Sales, www.cbsd.com
In the UK, Turnaround Publisher Services, www.turnaround-uk.com
In Canada, Publishers Group Canada, www.pgcbooks.ca
All other countries, Ingram Publisher Services International, ips_intlsales@
ingramcontent.com

Cover design by Jamie Kerry and Ragina Johnson.

This book was published with the generous support of Lannan Foundation
and the Wallace Action Fund.

Printed in United States.

10 9 8 7 6 5 4 3 2 1

Library of Congress Cataloging-in-Publication Data is available.

Contents

Preface

Victoria Carty with Daniele Struppa, Jerry Price, and Bishop Kevin William Vann

This volume is the product of a conference, "Breaking Borders: Dialoguing on Immigration," that was held at Chapman University in Orange, California, in April 2015. Scholars and students from various universities, Chapman University administrators, community organizers, and those active in pastoral life attended and presented their work. Below are samples of commentary by three of our distinguished conference speakers: Daniele Struppa, the president (then chancellor) of Chapman University; Jerry Price, Chapman's vice chancellor for student affairs and dean of students; and Kevin William Vann, the bishop of the Roman Catholic Diocese of Orange County, one of the largest diocese in the United States.

President Struppa opened the conference with an invitation to view the current crisis of immigration through a global, contemporary, and compassionate perspective. Vice Chancellor Price cited many of the unique challenges that undocumented students in higher education face and noted how the story of undocumented students remains just that, "undocumented," as many students must hide their stories and situations. Expanding on both of these themes, Bishop Vann emphasized the need to put a human face on our undocumented friends and called for all of us to recognize those who are struggling in our midst but are easily ignored. These three pieces exemplify public sociology, which was at the root of the conference and is central to this collection (Burawoy 2005). What the contributors to this preface, as well as the other authors in the volume, attempt to do is demystify some of the fallacies and rhetoric surrounding current immigration debates, depoliticize them, take them out of the academy, extend a plea to our better selves to desist from passing judgment on those fleeing their home countries for various reasons, and encourage all of us to be mindful of the burdens they carry and perhaps even help carry the load as allies.

The Global Immigration Crisis and a Call for Compassion

Immigration requires immediate and urgent attention. It is a topic for political scientists, sociologists, law scholars, and economists, but in a way it is a topic for anybody who feels the responsibility of what we like to call "global" citizenship. While the authors of the essays in this book have significant expertise, I believe that the discussion on immigration has an importance that goes way beyond the confines of the ivory tower that is known as academia. This is not an academic discussion but a discussion that centers on the lives of our brothers and sisters who reach out across borders (not just across the U.S.–Mexico border) for a better life. Nor is it solely a political issue. Our moral obligation to engage in dialogue on this topic cannot be delayed and, frankly, cannot be left in the hands of politicians.

I am just a mathematician: I am good at what I do, but I cannot offer insightful words in the legal, economic, social, and political issues that are discussed and analyzed in this volume and I cannot offer solutions to the complex problems posed by immigration. But as a human being, I am beyond despair when I hear politicians (around the world, and of any political conviction) taking such an important issue and turning it into an instrument for their agenda. I am also Italian. I come from a country with a history of migrations. Italians used to leave their land, looking for opportunities elsewhere, immigrating to Belgium, the United Kingdom, Germany, Switzerland, South America (Argentina, Brazil, Uruguay), and North America, where many found the opportunities they were seeking.

Even though I did not leave Italy out of desperation, I am an immigrant to the United States, and with other immigrants I have shared the unpleasant experience of dealing with the Immigration and Naturalization Service (INS), an agency that does not serve American citizens (probably the only federal agency not to do so), and as a consequence has a customer service approach quite different from other agencies whose clients are citizens. Like many other immigrants, I have been stuck in long lines at INS offices; I have had to fill out paperwork; and I have had to answer a variety of questions about my past, my present, and my future. Most of the time I have been treated with respect and friendship, but sometimes that has not been the case. At the same time, as a relatively recent immigrant, I have a huge debt of gratitude to a country that has welcomed me in my younger years and that has given me access to many educational and career opportunities.

Immigration is now a big political issue in the United States and played an important role in the 2016 presidential election. While immigrants reach this country from many parts of the world, it is mostly the issue of "illegal immigration" from Mexico and Central America that is taking center stage in the policy arena. Paradoxically, the European Union is now facing an even harsher reality; as oppressive regimes in northern Africa are disintegrating, without anything sustainable to replace them, men and women often with children in tow from this region are fleeing pain, hunger, and fear. Many board unsafe vessels in the desperate hope to find a different and better life. On April 20, 2015, just a few miles from the Italian waters, nine hundred migrants drowned in the Mediterranean, a sea our ancestors used to call Mare Nostrum (Our Sea); now we are unable to turn this sea from an instrument of death into an instrument of salvation (Yardley 2015). Based on reports of the International Organization for Migration, at least 5,400 migrants died trying to cross national borders in 2015, and 3,100 lost their lives in the first five months of 2016. Europe in particular is on the cusp of a major immigration disaster. Those trying to cross the Mediterranean Sea to get to Europe do so at very high risk, as an estimated 3,770 died in 2015 trying to migrate (Sengupta 2016). The response we see in Europe is, to say the least, underwhelming.

On July 8, 2013, Pope Francis visited the Italian island of Lampedusa (the most southern tip of Italy, located 205 miles south of Sicily but only 113 miles north of the African coast). He officiated mass there, in the presence of all the people from Lampedusa, mostly fishermen, who know the difficulty of making a living on the sea. His mass occurred just a few days after a boat full of refugees capsized off the coast of Sicily in late June. Several of the refugees clung to the fishing nets of a Tunisian vessel before the fishermen cut the nets loose, sending at least ten people to their death. In his homily, Pope Francis used words that cannot be improved upon, and therefore I hope you will forgive me if I just quote them, rather than paraphrase them. It is a long quote, but a beautiful one.

> "Adam, where are you?" This is the first question which God asks man after his sin. "Adam, where are you?" Adam lost his bearings, his place in creation, because he thought he could be powerful, able to control everything, to be God. Harmony was lost; man erred and this error occurs over and over again also in relationships with others. "The other" is no longer a brother or sister to be loved, but simply someone who disturbs my life and my comfort. God asks a second question: "Cain, where is your brother?" The illusion of being powerful, of being as great as God, even of being God himself, leads to a whole series of errors, a chain of death, even to the spilling of a brother's blood!
>
> God's two questions echo even today, as forcefully as ever! How many of us, myself included, have lost our bearings; we are no longer attentive

to the world in which we live; we don't care; we don't protect what God created for everyone, and we end up unable even to care for one another! And when humanity as a whole loses its bearings, it results in tragedies like the one we have witnessed.

"Where is your brother?" His blood cries out to me, says the Lord. This is not a question directed to others; it is a question directed to me, to you, to each of us. These brothers and sisters of ours were trying to escape difficult situations to find some serenity and peace; they were looking for a better place for themselves and their families, but instead they found death. How often do such people fail to find understanding, fail to find acceptance, fail to find solidarity. And their cry rises up to God! Once again I thank you, the people of Lampedusa, for your solidarity. I recently listened to one of these brothers of ours. Before arriving here, he and the others were at the mercy of traffickers, people who exploit the poverty of others, people who live off the misery of others. How much these people have suffered! Some of them never made it here.

"Where is your brother?" Who is responsible for this blood? In Spanish literature we have a comedy of Lope de Vega which tells how the people of the town of Fuente Ovejuna kill their governor because he is a tyrant. They do it in such a way that no one knows who the actual killer is. So when the royal judge asks: "Who killed the governor?" they all reply: "Fuente Ovejuna, sir." Everybody and nobody! Today too, the question has to be asked: Who is responsible for the blood of these brothers and sisters of ours? Nobody! That is our answer: It isn't me; I don't have anything to do with it; it must be someone else, but certainly not me. Yet God is asking each of us: "Where is the blood of your brother which cries out to me?" Today no one in our world feels responsible; we have lost a sense of responsibility for our brothers and sisters. We have fallen into the hypocrisy of the priest and the levite whom Jesus described in the parable of the Good Samaritan: we see our brother half dead on the side of the road, and perhaps we say to ourselves: "poor soul...!" and then go on our way. It's not our responsibility, and with that we feel reassured, assuaged. The culture of comfort, which makes us think only of ourselves, makes us insensitive to the cries of other people, makes us live in soap bubbles which, however lovely, are insubstantial; they offer a fleeting and empty illusion which results in indifference to others; indeed, it even leads to the globalization of indifference. In this globalized world, we have fallen into globalized indifference. We have become used to the suffering of others: it doesn't affect me; it doesn't concern me; it's none of my business!

"Adam, where are you?" "Where is your brother?" These are the two questions which God asks at the dawn of human history, and which he also asks each man and woman in our own day, which he also asks us. But I would like us to ask a third question: "Has any one of us wept because of this situation and others like it?" Has any one of us grieved for the death of these brothers and sisters? Has any one of us wept for these persons who were on the boat? For the young mothers carrying their babies? For these men who were looking for a means of supporting their families? We are a society which has forgotten how to weep, how to experience compassion—"suffering with" others: the globalization of indifference has taken from us the ability to weep!

Today too, Lord, we hear you asking: "Adam, where are you?" "Where is the blood of your brother?"

POPE FRANCIS 2013

This was back in 2013, but over three years later we have come to realize how unprepared Europe is to deal with the major influx of immigrants escaping the violence and desperation in northern Africa and the Middle East, most notably. Europe's inability to come up with a realistic plan for what appears to be an unexpected (but shouldn't it have been expected instead?) surge of immigrants is laying bare a form of xenophobia that is increasingly transparent as governments in the European Union are beginning to close borders with other EU member countries in order to block the influx of African migrants. There is even discussion of the European Union dissolving as countries begin to build fences to thwart migrant crossings, which is causing bottlenecks and other logistical nightmares, especially across regions of Greece, Macedonia, and Turkey. Recently, in June 2016, voters in the United Kingdom decided to leave the European Union, partly in response to the migration surge, which may lead to further challenges for migrants.

As we reread Pope Francis's words (now made even more powerful by the public posture that he has adopted over the last two years on a variety of issues related to economic disparities), we see that they are not limited to the desperate immigration from northern Africa to Europe, but they could apply to any other migratory phenomenon. They certainly could apply to the desperation of our brothers who cross the border through tunnels under Tijuana, preyed upon by the coyotes. They apply to the suffering of men and especially women in Ciudad Juárez, Mexico, women who are being exterminated by the narcos, as our friend Rafael Luévano (2012), one of the editors of this volume, has researched in his last book *Woman-Killing in Juárez*.

For this different migration, not necessarily less desperate, though different in many specific aspects, I would like to offer another quotation, less sublime than the one by Pope Francis but full of significance as well. I want to remind all of us of a beautiful song of musician Manu Chao, "Desaparecido," which talks about a young man who illegally crosses the border at Tijuana, and because he has no papers, he has to hide and escape from the police. Released in 1998, this song is a beautiful testament to the pain that follows those brothers of ours who try to make a better life for themselves. In one of the opening stanzas, the singer tells us that his pain is difficult to withstand, but his convictions help him to overcome the pain. The pain that he makes reference to is not necessarily a physical pain but mostly a psychological one. It is the pain of those forced to leave the familiar for the unfamiliar, the known for the unknown. To these brothers, to these sisters, we should dedicate our thoughts (from the protected halls of academia) as we investigate how borders can be turned from instruments of segregation and pain into pathways to a new life.

Daniele Struppa

Undocumented Immigrants in Higher Education: Invisible Obstacles

Prior to coming to Chapman seven years ago, I served as dean of students at the University of Texas–Pan American in Edinburg, Texas (UTPA). UTPA is located in Hidalgo County in the Rio Grande Valley, some twelve miles from the Mexican border. Of our seventeen thousand students, hundreds were undocumented. They were brought into Texas as children and their families settled in Hidalgo County, often with extended family members. However, since 90 percent of our students were from Hidalgo County and 96 percent were Hispanic, our undocumented students looked just like everyone else. Their college experience, for the most part, was similar to other students' experiences. Yet, over the years, I learned that in some ways their experiences were very different. At times, because of their undocumented status, routine situations became anything but. Here are just a few examples:

- A student who was being aggressively harassed by a classmate refused to report it to campus police because her family had a strict rule about involving legal authorities.
- A group of students had an opportunity to present their projects at a regional academic conference, but one could not attend because he would have to travel through an immigration checkpoint.
- Our women's mariachi group received an invitation to perform at the White House, but three members could not travel because of their undocumented status.
- A student leader was elected student body president but inexplicably resigned shortly after the election; it turns out that the university changed its compensation from a stipend (which is applied as financial aid) to an hourly wage, for which she was ineligible.

These are just a few of the many examples that I can provide from my time at UTPA. During my five years at UTPA I had a chance to see the paradoxical nature of undocumented students' experiences. They are among our most financial needy yet are not eligible for most forms of financial assistance. They are lifelong residents of the community yet have fewer rights than visitors coming to study from other countries. Many are driven by their career aspirations for a better life yet are ineligible for employment once they graduate. In many ways they need us the most yet trust us the least.

This collection of essays, and the conference on which it is based, examines immigration issues through the lens of public sociology, an approach that encourages exchange between scholars, community leaders, and the persons affected by the very issues we are studying. Such dialogue is necessary because our students, who face challenges, do not exist in an academic bubble. They are in need of support not only from university administrators, counselors, professors, and fellow students but also from the communities in which they reside and in which they often feel invisible.

Jerry Price

Humanizing Immigration from a Pastoral and Community Perspective

When the topic of immigration comes up, it often emerges in the politicized culture and context where we live and brings to the surface many emotions and reactions that, in fact, lack a human face. I approach this "issue" of immigration with how I try to live and approach other pastoral challenges that come my way—as a pastor. One of the pastors in the diocese I serve, Reverend Ed Poettgen of Immaculate Heart of Mary Parish in Santa Ana, describes this something like "immigrants and the church bells." That is my experience exactly because it has been within the sound of church bells and the Houses of God where I have been that the faces of so many men, women, and children naturally seem to gravitate to be free of fear and find a new beginning. I try to find the human face and experience beyond the labels that certainly are everywhere these days. Where the human face and reality is found, then dialogue and search for the common good is much more possible. This is also at the heart of public sociology, the main theme of the conference and the collection of essays.

I also come at this concern of immigration from a wider perspective as the chair of the board of the Catholic Legal Immigration Network, Inc. (CLINIC). This is a 501c3 corporation that originated with the United States Conference of Catholic Bishops. CLINIC has assisted dioceses and missions with obtaining religious worker visas for immigrants so that immigrant communities can have the benefit of priests and religious and lay workers ministering to them and helping them to find stability in their new home and legally earn a living. This process is getting increasingly difficult, probably in some ways at least indirectly influenced by current attitudes toward "foreigners." CLINIC now works or partners with 250 other agencies across the country that together work with and assist families in irregular situations and help educate immigrant families about the process for obtaining visas and becoming "legal." It is work that I very much enjoy and that has certainly widened my perspective about the life and situation of immigrant families and pastoral workers all over the United States.

From a historical perspective, I again and again have to refer to the fact that we are a nation built on immigrants, symbolized at a most basic level by the poem by Emma Lazarus, "The New Colossus," found on the Statue of Liberty, focusing on the "huddled masses yearning to be free." Yet, despite the rhetorical welcome, there is also, at the same time, a fear of "foreigners." I remember when I was the bishop of Fort Worth, Texas, a letter to the editor appeared in the local newspaper. The writer railed against certain car dealers that flew the flag of a "foreign country" along with the American flag. This "foreign country" was Mexico, and the car dealership was located in an area of the Diocese of Fort Worth where the Hispanic population (mostly from Mexico) made up about 40 percent of the total population. This attitude in Texas is ironic given the fact that Texas at one time (prior to the Mexican American War and the signing of the Treaty of Guadalupe Hidalgo in 1848) was Mexico's territory, not unlike here in Southern California.

I would like to make a brief reference to the words of Pope John Paul II in a 1999 "Apostolic Exhortation" titled *Ecclesia in America.* Then as now an apostolic exhortation follows a gathering of the synod of bishops (an advisory body to the pope, composed of bishops from various regions of the world). The pope's strong words are certainly reflected in our time by the words of Pope Francis. Pope John Paul II said in his exhortation:

> In its history, America has experienced many immigrations, as waves of men and women came to its various regions in the hope of a better future.
>
> With this in mind, the Synod Fathers recalled that "the Church in America must be a vigilant advocate, defending against any unjust restriction the natural right of individual persons to move freely within their own nation and from one nation to another. Attention must be called to the rights of migrants and their families and to respect their human dignity, even in the cases of non-legal immigration." Migrants should be met with a hospitable and welcoming attitude which can encourage them to become part of the Church's life, always with due regard for their freedom and their specific identity. (sec. 65)

With this as background I would like to introduce you to some of the human faces beyond the politicized and polarized rhetoric of the day of "aliens," "fences," and "let them learn English," along with other slogans and buzz words. I remember three brothers and their families in Decatur, Illinois. All three were from Guanajuato. I see their faces as they huddle together in the cold December evenings as we walk through some of the trailer parks and worse areas in Decatur to pray and sing *posadas* (songs or a celebration of Latin@ popular religiosity in December that recalls Mary, Joseph, and baby Jesus's pilgrimage to Bethlehem). I see their faces as they all sit together in my office trying to complete the necessary paperwork to become "legal" in one of the "amnesties" in the late 1990s. They could not speak English well, even though they had tried to learn, and my Spanish was not that great at that time, but together we attempted to deal with a complicated system. Behind those forms were real human lives, hopes, and desires. They tried to make a home in a new country and culture, while struggling to maintain their faith and culture to hold them together with what they knew and loved. In the shadow of the "church bells" of Our Lady of Lourdes in Decatur, they wanted to do the right thing, as difficult as it was.

In Fort Worth, I remember at least weekly I used to go to a garage on the north side of the city, in a poor area, to sing, pray, and have a meal with a large group of young people who were the *jovenes* (youth) group of one of the parishes. They were young adults, all in their early twenties. Why did they gather in a garage with the door closed? Because they were afraid that with all the praying and singing that they did to build a sense of family among themselves, they might be turned in. They lived "in the shadows" in constant fear. For all practical purposes, I was their chaplain, priest, friend, and spiritual guide. Even with fear and uncertainty, they had joy, because they firmly sensed the presence of God in their midst. I eventually celebrated three marriages out of this group, and one of them entered the seminary. After a day of working in the office or trying to deal with the major problems the diocese had at the moment, I received great joy from this group of young adults—none of them "legal." These are the real human lives and struggles behind the rhetoric of the day and the necessary "forms" of paper.

This discussion is often framed as a largely Hispanic issue: the "flag of the foreign country" that flew over the car dealers in north Texas! Yet, in a trip that I made to Kumasi, Ghana (because the Diocese of Fort Worth has a large population of Ghanians, it has a relationship with the Archdiocese of Kumasi), the first question I got in the Cathedral of Saints Peter and Paul in Kumasi from the lay leaders of the diocese concerned immigration. They asked what is being done to help their people who now have major problems because of nonrenewal of visas that was not their fault. It is not only Mexican immigrants who face challenges related to their immigration status.

I also became close to another family in Texas who had four children. The parents were active in both Cursillo (a Christian movement that stresses the need to educate laypeople on becoming Christian leaders) and their parish (a small mission in what had been a "barrio" at one time).[1] I often visited them in their small and crowded home in a rundown Fort Worth neighborhood. I prayed and often shared a meal with them, and they readily gave to me what they were serving. I eventually became the husband's spiritual director and advisor, and still am even at this distance. He was here legally but his wife was not. She (and they) lived in great fear of deportation. They would like to come see me here, but they are afraid of traveling to this part of California because they fear being stopped by police or immigration authorities. They do not wish to defy the law, but they are stuck for now, like so many others, in a broken immigration system. However, in spite of this, they live in hope and are very much aware of the presence of God in their lives.

---

1   For information on the Cursillo movement, see https://www.natl-cursillo.org/.

Here in Southern California these stories continue with new families and friends whom I have met. I spend a great deal of time in Santa Ana and Anaheim, and the southern part of the county where the stories are the same, the hopes and fears are the same. Every year in December, I often stop (unannounced) at homes in Santa Ana around the feast day of Our Lady of Guadalupe (December 12). I find people gathered together, praying and singing, and I join them as bishop, pastor, and friend, to try to help them understand, just as they do for me, that truly "God is here."

I have learned so much from all of these families and friends who have helped me to see beyond the labels and rhetoric of the moment. I share these when I can to try to help others do the same. When we know someone, or at least see their faces, we can no longer "demonize" them. These meetings and relationships are for me an example of what Pope Francis calls a "culture of encounter," which to me is an antidote to the current indifference, individualism, and rhetoric. And I believe that many of us have experienced these and therefore have an obligation to share these experiences of "encounter" with real human situations in our academic, ministerial, community, and work worlds.

In closing, I refer back to another reflection by Pope John Paul II when he said in his 1999 exhortation:

> The Church is well aware of the problems created by this situation and is committed to spare no effort in developing her own pastoral strategy among these immigrant people, in order to help them settle in their new land and to foster a welcoming attitude among the local population, in the belief that a mutual openness will bring enrichment to all. (sec. 65)

Bishop Kevin William Vann

All three contributors, Struppa, Price, and Vann, note and magnificently reflect the spirit of the conference and this volume, as will be evident in the proceeding chapters. The goal of this book, and our previous gathering, is to explore ways in which, through dialogue and open encounters and despite our differences, we can break down the barriers and misconceptions that separate us so that we realize we are all responsible for the struggle to provide dignity and compassion to those residing among us who are lacking both.

Bibliography

Burawoy, Michael. 2005. For public sociology. *American Sociological Review* 70, no. 1:4–28.

Luévano, Rafael. 2012. *Woman-killing in Juárez: Theodicy at the border*. Maryknoll, NY: Orbis.

Pope Francis. 2013. Visit to Lampedusa: Homily of Holy Father Francis. Vatican City: Libreria Editrice Vaticana, July 8. http://w2.vatican.va/content/francesco/en/homilies/2013/documents/papa-francesco_20130708_omelia-lampedusa.html.

Pope John Paul II. 1999. *Ecclesia in America*. Vatican City: Libreria Editrice Vaticana. http://w2.vatican.va/content/john-paul-ii/en/apost_exhortations/documents/hf_jp-ii_exh_22011999_ecclesia-in-america.html.

Sengupta, Somini. 2016. Reports tell a trail of migrant deaths across deserts and seas. *New York Times*, June 14.

Yardley, Jim. 2015. Rising toll on migrants leaves Europe in crisis; 900 may be dead at sea. *New York Times*, April 20.

Acknowledgments

Projects such as this collection of essays and the conference from which it stemmed require the collaboration of many people and resources from both within and outside of the university. Scholars, administrators, students, community activists, community practitioners, and migrants all came together to make the volume and gathering a successful endeavor in bridging the borders by engaging in fruitful discussions.

Several key individuals at Chapman University need be thanked for their support of both this collection and the conference. We extend our first thanks to our dear friend and esteemed colleague at Chapman, Tekle Woldemikael, professor of sociology, who helped conceive this project. He worked diligently on the organization of the originating conference as well as the initial stages of this volume. Chapman president Daniele Struppa, in his prior capacity as chancellor, offered us the requisite funding for the conference and this volume—along with lots of encouragement as well as a presentation at the conference and a written contribution to this volume. Patrick Fuery, dean of the Wilkinson College of Arts, Humanities, and Social Sciences, provided funding, professional support, and a warm welcome to our conference participants. Lynn Horton, director of the International Studies Program, made organizational as well as important financial contributions. Funding from the Huntington Endowment for our keynote speaker was made possible by members of the Religious Studies Department, especially the department chair, Nancy Martin. A host of graduate students also assisted with important conference details.

We offer our thanks to all the Wilkinson administrative and secretarial staff. They attended to every detail of organization for our conference, from food and guest services to the processing of financial requests. In particular, Barbara Piscitelli, Wilkinson's administrative director, never failed to respond to every inquiry and need with generosity, patience, and efficiency.

We offer our sincere appreciation to all who attended and participated in the conference, some of whom came great distances, crossed the Mexican border, and tackled the Los Angeles freeways. And we remind our readers that the essays in this volume are only a representative selection of many excellent conference presentations that led to energetic and productive dialogue. Of course we extend our thanks to all our contributing coauthors who responded to our rigorous critical review with openness and astute attention. Their work will provide fodder for continued dialogue in academia and in the community on breaking borders.

This volume would not have come to completion without the hard work of Basia Nowak, who served as our managing editor for these essays. Her superlative editorial eye reviewed every word, citation, and punctuation mark in this volume. Our contributing editors admired her diligence and stellar positive disposition. We cannot offer sufficient words of thanks for her respectful and generous service to our coauthors and to us.

David Fasenfest, our patient editor, oversaw all editorial production processes at Brill. We thank him for recognizing the importance of this topic and assisting us in the completion of the project.

Gracias

List of Illustrations

Maps

Tables

List of Contributors

Amelia Alvarez
is a practicing civil rights lawyer in Los Angeles, California. She graduated from the University of California, Irvine School of Law in 2015. While at UCI Law, she spent three semesters working in the Immigrant Rights Clinic and was among the first students to work on the clinic's Gang Injunction Advocacy project. Prior to attending law school, she earned a bachelor of arts in sociology from Dartmouth College.

Fawn Bekam
graduated from the University of California, Irvine School of Law in 2015. For three semesters, while a student at UCI Law, she worked in the Immigrant Rights Clinic and was among the first students to work on the clinic's Gang Injunction Advocacy project. Prior to law school, Bekam attended the University of California, Los Angeles, where she earned a bachelor of arts in political science.

Victoria Carty
is an activist scholar and associate professor of sociology at Chapman University. Her current interests focus on local issues in Southern California, which include immigration, restorative justice, and the sociology of gang prevention efforts. She coedited (with Rafael Luévano and Tekle Woldemikael) *Scholars and Southern Californian Immigrants in Dialogue: New Conversations in Public Sociology* (Lexington Books, 2014) and authored *Social Movements and New Technology* (Westview Press, 2015).

Kristin E. Heyer
is professor of theology at Boston College. She received her bachelor of arts from Brown University and her doctorate in theological ethics from Boston College in 2003. Her books include *Kinship across Borders: A Christian Ethic of Immigration* (Georgetown University Press, 2012) and *Prophetic and Public: The Social Witness of U.S. Catholicism* (Georgetown University Press, 2006), which won the College Theology Society's Best Book Award. She also coedited (with David E. DeCosse) *Conscience and Catholicism: Rights, Responsibilities, and Institutional Responses* (Orbis Books, 2015) and (with Mark J. Rozell and Michael A. Genovese) *Catholics and Politics: Dynamic Tensions between Faith and Power* (Georgetown University Press, 2008). Her articles have appeared in *Theological Studies, The Journal of Catholic Social Thought, The Journal of Peace and Justice*

Studies, Political Theology, and *America*. Heyer is co-chair of Catholic Theological Ethics in the World Church and an editor for the Moral Traditions series from Georgetown University Press. She taught at Santa Clara University from 2009 to 2015.

Patricia Huerta

is an adjunct professor through the Extended Education/College of Educational Studies Community Collaboration Program at Chapman University and serves as an instructor for the St. Ignatius of Loyola Rules of Discernment workshop at St. Peter Channel Catholic Church. She is also CEO and cofounder of Padres Unidos (United Parents), a nonprofit organization that helps build successful communities by providing educational and support services to families. Huerta earned her master's degree in social work from California State University, San Bernardino; served as senior social worker for Orange County for over ten years; and has over twenty-five years of experience working with Latin@ families.

Rusty Kennedy

is the founding CEO of the nonprofit OC Human Relations, established in 1991, whose mission is to promote understanding among diverse residents and to eliminate prejudice, intolerance, and discrimination. He is an advocate for immigration reform that includes a path to citizenship, family reunification, and protections for all workers. Kennedy has been organizing around humane immigration policy since founding the OC Coalition for Immigrant Rights in 1986.

Oliver Lopez

is a statistics and education consultant and a board member of a renowned research entity. He earned his doctorate in biostatistics from the University of Southern California in 2016. He attended Chapman University for his undergraduate education and California State University, Fullerton for his master's degree. Brought to the United States when he was four years old, Lopez has achieved much academic and professional success navigating through systems of higher education and government as an undocumented person.

Rafael Luévano

is associate professor in the Religious Studies Department at Chapman University. He also serves as the university's Roman Catholic chaplain and has been a priest since 1981 in the Diocese of Orange, California. He is the author of *Woman-Killing in Juárez: Theodicy at the Border* (Orbis Books, 2012), focusing on the feminicides in northern Mexico, and is currently conducting research on narco-related violence in Mexico. He coedited (with Victoria Carty and

Tekle Woldemikael) *Scholars and Southern Californian Immigrants in Dialogue: New Conversations in Public Sociology* (Lexington Books, 2014). Luévano was a Fulbright-García Robles Research Fellow for 2015–16. For the past thirty years, he has served as the chair of the Luévano Foundation, honoring his deceased parents, which offers scholarships to Catholic grade school children.

Raquel R. Marquez

is professor of sociology at the University of Texas at San Antonio (UTSA). She received her doctorate from the University of Texas at Austin. Her teaching expertise centers on issues of race relations, immigration, and border and Latin@ studies. Her research has addressed Latin@ issues related to labor, the border and immigration, and community change in San Antonio. Marquez served as UTSA Sociology Department chair for seven years and now serves as the associate dean for Graduate Studies and Research in the UTSA College of Liberal and Fine Arts. She is the coeditor (with Harriett Romo) of *Transformations of La Familia on the US–Mexico Border* (Notre Dame Press, 2008). Marquez currently is producing a feature-length documentary on the United Farm Workers of Texas. She is part of a research team examining social, political, and cultural issues related to UTSA and UT Austin students affected by the lack of Dream Act legislation.

Eileen McNerney, CSJ

is a sister of St. Joseph of Orange. In 1995, she founded Taller San Jose Hope Builders and served as its executive director for thirteen years. She is now president emeritus of this organization and serves on its board of directors. Sister Eileen is the author of *A Story of Suffering and Hope: Lessons from Latino Youth* (Paulist Press, 2005). In 2006, she received the James Irvine Foundation Leadership Award for her work.

Patrick Murphy, CS

is director of the Casa del Migrante in Tijuana, which provides hospitality to an average of 125 migrants per evening. He completed seminary studies in New York City, Chicago, and Toronto. Since 1976, he has been a member of the Scalabrinians, Missionaries of St. Charles, and over the years has served in a variety of locations, including Chicago, Los Angeles, and Kansas City. He has been a missionary for migrants for the last thirty-five years.

Jerry Price

is the dean of students and vice president for student affairs at Chapman University. Prior to coming to Chapman, he served as dean of students at the

University of Texas–Pan American in Edinburgh, Texas, from 2003 to 2008. He is the editor of *Understanding and Supporting Undocumented Students* (Wiley Periodicals, 2010).

Lisa D. Ramirez

is a California State Bar immigration and nationality law specialist and notably one of the first women and the first Spanish-speaking specialists in Orange County. She received her law degree from Loyola Law School, Los Angeles, in 2000. Before cofounding U.S. Immigration Law Group, LLP, Ramirez established a solo practice representing individuals through all aspects of the immigration process. She began her legal career serving as the director of Legal Services and Advocacy for Catholic Charities of Orange County, and served at the Public Law Center, where she developed the legal immigration services program.

Harriett D. Romo

is professor of sociology at the University of Texas at San Antonio (UTSA). She is also the director of the UTSA Mexico Center and the UTSA Child and Adolescent Policy Research Institute. She received her doctorate from the University of California, San Diego. She teaches courses on immigration, educational inequality, sociology of childhood, and border studies. Her most recent edited book (with Olivia Mogollon) is *Mexican Migration: Perspectives from Both Sides of the Border* (University of Texas Press, 2016). She has directed grant projects and published on transnationalism, youth with experiences in the child welfare system, and Latin@ education. Her book (with Toni Falbo), *Latino High School Graduation* (University of Texas Press, 1996), was a finalist for the C. Wright Mills Prize for research of value to the community. Romo has directed research projects on undocumented immigrants, dual-language learners, and the impact of lack of affordable housing on youth and families.

Suzanne SooHoo

is the Endowed Hassinger Chair in Education and the codirector of the Paulo Freire Democratic Project at Chapman University. She teaches classes in critical pedagogy and culturally responsive qualitative methodologies, the latter inspired by her book (coedited with writing partners Mere Berryman and Ann Nevin) *Culturally Responsive Methodologies* (Emerald Group Publishing Limited, 2013). She works with doctoral students and parents in her community who strive to be critically conscious and socially responsible and who are mutually inspired by Paulo Freire's philosophy. As a former school principal and now full professor, she has committed a lifetime to understanding and nurturing relationships, listening authentically to marginalized voices, and engaging dialogically toward the development of a more humane and socially just world.

Madeleine Spencer

is a postdoctoral student at Pacifica Graduate Institute and is finishing her dissertation with an emphasis on community psychology, eco-psychology, and liberation psychology. She earned her bachelor of arts in philosophy and critical theory in 2008 from Chapman University and her master's degree in depth marriage and family therapy in 2011 from Pacifica Graduate Institute. Her most recent interests include community building and research models of community resistance. Spencer has worked in the Los Angeles Department of Corrections with incarcerated youth, at Project Hope with homeless children, and at the Isaiah House with homeless women ages thirty to fifty. She participates actively in the community, consults with the Santa Ana Business Council, and works as a learning facilitator for the Humanities Department at Santiago Canyon College.

Daniele Struppa

is the president of Chapman University and professor of mathematics. From 2007 to 2016, he served as the chancellor at Chapman. His articles have appeared in numerous periodicals and he has edited or coauthored more than ten books in the field of mathematics. An immigrant from Italy, Struppa understands firsthand the challenges that immigrants face.

Bishop Kevin William Vann

serves as the bishop of the Roman Catholic Diocese of Orange, California. Ordained as a priest in 1981, Bishop Vann was appointed as bishop in 2012 by Pope Benedict XVI. He is a member of the United States Conference of Catholic Bishops Committee on Migration and serves as chairman of the board of directors of the Catholic Legal Immigration Network, Inc. (CLINIC).

Introduction

Victoria Carty

I'm helping José, Mario, and Lalo, three migrant boys, seven or eight years old, with their homework at Higher Ground, a nonprofit organization focused on gang prevention located in a distressed part of Anaheim, California.[1] Suddenly the school bell rings. *"¡La migra, la migra!"* the *muchachos* shout, and then break into laughter. *"¡La migra, la migra!"* In the last two years working with Higher Ground I have witnessed this time and again: migrant children's fear of the local police and the United States Immigration and Customs Enforcement (ICE).

The kids only know ICE as *"la migra,"* and they channel their fears of *la migra* into laughter—sometimes their anxiety and shame too. What other way do they have of protecting themselves? What resistance do they have? After all they're just *muchachos*. Do the white kids in the privileged part of Anaheim Hills even have a clue what *la migra* is? I wonder. Do they worry about losing their dad, mom, brother, or sister on an Anaheim city street, home raid, or work raid through deportation? In the flatlands, José, Mario, and Lalo wonder why their parents won't even walk them to school, or if there will be food on the table when they get home because their *papi*, as a day laborer, couldn't find work that day. As an activist-scholar working at Higher Ground I have come to realize what public sociology means in practice (Burawoy 2005). José, Mario, and Lalo have taught me.

Public sociology is grassroots and demands activity in our local communities. My relationship with Higher Ground began when I first met the founder, Joe Baldo, at a community meeting as he spoke about his need for mentors at Higher Ground. Talking to him after the meeting, I told him that some of my sociology students could do experiential learning at the site; this is a type of pedagogy through which students spend several hours in the community for course credit. As my students and I began to engage in this community work just a few miles from our campus, we increasingly came to understand the bizarre duality of where we live, work, and go to school—a tale of two cities, with immigration issues at its core.

As we know, Disney's claim to fame is the "happiest place on earth." Surrounding the resorts and fancy hotels is the "crappiest place on earth," as I once heard Baldo say. At Lincoln Elementary, the location of Higher Ground,

---

1   For more information on Higher Ground, see http://www.highergroundoc.org/.

92 percent of the children qualify for free lunch, and homelessness, crime, violence, and gangs abound on all sides of the school. Lalo and his *amigos* must navigate this environment every day going to and from school. The *muchachos* and their families reside right outside of Disney's gates; get bounced from school to school, motel to motel, and shelter to shelter; and sometimes live on the streets. The Marios, Josés, and Lalos who attend Higher Ground live in families whose *papis* and *mamis* clean the Disney resorts, sell the tickets, blow the leaves, and manicure the landscaping, all for poverty wages.

My students write in their course papers that they observe José and his friends congregating on the sidewalk across from the school, playing improvised games or just hanging out, once the program at Higher Ground ends for the day. They are clearly stalling to go home. In addition to the fear of *la migra* is one that looms at home. It may be the motel where they are temporarily staying, and where the only place to play is a parking lot where gang members congregate. Or, maybe in the single bedroom apartment they are heading home to, ten relatives live in a tight space; there is no privacy, a space of quiet to do homework, or a safe place to play. Hopefully, they got an extra snack at Higher Ground that can tide them over until lunch tomorrow at school since it is hit or miss whether their parents can give them anything to eat that evening.

Mario, Lalo, José, and a few dozen other kids from Higher Ground and their older siblings and families visit Chapman University for a day of fun activities for the kids and workshops emphasizing the importance of higher education for the parents and junior high and high school siblings. Here, they have some reprieve from their violent and impoverished neighborhood. The campus has many lovely fountains, beautiful brand new buildings and facilities, impeccably manicured lawns and flowers—a very serene place especially on a Saturday. On their exit surveys, the kids tell me that their favorite part of their campus tour was seeing a piece of the Berlin Wall that is prominently displayed in one of the fountains. German writing is spray-painted on it; the kids do not know what it says, but it resembles graffiti, so for them, it is something familiar in a very unfamiliar environment. They remind me of these two realities, just separated by a city border.

Another example of the two realities is that when we invite parents of Higher Ground students to come to Chapman for workshops, many sign up to attend but only a few actually come. Over lunch the mothers speak to me about the overshadowing fear that permeates their lives and limits their choices, not of *la migra* this time but of going into a space where they are not sure they will feel welcomed. Why would they think otherwise, I realize. Like at Disney, Latin@s are welcomed at Chapman to serve and clean up after many white privileged patrons but not to be seen as students. Through dialoguing efforts with parents at the Higher Ground site, in their own space of familiarity and security, we have been able to gain their trust. As a result, their attendance at campus events has increased. We have shown our commitment to them and we have come to understand and address some of their fears—once again public sociology in practice.

This is why I love sociology—public sociology in particular. I work in the academy, but I live and breathe in the community. I am blessed to be able to do both. Many of the contributing authors in this volume I have met through my activist work. I came to know about Sister Eileen McNerney after I located Taller San Jose (now Taller San Jose Hope Builders)—a local program that gives youth a second chance upon getting out of prison or out of a gang, or just wanting a better life—and read her book about her work (2005). I met Oliver Lopez at a church event where he gave his testimony as an undocumented student. Since then we have served together on various conference panels on immigration. The chapter that I coauthor with Madeleine Spencer is also due to a community connection. I originally met her through a coalition, Orange County May Day Coalition, in which we both are members, representing our perspective community groups. I was representing a group called Chicanos Unidos and Madeleine was representing Santa Ana Collaboration for Responsible Development (SACReD). We have marched together in the streets during May Day festivities and we see each other regularly at various community meetings and events.

Thus, public sociology is important to those inside and outside of academia. It embraces the community and treats people as having an equal voice in the process of learning about ourselves and our social conditions through rich engagement with our neighbors and their struggles. This, in turn, allows us to come together to work on solutions and policies to rectify social problems. It is a practice through which José, Mario, and Lalo are not objects of our study but our friends—and partners—with their own histories, experiences, and challenges. Public sociology is also inherently interdisciplinary and different scholars can use it in a variety of ways as a method to understand our social world. In this volume, we see how scholars and activists address the issue of immigration, informing each other and working side by side with some of the most vulnerable in our community, such as those who are undocumented.

As Rafael Luévano alludes to in the conclusion, in addition to promoting dialogue, public sociology is a form of narrative, a bringing together of sometimes seemingly two different worlds or realities. Through what Luévano refers to as "public sociology narrative," in this text, we open up space for migrants to give testimony to their own struggles and to inform us about solutions to the dilemmas they face on a daily basis. By hearing each other's stories and perspectives on issues, we see the humanity in all of us, which can lead to learning experiences that are horizontal and transformative in nature.

The Historical and Recent Tension on the U.S.–Mexico Border

The border between the United States and Mexico has served as one of the largest immigration focal points for nearly two hundred years. In this section, I contextualize the relevance of public sociology by providing a brief overview of the historical tension between the United States and Mexico. This tension has led to the discussion of the unresolved issue of immigration between the two countries and most recently those fleeing Central America, many of whom are unaccompanied minors.

Without covering the entire history, a few major dynamics are worth noting, all of which operate within the framework of U.S. imperialism and the quest for profit and political power. For example, Manifest Destiny led to the 1848 Mexican American War and the ultimate signing of the Treaty of Guadalupe Hidalgo in 1848 under which one-half of Mexican territory was seized by the United States. U.S. interventionist policies throughout Latin America (including financially and militarily supporting coups and dictators to ensure safe havens for American businesses) have promoted U.S. imperialism. And trade deals, such as the North American Free Trade Agreement (NAFTA), made the border porous for the flow of goods but not people. Simultaneously NAFTA has forced people to flee as cheap American agricultural products flooded the market in Mexico, pushing farmers to migrate to border cities to work in U.S.-owned factories, or *maquiladoras*. Many of these factories were created as part of NAFTA and previous trade agreements. However, as migrants to the border regions within Mexico soon realized, wages were too meager to support themselves and their families, and they therefore looked for opportunities north of the border. Most recently, the failed U.S.-backed War on Drugs—which has spurred the growth of drug cartels and massive crime, violence, gang activity, and government and police corruption throughout much of Mexico—has energized migration, especially of those seeking asylum, over the last few years.

U.S. policies are also largely responsible for the influx of immigrants from Central America. Between 2014 and 2016, more than one hundred thousand refugees arrived in the United States, mostly mothers with young children seeking asylum and trying to escape gang violence and human trafficking generated by the narcos who operate with virtual impunity, especially in El Salvador and Honduras (Chen 2016). The civil wars that raged in much of the region during the 1980s, in which the United States provided financial and military aid to authoritarian governments and right-wing death squads who terrorized the population across El Salvador, Guatemala, and Nicaragua, and much of it as a proxy war during the Cold War to "save" countries from socialism and protect U.S. business interests, have left much of Central America in a state of disarray. El Salvador is now the deadliest country in the world when it comes to gang violence, and Honduras is considered the murder capital of the world (Isacson, Meyer, and Morales 2014). Additionally, the 2009 coup in Honduras, backed by the U.S. government, has played a large role in the failed state that cannot contain the growing violence related to gangs and drug cartels.

Though the number of migrants from Central America is increasing, with a major surge beginning in 2012, illegal crossings from Mexico are at their lowest levels in nearly five decades. Many are leaving the United States because of the recession that began in the U.S. in 2008 and because of their desire to reunify with family members. The year 2014 marked the first time that more non-Mexicans than Mexicans were apprehended at the border (Passel et al. 2014). Ironically, but also strategically, Mexico is now deporting more children from Central America than the number of children the United States is deporting from Mexico. In fact, the United States has been giving Mexico millions of dollars a year to enforce the control of its southern border, thus alleviating the United States from doing much of the dirty work (Isacson, Meyer, and Morales 2014).

To complicate matters, due to the building of fences and the militarization of the U.S.–Mexico border, migrants from both Mexico and Central America are forced to travel routes that are more difficult, longer, and more isolated than in the past, and they often have to navigate through drug cartel territory. Between 1998 and 2015, 6,571 bodies were found in the United States close to the border (Sengupta 2016). To circumvent the risks and dangers, most rely on coyotes that can cost up to eight thousand dollars (Isacson, Meyer, and Morales 2014). Many of those escaping Central America manage to survive the arduous and expensive journey on foot and on top of fast-moving and unsafe trains. Along the way, unfortunately, many are victims of robbery, extortion, and rape, and go days without food.

Stereotypes and blatant xenophobic attitudes have continued to escalate. For example, upon their arrival from Central America, unaccompanied minors are met with attitudes rooted in intolerance and indignation. One of the most notable cases was in the summer of 2015 in Murrieta, California. Immigrants, mostly unaccompanied minors, were met with signs reading, "Return to Sender," "Save Our Children from Diseases," "Bus Illegal Children to the White House," and "Not Our Children Not Our Problem," as protesters impeded buses trying to get the migrants to the border patrol processing station (Larson

2014). During the 2016 presidential election, immigration was one of the most controversial topics, and many Republican candidates took an extreme and xenophobic stance. The most brazen was the one proposed by the presidential Republican nominee, Donald Trump, who, during the primaries, stated that Mexico is emptying its prisons of rapists, murderers, and the mentally ill, and who ran on a platform of building a bigger wall (which Mexico would pay for) to separate the two countries and to stop Mexican and Central American immigrants from stealing American jobs.

This anti-immigrant sentiment rooted in stereotypes and demagoguery among Republican candidates and their supporters clearly preceded the 2016 election. Political pundit and conservative radio host Glenn Beck, for example, stated on September 4, 2007, that "every undocumented worker is an illegal immigrant, a criminal, and a drain on our dwindling resources" (Waldman et al. 2008). However, less than 6 percent of prisoners are foreign born, and only some of those are undocumented immigrants. A study released in July 2015 found that, according to Federal Bureau of Investigation (FBI) data, between 1990 and 2013, a period in which the foreign-born in the United States nearly doubled and the number of undocumented immigrants more than tripled, violent crime decreased by 48 percent and property crime by 41 percent. The study also found that incarceration rates of native-born Americans are much higher than those of immigrants (Gladstone 2016).

Internal Borders of Discrimination within the Confines of Orange County

There has been a long history of segregation and discrimination against Mexican immigrants in Orange County, dating back to the first half of the twentieth century, and the city of Orange, where Chapman University is located and the conference was held (of which this volume is a product), is no exception. For example, Hart Park, about a mile south of the university featured "Mondays for Mexicans," the one day that Mexicans were allowed to swim in the public swimming pool, which would then be drained and cleaned on Tuesday morning so as not to contaminate the Anglos who then had access to the pool for the next six days (Tobar 2010). Directly across from the university is the Son Light Christian Center, which in the first half of the twentieth century was the Orange Theatre. Mexicans were segregated to the balcony section in the back of the theater, while whites sat in the front area. And, in Orange you can still find one of the segregated "Mexican schools" that children of Mexican immigrants were forced to attend, which has been preserved as a historical site.

These segregated schools went unquestioned, as did the whole segregation system, until the historic 1947 case of *Mendez v. Westminster* that went before the United States Court of Appeals for the Ninth Circuit. Westminster is a city a few miles from Orange. The Mendez family was told that their lighter skinned children, but not their darker children, could attend the white schools (Gonzalez 1990). The court ruled this unconstitutional. As an interesting side note, I teach courses on immigration, social movements, and social inequality. Each semester I query my students if anyone has heard of the *Mendez v. Westminster* case. Maybe one or two hands go up, but typically students stare at me blankly. I then ask if anyone is familiar with the 1954 *Brown v. Board of Education* case that was heard by the Supreme Court, with a favorable ruling on the side of black Americans presumably guaranteeing equal access to educational facilities. All hands go up immediately.

I find this curious as Chapman is located a few minutes from Westminster and this is a major historical case, one that the lawyers during the *Brown v. Board of Education* trial used as a precedent. Perhaps it is because Mexicans complicated the black/white dichotomy since they were perceived as neither. Or, we could surmise that given the extreme conservative nature of Orange County at the time, the media and other politicians made sure the story was not well spread, and certainly not incorporated into classroom textbooks. Or maybe it has been largely overlooked to protect other institutions or businesses that used similar forms of segregation from further lawsuits or court cases. These questions do not have definitive answers but do magnify the lack of interest or understanding of the difficulties Mexican immigrants have suffered in Southern California, as they have in much of the Southwest.

A More Compassionate Perspective on a Global Scale

Pope Francis has been one of the most prominent voices pleading for empathy toward those either fleeing horrific conditions in their home countries or seeking a better life for themselves and their families. For instance, on February 16, 2016, during a papal visit to Mexico, Pope Francis prayed for compassion toward immigrants on the border of the Rio Grande, from the Mexican side (Yardley and Ahmed 2016). He held a mass on the U.S.–Mexico border, in Ciudad Juárez, while onlookers in El Paso, Texas, on the other side of the river in the United States, listened to his talk. His homily commemorated and prayed for those who have transitioned from this life to another trying to cross the border. During his visit, Pope Francis also stated (in reference to trade deals such as NAFTA), "The flow of capital cannot decide the flow and life of people" (2016a). He further elaborated in his homily,

We cannot deny the humanitarian crisis which in recent years has meant the migration of thousands of people. The human tragedy that is forced migration is a global phenomenon today. The crisis, which can be measured in numbers and statistics, we want instead to measure with names, stories, families. (2016b)

There is a consistency in his message that dates back to his first days serving as pope when he stressed to all of those in pastoral positions "to be shepherds that smell like sheep." In other words, stop trying to be a vanguard, an expert, but rub elbows with the common people and hear their stories, get your hands dirty, work alongside people, and be available to offer gentle guidance and assistance as a shepherd. In sum, Pope Francis has, on a regular basis, implored all of us to move away from attitudes of fear and indifference and instead to engage in compassionate dialogue. These expressions were at the core of the conference, "Breaking Borders: Dialoguing on Immigration," that we held at Chapman University on April 24, 2015, and are an essential part of this volume. Both the conference and the volume are an attempt to understand our current social condition through interaction between academics, community activists, community practitioners, and those who are marginalized and excluded.

Outline of the Volume

Public sociology manifests itself in all of the chapters in this book. This approach calls scholars and community activists and practitioners to engage in dialogue and work together in the struggle for social justice. By engaging with the community, scholars can put a human face on the topics they are researching and analyzing, become active learners, and understand the grassroots community-based analyses of social problems. And activists can, through dialogue, trust some of the expertise of scholars who are trained to study, objectively, some of the most pressing issues of our communities.

This book is divided into two sections—"Immigrant Oppression and Resistance Movements" and "Immigrants and Community Narratives"—that reflect the theme of the conference in an effort to combine academic work with community activism. The first section is more research-oriented. It examines some of the racial implications of tools that the criminal justice system relies on, gentrification processes that also have a racial and class dynamic, border issues and U.S. policies that lead to unnecessary deaths of those fleeing from terrible conditions in their home countries, and Dreamers' attempts to find their way through higher education. All of these topics are directly related to immigration issues.

In the first chapter, Amelia Alvarez and Fawn Bekam offer a critique of the collaboration between federal immigration authorities and local law enforcement, and in particular examine the effect that this has on Latin@ youth who are suspected of being gang members. They note the racialized and unreliable processes that underlie the creation of gang databases and the fact that many of those living in areas with a high concentration of gangs are discouraged from applying for immigration relief, such as Deferred Action for Childhood Arrivals (DACA), because they may be listed in a gang database without their knowledge. Therefore, those residing in Latin@ communities are at risk of suffering adverse immigration effects even in the absence of a criminal conviction or actual gang membership due to racial profiling and stereotypes.

In a continuation of some of these themes, in the following chapter, Madeleine Spencer and Victoria Carty examine how the political reproduction of power relations, as expressed in zoning and land use laws, as well as segregation through gentrification processes and gang injunctions, serves as a form of control for certain demographic populations. They use a case study of the city of Santa Ana, California, located adjacent to the city of Orange, to explore how systems of power affect not only the physical but also the psychological life of communities by instilling a perpetual state of insecurity and fear of displacement (through gentrification) or punishment (through the implementation of gang injunctions) among residents. This is of particular concern for immigrants whose families and livelihoods are now threatened by a proposed streetcar project that would run through Santa Ana in an area consisting primarily of low-income immigrant neighborhoods and that works in concert with a gang injunction in the neighborhood through which the new transit line will run. Meanwhile, this project benefits private investors and the local government at the expense of poor, less politically powerful, and marginalized communities. Thus, Spencer and Carty consider the term "development" as used by city planners to be a euphemism that introduces and reinforces processes of gentrification and sorting by race and class.

In Chapter 3, Kristin E. Heyer embraces a broader view of the dynamics surrounding immigration by focusing on border issues and a counternarrative rooted in Catholic social teaching. Her interdisciplinary approach combines theological and sociological perspectives to address the nuances surrounding the immigration debate. She begins by highlighting the paradox that shows that while the death toll of migrants crossing from Mexico into the United States is increasing, border crossing attempts are decreasing. Her essay offers a counter to the backlash against immigrants that espouses an ethic of kinship across borders and embraces solidarity rather than exclusion. In doing so, she challenges us to be wary of individualist paradigms and absolutist categories by taking into consideration the social context of the plight of those attempting to cross the border.

Harriett D. Romo and Raquel R. Marquez, in the next chapter, employ ethnographic research rooted in fieldwork and in-depth interviews with Dreamers, those brought to the United States by their parents but who do not have proper documents to qualify as U.S. citizens. At the crux of their research is an attempt to understand how Dreamers navigate higher education despite the many obstacles they face. At the same time, they develop a sense of civic engagement that helps them to foster a sense of agency, collective identity, connectivity, and inclusivity. Romo and Marquez's essay illuminates the persistence of these young people to succeed through organizing efforts despite the setbacks at the federal level to pass the Dream Act, as it was stalled and then rejected in the House of Representatives in 2012.

In the second section, contributors write about their experiences finding proactive ways to assist immigrants in various ways, especially given the absence of a comprehensive response at the federal level. Lisa D. Ramirez, a California State Bar certified specialist in U.S. immigration and nationality law, is certainly on the front line of immigration issues, particularly as it relates to minors. In Chapter 5, her voice lends credence to the difficulties underlying immigration given the outlandish complexity of the ever-changing laws that even lawyers cannot understand. She laments how immigrants, especially unaccompanied children seeking asylum, must go before a judge to plead their case with no legal representation (in most cases). Her chapter also discusses the disillusionment that many children of immigrants face when they come to realize, typically when they reach their teenage years, that they were not born in the United States and therefore are not documented. Despite living their whole lives in the United States and having assimilated the American dream into their psyche, they become disillusioned once they understand they lack a legitimate social security number that deprives them from many rites of passage as a young person pursuing work or higher education.

Rusty Kennedy, like Ramirez, is also a practitioner in the field of immigration, serving as a community organizer and executive director of the governmental Orange County Human Relations Commission and now the CEO of the nonprofit organization Orange County Human Relations. In Chapter 6, he acutely unveils the "love-hate" relationship that the Orange County environment affords to recent immigrants from a historical perspective. He highlights the evolution of far right-wing groups that have been integral to the local history of Orange County and the ways his organization has responded through a wide range of initiatives to this negative attitude toward immigrants.

In the next chapter, Sister Eileen McNerney writes about her work with youth (most of them immigrants or children of immigrants). She began her activism on the streets of Santa Ana, moved into the barrio to reside in their environment, and then ultimately opened up a facility in 1995 called Taller San Jose (Saint Joseph's Workshop), now called Taller San Jose Hope Builders. Although she is not a sociologist herself, she offers a sociological perspective. Through her interactions with youth, she has come to understand that many of these young people, as recent immigrants, are trapped between two cultures; they are not accepted as American, but having lived in the United States most if not all of their lives, they cannot identify as Mexican either. The young people who come to Taller San Jose Hope Builders try to navigate this hybrid status. They live in impoverished, violent, and gang- and crime-infested barrios, and they are stereotyped and constantly harassed by police. Hope Builders offers them a second chance to escape the labels of "dropouts," "mess-ups," and "felons" by offering education, job training, and life skill courses.

Father Patrick Murphy's essay in many ways dovetails with Sister McNerney's. He runs the Casa del Migrante (House of the Migrant) in Tijuana, Mexico, where many of those deported from the United States are now sent. He explains that the Casa was originally established to assist immigrants, almost exclusively young men, going to the United States to find work, with the intention of returning within a few years. The initial purpose of the Casa was to provide food and lodging for migrants for a day or two. However, as immigration laws have changed over the years, as the border has been militarized making it impossible to pass through Tijuana, and as increasing numbers of people are either being deported to the Mexican border or seeking refuge during the increasingly arduous trip to the United States from both Mexico and Central America, the goals and missions of the Casa have changed. At the crux of his argument (very similar to Ramirez's and Kennedy's pieces) is how insane immigration policy and enforcement in the United States has become, as many of the people who seek reprieve at the Casa have no recollection of Mexico (those brought by their parents at a young age) or have not visited in decades. Today, the refuge spot is called Casa de los Deportados (House for Deportees).

In Chapter 9, Oliver Lopez gives a firsthand account of the lived experience of an undocumented youth navigating the system of higher education in hopes of landing a job after getting two bachelor's degrees at Chapman University, a master's degree from California State, Fullerton, and finally a doctorate from the University of Southern California. What is very interesting about his testimony, and which helps us to reconsider some of the generalizations that many have about people coming to the United States without proper documentation, or who overstay their visas, is his honesty and clarity about his own family's situation. He acknowledges that his parents, successful entrepreneurs in Mexico who enjoyed a comfortable middle-class lifestyle, had a plan: obtain a visa to enter the United States, have Oliver and his older brother stay in the United States long enough to learn English, and then return to Mexico where they would study at top-tier universities and go on to become successful entrepreneurs themselves. As the chapter reveals, this plan backfired and the family stayed in the United States. However, despite the different reasons for leaving Mexico than many other migrants, Oliver shares the experience of most children of immigrant parents who lack proper documents, which causes stress, fear, and anxiety at times. Even though he feels "American," as this is the only country he has known, and is highly educated, he still has the stigma of an outsider as he lacks the magical nine-digit number to attain employment.

The last chapter, by Suzanne SoHoo and Patricia Huerta, encapsulates the spirit of the conference and the theme of this volume. Their essay focuses on a thriving community/university relationship between Chapman University and a community group called Padres Unidos (United Parents), an organization that Huerta cofounded in 1996. As they detail, this partnership is truly public sociology at its core, bringing the community to the university and the university to the community. The partnership, which began in 2010, between the university and this grassroots community organization is dedicated to train and certify parents, most of them from poor immigrant families who face the tough challenges of barrio life in terms of poverty, crime, and the allure of gang life, to empower themselves and their communities to be agents of change in the midst of turmoil.

This is the same kind of dedication manifested by Chapman's partnership with Higher Ground. Higher Ground works with families that include the Marios, Lalos, and Josés who reside in the barrio neighborhoods; physically they are close to the wealthy and privileged in Orange County, yet they might as well be a thousand miles away in terms of concern for their struggles, especially those who are undocumented. It is a population not only vilified in many circles but also deemed invisible. I read somewhere, "the greatest sin is not to bother." Or, we can take this to mean that we need to care for our brothers and sisters who need allies and figure out ways to serve them, either from the academy, or our work on the streets, or both. This gets sociology back to its roots, studying and trying to resolve social problems in an organic way through our interaction with the community, while also using the tools of our trade as trained researchers. The conference that we held at Chapman and this volume are efforts to do both.

Bibliography

Burawoy, Michael. 2005. For public sociology. *American Sociological Review* 70, no. 1:4–28.

Chen, Michelle. 2016. Obama's new plan for detained migrant children militarizes immigration policy. *The Guardian*, July 9.

Gladstone, Rick. 2016. Research doesn't back a link between migration and crime in the United States. *New York Times*, January 13.

Gonzalez, Gilbert G. 1990. *Chicano education in the era of segregation*. Repr., Denton, TX: University of North Texas Press, 2013.

Isacson, Adam, Maureen Meyer, and Gabriela Morales. 2014. Mexico's other border: Security, migration, and the humanitarian crisis at the line with Central America. Washington Office on Latin America, June. http://www.wola.org/files/mxgt/report/.

Larson, Leslie. 2014. California town blocks illegal immigrant transfer: "Go home—We don't want you." *New York Daily News*, July 2.

McNerney, Eileen, CSJ. 2005. *A story of suffering and hope: Lessons from Latino youth*. New York, NY: Paulist Press.

Passel, Jeffrey S., D'Vera Cohn, Jens Manuel Krogstad, and Ana Gonzalez-Barrera. 2014. As growth stalls, unauthorized immigrant population becomes more settled. Pew Research Center, Hispanic Trends, September 3. http://www.pewhispanic.org/2014/09/03/as-growth-stalls-unauthorized-immigrant-population-becomes-more-settled/.

Pope Francis. 2016a. Address of His Holiness Pope Francis: Apostolic journey of His Holiness Pope Francis to Mexico (12–18 February 2016): Meeting with the World of Labor. Vatican City: Libreria Editrice Vaticana, February 17. https://w2.vatican.va/content/francesco/en/speeches/2016/february/documents/papa-francesco_20160217_messico-lavoro.html.

Pope Francis. 2016b. Homily of His Holiness Pope Francis: Apostolic journey of His Holiness Pope Francis to Mexico (12–18 February 2016): Holy Mass. Vatican City: Libreria Editrice Vaticana, February 17. https://w2.vatican.va/content/francesco/en/homilies/2016/documents/papa-francesco_20160217_omelia-messico-ciudad-jaurez.html.

Sengupta, Somini. 2016. Reports tell a trail of migrant deaths across deserts and sea. *New York Times*, June 14.

Tobar, Hector. 2010. Civil rights history—in Orange County. *Los Angeles Times*, December 3.

Waldman, Paul, Elbert Ventura, Robert Savillo, Susan Lin, and Greg Lewis. 2008. Fear and loathing in prime time: Immigration myths on cable news. Media Matters Action Network. http://mediamattersaction.org/reports/fearandloathing/online _version.

Yardley, Jim, and Azman Ahmed. 2016. Pope Francis steps into U.S. immigration debate: At the edge of the Rio Grande, he prays for compassion toward "forced migration." *International New York Times*, February 19.

PART 1

Immigrant Oppression and Resistance Movements

∵

Collaboration between Federal, State, and Local Law Enforcement: Gang Injunctions, Gang Databases, and Immigration Consequences

Amelia Alvarez and Fawn Bekam

The United States Immigration and Customs Enforcement (ICE) removed 357,422 noncitizens in 2013. Of the noncitizens removed, 347,913 were from Mexico, Guatemala, Honduras, and El Salvador. During that same year, ICE also detained approximately 441,000 individuals. Fifty-six percent were Mexican, 13 percent Guatemalan, 12 percent Honduran, and 9 percent Salvadoran nationals, and in total, 90 percent of detainees were from these four countries (ICE 2013, 4). A number of these Latin@ noncitizens were exposed to ICE after interactions with state and local law enforcement. The increasing overlap between the criminal justice and immigration systems has resulted in adverse consequences for noncitizen Latin@s, and particularly for noncitizen Latin@ youth accused of gang affiliation or membership, through the employment of gang injunctions and gang databases.

Gang injunctions are civil court orders that prohibit defendants, or those individuals against whom the injunction is sought, from engaging in certain activity within a designated geographical area called a "safety zone" (for example, see Atkinson 2006, 1693–95). They are obtained by prosecutors who sue a gang and its suspected members in civil court, alleging that the gang constitutes a public nuisance and its members should therefore be forbidden from engaging in conduct that contributes to the nuisance. Such conduct often includes already illegal activity, but it can also include innocent and lawful activity, such as associating with "other gang members," being out past curfew, or wearing particular colors. Individuals named in the initial request for a gang injunction are given notice and opportunity to object to the injunction in court. However, more individuals can be added onto the injunction after it has been approved, and they are not ordinarily given the opportunity to challenge their inclusion in court until they have already been charged with violating it.

Despite the potential for criminal consequences, because injunctions are civil orders, individuals are not entitled to court-appointed counsel when challenging their inclusion in a gang injunction.[1] In addition, criminal

---

1 See *Iraheta v. Superior Court of L.A.*, 83 Cal. Rptr. 2d 471 (1999).

consequences may result if an individual is found to have violated the gang injunction. Individuals who violate the expansive terms of an injunction may be arrested and charged with criminal contempt of court. Criminal contempt may be charged as a misdemeanor punishable by six months in jail and/or a fine up to one thousand dollars.[2]

Gang databases are law enforcement investigative tools (Valentine 1992, 2–3). Because they are not designed to act as judgments and verdicts, they are often over-inclusive and constitutionally defective when used for immigration purposes (Reiner 1992, 111; Katz 2003, 512; Wright 2005, 115; Brown 2009, 293, 320). A few gang databases include only individuals involved in gang-related crimes, but others use much broader criteria that are met without any type of gang-related activity (Brown 2009, 302–5). The information is often obtained through field interviews unrelated to a criminal arrest or investigation (Wright 2005, 121). These field interviews are overwhelmingly conducted by patrol officers, not gang-unit officers specially trained to identify and document gang membership. This is because patrol officers more regularly come into contact with individuals in the course of their duties. Officers then record information obtained during the field interview on a card, which is submitted for documentation into a gang database (Hufstader 2015, 672).

Gang injunctions and gang databases currently allow local and state agencies to label an individual as a gang member without offering a meaningful opportunity to challenge that designation. This information is often unreliable and highly racialized (Muñiz and McGill 2012), and is particularly concerning when individuals are erroneously labeled as gang members. Inclusion on a gang injunction or database affects all stages of the immigration process: the decision to initiate removal proceedings, the decision to detain an individual pending his immigration proceedings, and the availability of or the decision to grant immigration relief. This approach has led to the criminalization of individuals, particularly Latin@ youth, who are not gang members and not engaged in unlawful activities.

In this chapter, we suggest that to combat the immigration consequences of erroneous gang labels, state and federal law enforcement agencies should implement adequate and meaningful opportunities for individuals to challenge their inclusion on a gang injunction or database. Civil rights groups, students, advocates, and community-based organizations have long questioned these law enforcement tactics. By taking these issues out of academic discussion and into reality, community-based grassroots organizations can continue to work with Latin@ immigrants to challenge the systems depriving them of their

---

2   See Cal. Penal Code §166(a)(4) at §19.

rights. Scholars working as intermediaries in these endeavors help to promote the field of public sociology (Burawoy 2005).

The Roots of the Criminalization of the Immigration System and Its Overlap with the Criminal Justice System

In the mid-1960s, President Lyndon B. Johnson declared a War on Crime, in response to the perceived lawlessness of civil rights protestors. This initiated a series of federal laws aimed at making crime control a national priority through an increase in federal law enforcement programs and the criminal justice system (Hinton 2015). As a result, the number of individuals incarcerated in the United States rose dramatically over the next decades. Between 1980 and 1996, state and federal incarceration rates increased by over 200 percent. During this same period, Latin@s were the fastest growing minority group among the incarcerated, ultimately rising to 17.6 percent of all inmates. Overall, the number of Latin@s sentenced to a year or more in a state or federal prison increased by 554 percent (Blumstein and Beck 1999, 17, 22–23). Based on these and similar figures for black communities, scholars have suggested that these trends, although depicted by politicians as a "cracking down on crime," actually occurred with significant racist undertones (García Hernández 2014, 1457, 1495; Alexander 2010, 42–43).

As the criminal justice system expanded, the immigration system also became more criminalized.[3] Beginning in the 1980s, the federal government passed a flurry of legislation that increased the criminal bases for deportation and, accordingly, the grounds for immigration detention. In the Anti-Drug Abuse Act of 1986, for instance, Congress expanded bases for deportation when it replaced the provision of the Immigration and Nationality Act (INA), allowing for deportation based on a conviction for an "addiction-sustaining opiate" with one authorizing deportation based on conviction of any controlled substance under state, federal, or a foreign state's law.[4] Only two years later in the Anti-Drug Abuse Act of 1988, Congress again amended the INA to require the deportation of those noncitizens convicted of an "aggravated felony." The definition of aggravated felony included convictions for murder, narcotics trafficking, and unlawful firearms trafficking, but Congress continued to expand

---

3   Scholars have termed the criminalization of the immigration system "crimmigration" (Stumpf 2006; García Hernández 2014).

4   See Anti-Drug Abuse Act of 1986, Pub. L. No. 99–570, § 1751, 100 Stat. 3207; and INA § 237(a) (2)(B)(i), 8 U.S.C. § 1227(a)(2)(B)(i).

the definition to include more crimes with the passage of the Antiterrorism and Effective Death Penalty Act (AEDPA) and the Illegal Immigration Reform and Immigrant Responsibility Act (IIRIRA).[5]

These legislative changes significantly increased the likelihood that removal proceedings would be triggered as a "collateral consequence" of a criminal conviction. The changes also occurred at a time when the nation was increasingly convicting Latin@s and the media was negatively depicting Latin@ immigration as the "Latin@ threat" (Chacón 2007, 1827, 1844; Blumstein and Beck 1999; Massey and Pren 2012, 1, 5–6). In addition, this move toward convictions-based removals tightened the link between the immigration and criminal justice systems, and specifically, state and local law criminal justice officials.

The overlap between these two systems provided state and local law criminal justice officials with multiple opportunities to affect a noncitizen's immigration consequences. Decisions by local prosecutors took on increasing importance. Law professor Stephen Lee has explained that this phenomenon results in state courts behaving as "de facto immigration courts." More precisely, he contends that the power afforded to prosecutors has contributed to a criminal justice system in which prosecutors' decisions concerning whether to charge noncitizens and what to charge them with generally dictates what will occur in immigration courts (2013).[6] But even before noncitizens interact with local prosecutors, they face the law enforcement officials policing their communities who are part of a criminal justice system that has disproportionately affected Latin@s (Walker et al. 2004, 17).

Collaboration between Federal Immigration Authorities and State and Local Law Enforcement

Collaboration between ICE and state and local law enforcement increases the chances for noncitizens to be exposed to adverse immigration consequences. Several programs have been introduced to facilitate this collaboration. Section 287(g) of INA, adopted as part of the IIRIRA in 1996, allows ICE to delegate its authority to state and local law enforcement officers. Through 287(g),

---

5   Anti-Drug Abuse Act of 1988, Pub. L. No. 100–690, § 7342, 102 Stat. 4181, 4469–70 (amending INA § 101(a), 8 U.S.C. 1101(a)); AEDPA, Pub. L. No. 104–132, 110 Stat. 1214; and IIRIRA, Pub. L. No. 104–208, Div. C, 110 Stat. 3009–546.

6   Lee states: "Immigration law's increasing dependence on criminal convictions to identify potentially removable migrants has transformed many state courts into de facto immigration courts" (2013, 596).

over 1,500 state and local law enforcement officers have been trained to enforce immigration law. Its usefulness as an immigration tool is clear. ICE claims that between January 2006 and September 2014, more than 373,800 potentially removable noncitizens were identified through 287(g), mostly in local jails (ICE, n.d.). Most significantly, separate reports by the Department of Justice have found that the 287(g) program has resulted in widespread racial profiling of Latin@s.[7]

Through the Criminal Alien Program (CAP), federal immigration agents, instead of local law enforcement officers, interview arrestees in state and local jails to identify removable noncitizens (Cox and Miles 2013, 87, 93). Under this program, established in 1988, local law enforcement officers hold individuals until an ICE officer can interview them and determine whether to issue an immigration detainer (Barry 2009). CAP has been criticized for racially profiling Latin@s. A study conducted by the Chief Justice Earl Warren Institute on Race, Ethnicity, and Diversity (at the University of California, Berkeley Law School), for example, found that a local police department's discretionary arrests of Latin@s of petty offenses, including traffic violations, rapidly increased following the department's partnership with ICE through CAP (Gardner and Kohli 2009, 5, 1).

While Section 287(g) and CAP have received significant critique from academics and civil rights advocates, the most controversial collaboration between federal immigration authorities and state and local law enforcement has been the Secure Communities program. Created in 2008, Secure Communities, an information sharing program, sought to "more effectively identify and facilitate the removal of criminal aliens in the custody of state and local law enforcement agencies" (Department of Homeland Security [DHS] 2014c, 1; see also Kohli, Markowitz, and Chavez 2011, 1). Pursuant to Secure Communities, local law enforcement uploads an arrestee's fingerprints to the Federal Bureau of Investigation (FBI) criminal justice database. Upon receiving this information, ICE searches to see whether the arrestee's information could be found within the DHS immigration database. Based on the results of this search, ICE can then issue a detainer, which is a request to hold the arrestee until he or she could be taken into ICE custody (DHS 2011).

---

7 On Arizona, see a December 15, 2011, letter regarding the United States' investigation of the Maricopa County sheriff's office from Thomas E. Perez, the assistant attorney general, to Bill Montgomery, the Maricopa County attorney (Perez 2011). On North Carolina, see a September 18, 2012, letter regarding the United States' investigation of the Alamance County sheriff's office from Perez to Clyde B. Albright, the Alamance County attorney, and Chuck Kitchen, from the Turrentine law firm (Perez 2012).

Although the stated goal of Secure Communities was to identify and remove noncitizens convicted of serious crimes, the program has resulted in the removal of noncitizens arrested or convicted of minor offenses. In light of the critique of Secure Communities, DHS announced in November 2014 that it would terminate the program and replace it with the Priority Enforcement Program (PEP). However, this new program continues ICE's reliance on "fingerprint-based biometric data submitted during bookings by state and local law enforcement agencies to the Federal Bureau of Investigation for criminal background checks" (DHS 2014c, 2).[8] PEP was only recently implemented in January 2015, and there is no indication that it will function significantly differently than Secure Communities or better avoid the removal of noncitizens arrested for minor crimes. In response, immigrant rights' activists, such as the Orange County Immigrant Youth United (OCIYU), have demonstrated against PEP in attempts to keep it from being a mere continuance of Secure Communities, while others, such as the National Day Laborer Organizing Network (NDLON), have filed suit against DHS and ICE to require these government agencies from disclosing how they are implementing the new program (San Roman 2015; Kowalski 2016).

Secure Communities and its successor, PEP, epitomize the problem of collaboration between federal immigration authorities and state and local law enforcement. As a result of these collaborative programs, noncitizens have become subject to removal proceedings and detention not only following a criminal conviction but also after a mere arrest (without a subsequent conviction) or a traffic violation, and even after calling the police as a victim of crime (DHS 2014c, 2). In 2013, pressure from activists and community organizations (Molina 2012; Richman 2013; Barnes 2012) from all over the state prompted the California legislature to pass a law known as the TRUST Act, which limits state cooperation with federal immigration authorities. The TRUST Act prohibits state and local law enforcement agencies, through Secure Communities, from detaining individuals for additional time in order to allow ICE to take them into custody unless they have been charged or convicted of certain crimes.[9] However, removal is not the only consequence of this type of collaboration; an individual's eligibility for citizenship or permanent residence is also jeopardized when they have come into contact with law enforcement.

---

8 The DHS memorandum states: "But the reality is the program has attracted a great deal of criticism, is widely misunderstood, and is embroiled in litigation; its very name has become a symbol for general hostility toward the enforcement of our immigration laws" (2014c, 1).

9 2013 Cal. Stat. 4650.

Local Law Enforcement Tactics, Gang Injunctions and Databases, and Immigration Effects

Local law enforcement officers can affect a noncitizen's immigration outcomes, particularly when the noncitizen is accused of gang activity. Indeed, when gang activity is involved, even if state courts are not, what happens at the local level largely affects an individual's immigration consequences. Section 212 of the INA addresses the "general class of aliens ineligible to receive visas and ineligible for admission," in addition to available waivers of ineligibility. Although Section 212 does not explicitly mention gang membership, it deems individuals who have participated in terrorist activity as inadmissible to the United States, and it is often the means by which suspected gang members are barred from any type of pathway to lawful immigration status. Terrorist activity is defined as including "the highjacking or sabotage of any conveyance (including an aircraft, vessel, or vehicle)" and "the seizing or detaining, and threatening to kill, injure, or continue to detain, another individual in order to compel a third person to do or abstain from doing any act."[10] A gang's activities may very likely meet this definition by stealing cars or threatening to kill one person in order to get another person to do something. Even if an individual has never participated in this type of conduct, it is likely that suspected gang membership will still bar them from immigration benefits.

In addition, in a series of memoranda offering guidance on President Barack Obama's new immigration policies, DHS laid out its new enforcement priorities. Of the highest priority "for the apprehension, detention, and removal of aliens in this country" are threats to national and border security and public safety. Included in this category are "aliens convicted of an offense for which an element was active participation in a criminal street gang, as defined in 18 U.S.C. §521(a), or aliens not younger than 16 years of age who intentionally participate in an organized criminal gang to further the illegal activity of the gang" (DHS 2014b).

These immigration statutes and policies heighten the consequences for noncitizens labeled "gang members." At the same time, collaboration between ICE and state and local law enforcement officials has focused its efforts on gang members. It is essentially a collaboration in which federal agencies aim to curb gang activity through intervention with state and local law enforcement (Kingsbury 2006). Additionally, ICE officials rely on information provided by local law enforcement and arrests made at the local level. This collaboration and the tactics used by local law enforcement can directly affect an undocumented

---

10   INA §212(a)(3)(B)(ii)(I); and INA §212(a)(3)(B)(iii)(II).

individual's status, particularly if that individual is suspected of gang activity. Furthermore, suppression tactics used by local law enforcement, especially gang injunctions and gang databases, are problematic because they result in the official labeling of youth as gang members.

As explained above, criminal convictions frequently lead to immigration consequences, and this is even more detrimental if one is suspected of being a gang member or having gang affiliation. Some counties in California have implemented procedures through which individuals can be removed from the injunction.[11] These administrative removal options require individuals to submit evidence to the district or city attorney proving that they have been wrongly identified on the injunction. Few have attempted this removal process, possibly because the procedure currently requires individuals to argue against their inclusion on an injunction in front of the agency that placed them on the injunction in the first place. In addition, as this is an administrative proceeding, individuals challenging their placement are not entitled to counsel and the evidence that would otherwise be inadmissible in court can be used against the individual (Vannoy 2009, 317).

ICE currently operates and maintains a computerized database, ICEGangs, that identifies and records information about suspected gang members and associates (DHS 2010). ICE has not revealed what criteria it uses to identify gang members, but ICEGangs users have access to the CalGang database through use of the same commercial software. CalGang is the hub for all state gang databases and currently contains information on an estimated 250,000 to 300,000 individuals (O'Connor 2000). The information contained in CalGang is not publicly available, which means there is no way for individuals to know if they have been suspected of gang affiliation or to contest it. California offers little to no due process with respect to CalGang; there is no right to notification for adults, no right to an appeal, and no right to be removed.

Advocates and civil rights groups, including the American Civil Liberties Union (ACLU) have denounced CalGang for its lack of uniform standards regarding collecting and entering information, its lack of significant oversight, and the minimal protection of individuals' rights (Munoz 1997; Garcia-Leys, Thompson, and Richardson 2016, 1). CalGang has also been condemned for containing erroneous or obsolete information. A recent audit of CalGang that found errors and unsubstantiated entries seems to support these critiques (Winton 2016).

---

11   Vannoy (2009, 285) describes Los Angeles' administrative removal process; *Vasquez v. Rackauckas*, 734 F.3d 1025, 1049 (2013) describes Orange County's administrative removal process; and San Diego County District Attorney's Office (n.d.) describes San Diego County's removal process.

Gang databases have also been criticized for leading to racial profiling of Latin@ youth, who are disproportionately represented in these databases. Similarly, gang injunctions can serve to control individuals not involved in gangs by criminalizing some conduct that would otherwise be lawful. Although civil in nature, gang injunctions result in criminal charges if violated, which can lead to adverse immigration consequences. Because the processes for seeking removal from an injunction or database can be difficult to figure out, those individuals who have been erroneously labeled as gang members often remain on these lists.

Response from Community Advocates

The imposition of extensive restrictions on civil liberties has not gone unnoticed by community-based grassroots advocates. In 2009, an injunction was filed against the Orange Varrio Cypress (OVC) gang in Orange, California. Community advocates, such as the local group Chicanos Unidos, rallied and contacted the ACLU to challenge its constitutionality. These advocates gathered community support and encouraged nearly half of the individuals named on the injunction to challenge their inclusion in court. The Ninth Circuit Court of Appeals struck down the OVC gang injunction as unconstitutional, and found that the process by which the Orange County district attorney determined gang affiliation was inadequate (San Roman 2013). Although the holding was limited to the OVC injunction, it is an illustration of how community-based grassroots advocates can succeed in encouraging communities to assert and protect their rights.

There are currently thirteen gang injunctions in effect in Orange County (Cabrera 2014). Unfortunately, the San Juan Capistrano and San Clemente injunctions in particular have garnered little to no attention. This could be in large part because, until recently, there has been an absence of community-based grassroots advocacy groups in the southern parts of the county. During the summer of 2014, We Are San Juan, a group formed in response to this void, canvassed door to door to ask San Juan Capistrano residents living in predominately Latin@ areas what they believe the biggest problems facing the community are. Overwhelmingly, the answer was gangs, and overwhelmingly, there was support for the gang injunction.[12]

The lack of knowledge about gang injunctions and gang databases in San Juan Capistrano has resulted in real immigration consequences for Latin@ youth in the community. The Immigrant Rights Clinic at the University of

---

12   We Are San Juan shared the results of their canvassing interviews with us in fall 2014.

California, Irvine School of Law represented one such youth during a bond hearing in his immigration case. The young man had recently received his high school diploma and was offered a scholarship to attend community college when he was served with the San Juan Capistrano gang injunction.[13] His father has serious health issues and, at the time, this young man was his primary caretaker. Among other things, he was forbidden from being out past 10 p.m. and from associating with "other gang members." "Other gang members" does not simply mean other individuals named on the gang injunction, but anyone who the police suspect to be a gang member. For example, the young man was arrested at an annual parade for violating the gang injunction because he was there with a family friend. The young man denies any gang involvement, though he knew people in gangs by virtue of growing up in San Juan Capistrano. Unfortunately, he was unable to avoid violating the strict terms of the injunction and was arrested several more times. As a result, he was unable to attend college and has been fighting deportation while in immigration detention since 2013.

This young man's story demonstrates why community-based grassroots advocacy is so important. When San Juan Capistrano residents expressed their support of the gang injunction, they showed a lack of understanding of its consequences. This particular injunction has been in place for more than eight years, yet gang activity continues to be a problem. Meanwhile, young people in the community have had basic liberties stripped from them with little to no due process. The lack of community activism could very likely be the reason that those living in immigrant communities support police tactics that lead to deportation. Had there been more advocacy when the gang injunction was proposed, it might have been struck down for containing the same constitutional defects as the OVC injunction, which was introduced years later.

Implications for Immigrants and the Threat of Deportation

ICE officers exercise prosecutorial discretion in deciding which cases to pursue. This includes the decision of whether to issue or cancel a Notice to Appear; who to question and detain for an immigration violation; whether to settle, dismiss, appeal, or join a motion in a case; and whether to grant deferred action, parole, or stay of removal in lieu of seeking a formal order of removal. Prosecutorial discretion is also exercised when an ICE officer determines whether compelling factors exist that indicate an individual is not a threat to public safety and therefore not an enforcement priority (DHS 2014b).

---

13   To protect this individual's privacy, any identifying information has been withheld.

This means that inclusion in a gang database or gang injunction would operate against an individual seeking an exercise of favorable prosecutorial discretion in their immigration case. DHS has referred to gang participation as a disqualifying bar for the various forms of prosecutorial discretion, including relief under the Deferred Action for Childhood Arrivals (DACA) policy.

DACA was announced on June 15, 2012 (DHS 2012). DACA is an executive immigration policy, a form of prosecutorial discretion, granting renewable two-year periods of deportation relief and work authorization to some young undocumented immigrants (U.S. Citizenship and Immigration Services [USCIS] 2015). More than two years later, Deferred Action for Parents of Americans and Lawful Permanent Residents (DAPA) was announced. This action has met considerable opposition in Texas, where a federal judge issued an injunction claiming that the president had failed to comply with federal requirements (Mullen and Diamon 2015). The decision was upheld by the Supreme Court of the United States in 2016, and it is not clear if or when DAPA will take effect.[14] DAPA, similar to DACA, offers deportation relief and work authorization for three-year periods. To be eligible, an applicant must have been a parent of a U.S. citizen or lawful permanent resident child on November 20, 2014, and must have continuously resided in the United States before January 1, 2010 (DHS 2014a).

Applicants who are otherwise eligible for DACA will be barred if they have serious criminal records or if USCIS determines that they are a threat to public safety. Threat to public safety includes suspected gang membership. Although information contained in a DACA application is usually kept confidential, USCIS is required to refer an applicant to ICE for removal if that applicant is a public safety threat. Similarly, otherwise eligible applicants might still be denied DAPA if they have serious criminal records, but the other criminal bars vary from that in DACA. Instead of a broad public safety exception, an applicant who has been convicted of an offense for which one of the elements is active participation in a criminal street gang will be denied DAPA. DAPA is also barred to any individual who purposefully participated in a criminal street gang to further the gang's illegal activity (DHS 2014a). Similar to DACA, if an applicant is denied because of a gang conviction or because of gang conduct, USCIS will refer him or her to ICE for removal (USCIS 2014).

DACA set aside expunged convictions and juvenile delinquencies, but there is no such assurance with DAPA (DHS 2014a). On the other hand, DAPA's gang bars are a slight improvement over DACA's public safety exception because DHS has finally articulated a standard for what constitutes a gang threat. These standards might potentially narrow the number of people who

---

14   *United States v. Texas,* 579 U.S. (2016).

are excluded based on gang membership, but there are also specific flaws in the way in which the government screens for gang affiliation and participation. This means that Latin@ communities are left dealing with the reality of these flaws and the threat of deportation as a result.

Advocates hope that the standards articulated by DHS about what constitutes a gang threat will foreclose denials based solely on inclusion on a gang list, gang injunction, or association with gang members. However, DHS has not addressed whether gang association outside of those terms may nonetheless result in a denial on the basis of discretion. There is nothing stopping DHS from looking at other factors, even if they do not technically meet the gang-based bars to DAPA.

The problem remains that DAPA and DACA adjudicators will be instructed to refer known or suspected gang members to ICE for removal. Without clear guidance, people will be scared to apply if they have any gang connection at all, because if they do apply and their application is denied, they may be placed in removal proceedings. This means that a significant sympathetic population cannot avail itself of administrative relief, and families and children will remain vulnerable. If these marginalized populations could receive deferred action, they might be more willing to work with law enforcement to end gang violence.

Conclusion

The consequence of collaboration between federal immigration authorities and local law enforcement is that little to no protections are afforded to individuals against the immigration consequences of being wrongly labeled as a gang member. Current practices can lead to innocent Latin@ youth being placed on a gang database or gang injunction by virtue of where they live, who they walk to school with, and what color clothes they wear. The information in these databases is highly unreliable and often highly racialized, and Latin@ youth are at risk of suffering adverse immigration effects even in the absence of a criminal conviction or actual gang membership. With no way of finding out who exists on gang databases and inadequate processes for challenging the gang label, individuals who live in gang areas are discouraged from applying for immigration relief.

The solution is to educate Latin@ communities about the issues gang injunctions and gang databases present. With sufficient knowledge, community groups can draw broad attention to the tactics leading to the criminalization of Latin@ youth. Once the consequences of gang injunctions and databases are more widely understood, youth confronted with these law enforcement tools can turn to their community to help fight their inclusion. On a broader scale, communities can use this information to advocate for changes to the defective law enforcement tactics that lead to deportation based on suspected gang affiliation.

Bibliography

Alexander, Michelle. 2010. *The new Jim Crow: Mass incarceration in the age of colorblindness.* New York, NY: New Press.

Atkinson, Scott E. 2006. The outer limits of gang injunctions. *Vanderbilt Law Review* 59, no. 5:1693–1734.

Barnes, Brooks. 2012. California sheriffs oppose bill on illegal immigrants. *New York Times*, August 28.

Barry, Tom. 2009. Immigrant crackdown joins failed crime and drug wars. Center for International Policy, April 1. https://www.ciponline.org/research/html/immigrant-crackdown-joins-failed-crime-and-drug-wars.

Blumstein, Alfred, and Allen J. Beck. 1999. Population growth in U.S. prisons, 1980–1996. *Crime and Justice* 26:17–61.

Brown, Rebecca Rader. 2009. The gang's all here: Evaluating the need for a national gang database. *Columbia Journal of Law and Social Problems* 42, no. 3:293–333.

Burawoy, Michael. 2005. For public sociology. *American Sociological Review* 70, no. 1:4–28.

Cabrera, Yvette. 2014. Judge: Residents owed due process in gang injunction case. *Voice of OC*, November 20. http://voiceofoc.org/2014/11/judge-residents-owed-due-process-in-gang-injunction-case/.

Chacón, Jennifer M. 2007. Unsecured borders: Immigration restrictions, crime control and national security. *Connecticut Law Review* 39, no. 5:1827–91.

Cox Adam B., and Thomas J. Miles. 2013. Policing immigration. *University of Chicago Law Review* 80:87–136.

Department of Homeland Security (DIIS). 2010. Federal Register 75, no. 39, March 1. http://www.gpo.gov/fdsys/pkg/FR-2010-03-01/html/2010-4102.htm.

Department of Homeland Security (DHS). 2011. Task force on Secure Communities findings and recommendations. Homeland Security Advisory Council, September. http://www.dhs.gov/xlibrary/assets/hsac-task-force-on-secure-communities-findings-and-recommendations-report.pdf.

Department of Homeland Security (DHS). 2012. Secretary Napolitano announces deferred action process for young people who are low enforcement priorities. Press release, June 15. http://www.dhs.gov/news/2012/06/15/secretary-napolitano-announces-deferred-action-process-young-people-who-are-low.

Department of Homeland Security (DHS). 2014a. Exercising prosecutorial discretion with respect to individuals who came to the United States as children and with respect to certain individuals who are the parents of U.S. citizens or permanent residents. Memorandum, November 20. http://www.dhs.gov/sites/default/files/publications/14_1120_memo_deferred_action.pdf.

Department of Homeland Security (DHS). 2014b. Policies for the apprehension, detention and removal of undocumented immigrants. Memorandum, November 20. https://www.dhs.gov/sites/default/files/publications/14_1120_memo_prosecutorial_discretion.pdf.

Department of Homeland Security (DHS). 2014c. Secure Communities. Memorandum, November 20. https://www.dhs.gov/sites/default/files/publications/14_1120_memo_secure_communities.pdf.

García Hernández, Cèsar Cuauhtémoc. 2014. Creating crimmigration. *Brigham Young University Law Review* 2013:1457–1516.

Garcia-Leys, Sean, Meigan Thompson, and Christyn Richardson. 2016. *Mislabeled allegations of gang membership and their immigration consequences*. Irvine, CA: UCI School of Law Immigrant Rights Clinic, April. http://www.law.uci.edu/academics/real-life-learning/clinics/ucilaw-irc-MislabeledReport.pdf.

Gardner, Trevor, II, and Aarti Kohli. 2009. The C.A.P. effect: Racial profiling in the ICE Criminal Alien Program. Policy Brief. The Chief Justice Earl Warren Institute on Race, Ethnicity, and Diversity, University of California, Berkeley Law School, September 2009, 1–8.

Hinton, Elizabeth. 2015. Why we should reconsider the war on crime. *Time*, March 20.

Hufstader, Rebecca A. 2015. Immigration reliance on gang databases: Unchecked discretion and undesirable consequences. *New York University Law Review* 90, no. 2:671–709.

Immigration and Customs Enforcement (ICE). 2013. ERO Annual Report: FY 2013 ICE immigration removals. https://www.ice.gov/doclib/about/offices/ero/pdf/2013-ice-immigration-removals.pdf.

Immigration and Customs Enforcement (ICE). n.d. Delegation of immigration authority Section 287(g) Immigration and Nationality Act. http://www.ice.gov/factsheets/287g#wcm-survey-target-id.

Katz, Charles M. 2003. Issues in the production and dissemination of gang statistics: An ethnographic study of a large midwestern police gang unit. *Crime and Delinquency* 49, no. 3:485–516.

Kingsbury, Alex. 2006. Inside the feds' war on gangs. *U.S. News & World Report*, December 10.

Kohli, Aarti, Peter L. Markowitz, and Lisa Chavez. 2011. Secure Communities by the numbers: An analysis of demographics and due process. Research Report. The Chief

Justice Earl Warren Institute on Law and Social Policy, University of California, Berkeley Law School, October.

Kowalski, Daniel M. 2016. PEP FOIA lawsuit filed: NDLON v. ICE. *LexisNexis Legal Newsroom Immigration Law*, January 21. http://www.lexisnexis.com/legalnewsroom/immigration/b/outsidenews/archive/2016/01/21/pep-foia-lawsuit-filed-ndlon-v-ice.aspx.

Lee, Stephen. 2013. De facto immigration courts. *California Law Review* 101, no. 3: 553–608.

Massey, Douglas S., and Karen A. Pren. 2012. Unintended consequences of U.S. immigration: Explaining the post-1965 surge from Latin America. *Population and Development Review* 38, no. 1:1–29.

Molina, Alejandra. 2012. Inland immigration activists rally to support Trust Act. *Multicultural Empire* (blog). *The Press Enterprise*, August 29. http://www.pe.com/articles/-718112--.html (last updated August 18, 2014).

Mullen, Jethro, and Jeremy Diamon. 2015. Obama vows to abide by immigration court order. *CNN*, February 17. http://www.cnn.com/2015/02/17/politics/texas-obama-immigration-injunction/.

Muñiz, Ana, and Kim McGill. 2012. Tracked and trapped: Youth of color, gang databases and gang injunctions. Youth Justice Coalition's REALSEARCH Action Research Center, December. http://www.youth4justice.org/wp-content/uploads/2012/12/TrackedandTrapped.pdf.

Munoz, Lorenza. 1997. Gang database raises civil rights concerns. *Los Angeles Times*, July 14.

O'Connor, Anne-Marie. 2000. Massive gang member listed now clouded by rampart crime: Many of the names in the statewide database were compiled by LAPD's now-disbanded CRASH units. *Los Angeles Times*, March 25.

Perez, Thomas E. 2011. Assistant attorney general, U.S. Department of Justice, Civil Rights Division, letter to Bill Montgomery, Maricopa County (Arizona) attorney, December 15. http://www.justice.gov/sites/default/files/crt/legacy/2011/12/15/mcso_findletter_12-15-11.pdf.

Perez, Thomas E. 2012. Assistant attorney general, U.S. Department of Justice, Civil Rights Division, letter to Clyde B. Albright, Alamance County (North Carolina) attorney, and Chuck Kitchen, Turrentine law firm, September 18. http://www.justice.gov/iso/opa/resources/1712012918124624881908.pdf.

Reiner, Ira. 1992. Gangs, crimes, and violence in Los Angeles. County of Los Angeles: Office of the District Attorney.

Richman, Josh. 2013. TRUST Act activists target sheriffs in Sac, Oakland. *Political Blotter* (blog), September 18. http://www.ibabuzz.com/politics/2013/09/18/trust-act-activists-target-sheriffs-in-sac-oakland/.

San Diego County District Attorney's Office. n.d. Petition for removal from gang injunction enforcement. http://www.sdcda.org/preventing/gangs/petition-for-removal -from-gang-injunction.pdf.

San Roman, Gabriel. 2013. 9th Circuit Court rules OC DA's gang injunction in Orange violates due process. *OC Weekly* (blog), November 7. http://blogs.ocweekly.com/ navelgazing/2013/11/orange_varrio_cypress_gang_injunction_2013.php.

San Roman, Gabriel. 2015. Immigrant activists give a stern "pep" talk to Santa Ana City Council over new ICE program. *OC Weekly*, July 15. http://www.ocweekly.com/ news/immigrant-activists-give-a-stern-pep-talk-to-santa-ana-city-council-over -new-ice-program-6455895.

Stumpf, Juliet. 2006. The crimmigration crisis: Immigrants, crime, and sovereign power. *American University Law Review* 56, no. 2:367–419.

U.S. Citizenship and Immigration Services (USCIS). 2014. General information: How do I request consideration of Deferred Action for Childhood Arrivals? June. http:// www.uscis.gov/sites/default/files/USCIS/Humanitarian/Deferred%20Action%20 for%20Childhood%20Arrivals/daca_hdi.pdf.

U.S. Citizenship and Immigration Services (USCIS). 2015. Consideration of Deferred Action for Childhood Arrivals (DACA). August 3. http://www.uscis.gov/humanitarian/ consideration-deferred-action-childhood-arrivals-daca.

Valentine, Harold A. 1992. Law enforcement: Information on the Los Angeles County sheriff's department gang reporting, evaluation, and tracking system. Testimony before the Subcommittee on Civil and Constitutional Rights, Committee on the Judiciary, House of Representatives. United States General Accounting Office, GAO/ T-GGD-92-52, June 26. https://www.ncjrs.gov/pdffiles1/Digitization/151572NCJRS .pdf.

Vannoy, Brittany. 2009. Turning their lives around: California cities pioneer gang injunction removal procedures. *Journal of the National Association of Administrative Law Judiciary* 29, no. 1:283–323.

Walker, Nancy E., J. Michael Senger, Francisco L. Villarruel, and Angela M. Arboleda. 2004. *Lost opportunities: The reality of Latinos in the U.S. criminal justice system.* Washington, DC: National Council of La Raza.

Winton, Richard. 2016. California gang database plagued with errors, unsubstantiated entries, state auditor finds. *Los Angeles Times*, August 11.

Wright, Joshua D. 2005. The constitutional failure of gang databases. *Stanford Journal of Civil Rights and Civil Liberties* 2 (November): 115–42.

CHAPTER 2

Gentrification, Gang Injunctions, and the Impact on Latin@ Communities in Southern California

Madeleine Spencer and Victoria Carty

Civic development and planning policies and practices in Santa Ana, California, have contributed to creating and simultaneously concealing segregation and sorting (see map 2.1). Sorting is defined by psychiatrist Mindy Thompson Fullilove (2013) as the arrangement of residents in urban spaces according to race and class through the implementation of policies, laws, and customs that shape the urban environment and affect residents' access to resources. Law professor John A. Powell elaborates:

> Through the arrangement of space, we have translated our formerly explicit racist laws into an implicit and pervasive racial and economic segregation. It is now primarily through the use of space that we do our "racing." (2009, 24)

Over time, the United States has employed these practices through institutional structures, such as housing policies, bank loans and mortgages, and tactics implemented by the criminal justice system. One of the most recent tactics, we argue, is the implementation of gang injunctions in certain areas that are inhabited by low-income minority and immigrant populations.

Most city planners would deny their role in the spatio-political reproduction of power relations as expressed in zoning and land use laws, as well as segregation (i.e., sorting) through gentrification processes and gang injunctions as a form of control. In this chapter, however, we argue that these are indeed instruments used to segregate and control certain demographic populations. By using a case study of the city of Santa Ana in the heart of Orange County, we contend that systems of power affect not only the physical but also the psychological life of communities by instilling a perpetual state of insecurity and fear of displacement (through gentrification) or punishment (through gang injunctions) among residents.

This is of particular concern for immigrants whose families and livelihoods are now (2015–2019) threatened by a proposed project in Santa Ana—the

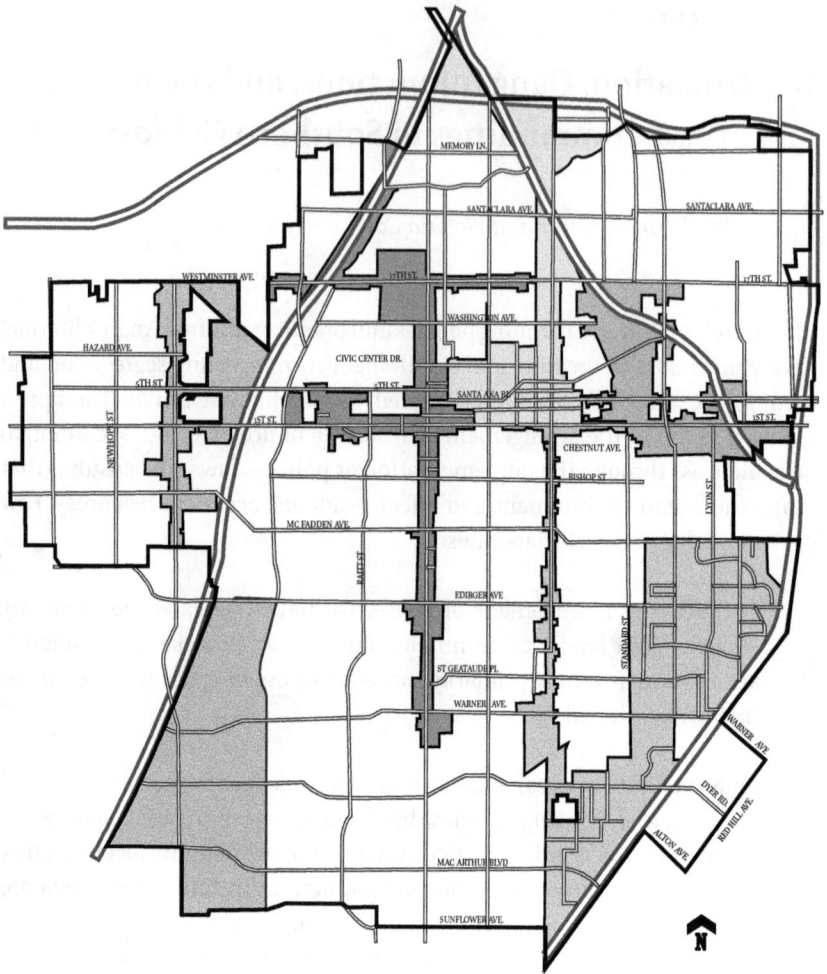

MAP 2.1   *Santa Ana community redevelopment agency implementation plan for July 1, 2010,*
            to June 30, 2015, for the Merged Santa Ana redevelopment project areas.
            SOURCE: COMMUNITY REDEVELOPMENT AGENCY OF THE CITY OF SANTA
            ANA, *FIVE-YEAR IMPLEMENTATION PLAN, JUNE 1, 2010–JUNE 30, 2015*
            (SANTA ANA, 2010), 10, HTTP://WWW.CI.SANTA-ANA.CA.US/CDA/DOCUMENTS/
            SAIMPLEMPLANFINALFINAL.PDF (ACCESSED MARCH 30, 2016).

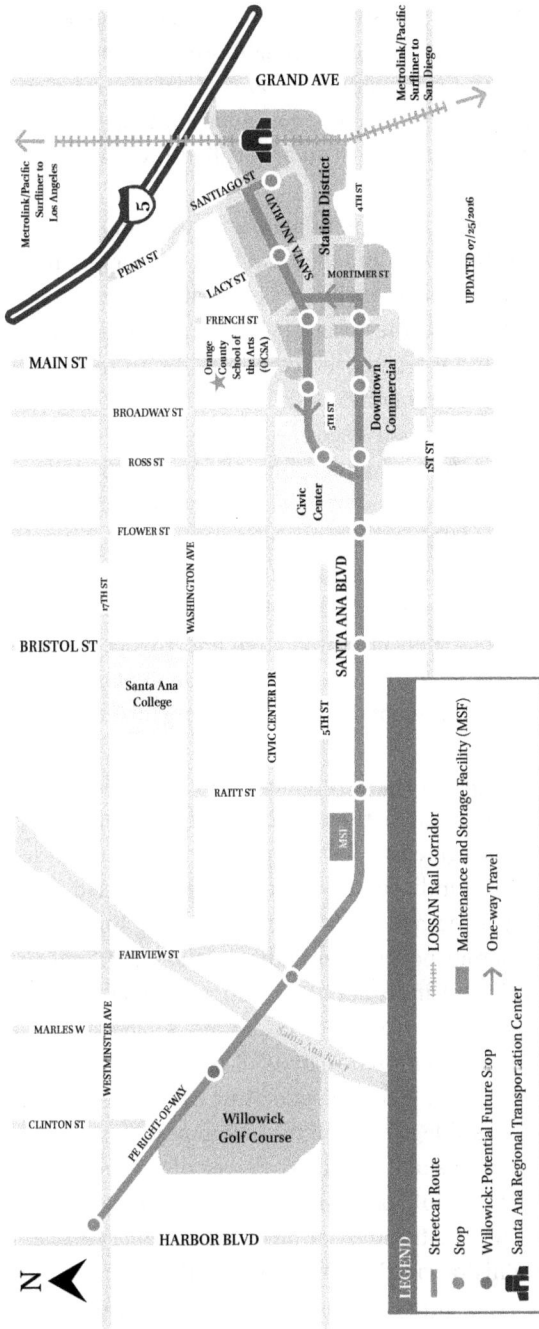

MAP 2.2   *Orange County streetcar.*

SOURCE: ORANGE COUNTY TRANSPORTATION AUTHORITY, HTTP://WWW.OCTA.NET/PROJECTS
-AND-PROGRAMS/ALL-PROJECTS/RAIL-PROJECTS/OC-STREETCAR/ (ACCESSED AUGUST 8, 2016).

development of a streetcar. The streetcar would run through an area consisting primarily of low-income immigrant neighborhoods (see map 2.2). Simultaneously, Latin@ youth face greater legal and social obstacles as the city is attempting to implement a gang injunction adjacent to the corridor through which the new transit line will run in an area called Townsend to purportedly "clean up" the neighborhood.

These efforts, we argue, are done in an attempt to entice investment and development within the city in order to increase property values of homes and businesses. The plan will intensify processes of gentrification, while benefiting private investors and the local government at the expense of poor, politically powerless, and marginalized communities. In this way, we understand "development" as a euphemism to introduce and reinforce processes of gentrification and sorting, by both race and class.

This analysis uses public sociology by combining scholarly work with community organizing at the level of local decision making (Burawoy 2005). We employ the spirit of Paulo Freire's call for liberation from the ground up (1998)—studying and writing about social issues while engaging in participatory action in the struggle for healthy and sustainable communities. For this essay, Madeleine Spencer participated and advocated in community meetings in which attendees discussed development plans and conducted interviews to elicit the sentiments of other local organizers, businesses, and residents.

We use Michel Foucault's theory of "biopower" to understand the forces of gentrification and gang injunctions that we argue are used to control urban space and certain segments of the population. Foucault described how, beginning in the eighteenth century, authorities increased techniques of maintaining order by using police forces and governing bodies within urban spaces. He cited numerous police reports that explained the requirements of city planning as significant in its ability to mitigate the effects of epidemics, revolts, and the overall preservation of important social mores of the time (Foucault 1977). This lent itself to the extended control over bodies and use of power in surveillance, which Foucault called "the microphysics of power." The state, he elaborated, was able to conceal the techniques of power and domination by invoking new forms of disciplinary power that served as mechanisms of control through the use of space and normalized procedures which were operationalized through institutions of law, government, politics, and other forms of social administration (Foucault 2003). Urban reorganization, growing inequality, and racialization of space, as seen in the case of Santa Ana, are representations of Foucault's concept of "biopower."

Sorting and Racing at the Federal, State, and Local Levels

An example of the role public policy has played in processes of gentrification, with racial implications at the federal level, is the construction of the interstate system, completed between the late 1950s and early 1970s. Historian Raymond A. Mohl documents the racial agenda behind the federal interstate system:

> When policy makers and highway engineers determined that the new interstate highway system should penetrate to the heart of the central cities, they made a fateful decision, but also a purposeful one. (2002, 1)

He states that "highway builders and downtown redevelopers had a common interest in eliminating low-income housing and ... freeing blighted areas for 'higher and better use'" (3).

At the state and local levels, one example of sorting and racing is redlining, a practice that limits access for minority groups to loans, mortgage lending, and housing (Sagawa and Segal 1999, 30). Restrictive mortgage lending programs and redlining of certain neighborhoods historically have created racially exclusive communities, and city planners have tended to neglect inner-city neighborhoods until they become aware that policy changes could yield profits (Palen and London 1984). Santa Ana is instructive in understanding these processes. This city has one of the highest concentrations of low-income households in Orange County and is the area that will be most affected by the city's proposed development plan. Its population is 80 percent Latin@, 50 percent of the residents are foreign-born, and per capita income is 16,891 dollars (substantially lower than the county's 34,550 dollars), placing it at a poverty rate of 16.5 percent (Kennedy Commission 2015). Additionally, Santa Ana has a weaker tax base than neighboring cities in the county because of high poverty levels.

The practices that initially determined Santa Ana's land use and zoning laws began in the 1900s and were cemented in the year 1927 with the inception of the city's first planning department, when codification was first written into government policies and enforced at the local level (Haas 1985). Robert A. Johnson and Charlene M. Riggens (2009) describe how, for many years, parts of Santa Ana consisted of racial covenants that were reserved for Caucasian people. These covenants emerged primarily as a byproduct of racial steering in real estate practices. Documenting city planning ordinances in the local newspaper, in 1925 the *OC Register* noted:

No person or persons other than a member of the Caucasian race shall be permitted to use or occupy any portion of said land, except a family servant.... The above mentioned conditions, covenants and restrictions shall be inserted in any deed hereinafter made, conveying any lot, piece or parcel of land front abutting upon said street.

quoted in JOHNSON and RIGGENS 2009, 13

This is a classic illustration of what M. Paloma Pavel (2009) and Fullilove (2013) have referred to in their writings as sorting and a new form of implicit rather than explicit racism expressed through the use of laws and policies that restrict urban space for certain groups. Racial spacialization also demonstrates Foucault's theory showing how planning and development agencies are used to preserve current social mores through the microphysics of power (2003; 1977).

Expansion of Migrant Groups in Santa Ana

As the need for (cheap) labor expanded when the city undertook a railroad construction project in the late 1800s, accompanied by a growing agricultural industry, Santa Ana experienced an influx of Chinese and Mexican immigrants (Gould 1995). They lived in a segregated neighborhood called Santa Anita, in part due to redlining laws and also for practical purposes as this area was close to their places of work (warehouses, industrial facilities, and agricultural centers).

Mexican and Chinese immigrants coexisted while marginalized spatially and racially from the white population in Santa Ana proper due to real estate practices that enforced segregation. This geographical breakdown of the housing in Santa Ana, along racial lines, again exemplifies Fullilove's conceptualization of sorting (2013). Through laws and city-planning development policies, migrants were forced into ethnic enclaves, living in substandard housing conditions and communities. It also embodies what several contributors to Pavel's collection (2009) describe as contemporary forms of "racing"— using space and economic segregation to reproduce forms of social inequality (Powell 2009; Shepard and Charles-Guzmán 2009; Chashin 2009). Currently, there is a relatively small Chinese population in Santa Ana (around 11 percent). This is in part because Chinatown, where the Chinese population resided, was burned down by city hall officials in 1906 amid national anti-Chinese sentiment, much of it fueled by the Chinese Exclusion Act of 1882. Most of the Chinese immigrants fled the city (Gould 1995, 10, 16). The Latin@ population continued to grow.

Resistance to Zoning Laws and Redlining

In such immigrant areas as Santa Anita and later in other areas as immigrants from Mexico continued to move into parts of Santa Ana (though still in segregated areas) that were zoned "industrial" (M2 zoning status), the housing built by residents was makeshift at best. Given the subpar living and housing conditions under legal processes of sorting and racing, many Latin@ immigrants began to challenge housing and zoning laws in the late 1970s.

One of the leaders of the early resistance movement was a longtime resident and business owner, Sam Romero. The first house he grew up in, located in the Logan neighborhood in central Santa Ana, was bought by his father in the 1930s for five hundred dollars. It was "a small shell of a house," with no heating or interior bathroom. Almost all of the homes in his neighborhood were also makeshift dwellings, lacking proper accommodations and necessities. The city tried to condemn these homes, and these Mexican families were not allowed to apply for loans to make repairs, while being redlined from purchasing homes in other areas of the city. Romero elaborates:

> The barrios were the only place where Latin@s like me were allowed to live, because the neighborhoods in Santa Ana were segregated. Logan, where I lived, was known as the worst barrio in Santa Ana. The community was zoned to have an M2 designation which meant that no banks would give out loans to fix, remodel, or rebuild our houses in that zone. So if you had a home it could be condemned by the city and there was nothing you could do about it.[1]

Residents in the neighborhood had few options to improve their living conditions (see map 2.3).

Residents turned to activism and lobbied against the city. In the late 1970s, the activism of the Logan neighborhood to combat segregated housing evolved into a community group called Santa Ana Neighborhood Organization (SANO), a group that was the inception of what in 1985 became the Orange County Congregation Community Organization (OCCCO).[2] Romero continues:

> Once we had formed SANO we began in the Logan neighborhood to fight against the city [of Santa Ana] to get the area rezoned so that folks could

---

1   Sam Romero, interview by Madeleine Spencer, May 20, 2015.

2   On the OCCCO, see http://www.occcopico.org/.

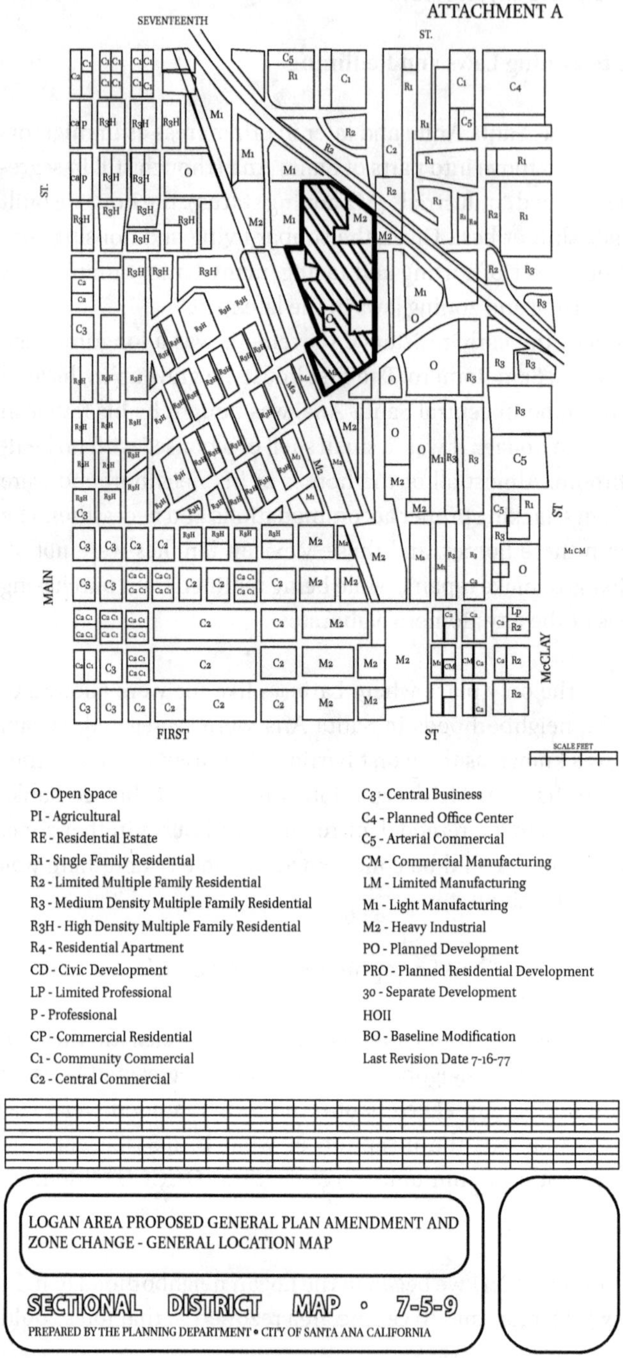

SEVENTEENTH ST.

ST.

MAIN

McCLAY

FIRST ST.

SCALE FEET

O - Open Space
PI - Agricultural
RE - Residential Estate
R1 - Single Family Residential
R2 - Limited Multiple Family Residential
R3 - Medium Density Multiple Family Residential
R3H - High Density Multiple Family Residential
R4 - Residential Apartment
CD - Civic Development
LP - Limited Professional
P - Professional
CP - Commercial Residential
C1 - Community Commercial
C2 - Central Commercial

C3 - Central Business
C4 - Planned Office Center
C5 - Arterial Commercial
CM - Commercial Manufacturing
LM - Limited Manufacturing
M1 - Light Manufacturing
M2 - Heavy Industrial
PO - Planned Development
PRO - Planned Residential Development
30 - Separate Development
HOII
BO - Baseline Modification
Last Revision Date 7-16-77

LOGAN AREA PROPOSED GENERAL PLAN AMENDMENT AND ZONE CHANGE - GENERAL LOCATION MAP

SECTIONAL DISTRICT MAP ∘ 7-5-9

PREPARED BY THE PLANNING DEPARTMENT • CITY OF SANTA ANA CALIFORNIA

MAP 2.3   *Logan arterial expansion proposal.*
SOURCE: SANTA ANA, 1977, IN PERSONAL POSSESSION
OF SAM ROMERO.

get bank loans and fix up their homes. This was the beginning of the war to change the zoning in our neighborhood. The city made it real hard for us in those days. We were in meeting after meeting till 2 a.m. in the morning working on this issue.... This was about thirty-five years ago now in the mid-1970s and this is how I got my start organizing.

In 1977, the city changed the zoning designation for the area from industrial (M2) to residential, allowing residents to get bank loans that they were previously denied. Thus, Romero notes, many homes within the Latin@ immigrant enclave were saved.[3]

These resistance efforts by SANO can be understood as ways in which individuals, through collective efforts, can and do challenge how city planners use urban space and normalized procedures (using Foucault's terminology) to segregate and control certain populations. More precisely, they illustrate how Foucault's description of the process of biopower and the normalization of control can be successfully contested.

Recent Demographic Shifts, Urban Renewal, and the Transit Line in Santa Ana

In the 1990s, Santa Ana experienced another large influx of Mexican immigrants. Between the 1970s and 1980s, the population of Latin@ immigrants in Santa Ana increased from 9 percent to 31 percent and reached 51 percent in the 1990s. One area (at the core of the new development plans for the streetcar and also at the heart of the gentrification already occurring) was transformed from a place that once symbolized white culture and commerce to one that became a thriving immigrant district known as La Calle Cuatro (Fourth Street). Latin@ shoppers throughout the city traveled to La Calle Cuatro to purchase fabrics, *quinceanera* dresses, shoes, and jewelry, as well as furniture. This area soon became one of the largest metropolises for immigrants in the United States (Gonzalez and Guaiana 2013, 538).

After the 2008 financial crisis, the demographics in Santa Ana began to shift once again as a new phase of gentrification started. The process had already begun before 2008 but was accelerated by the crisis. For example, spikes in foreclosures led to a 16 percent decline in the population of Latin@s in central Santa Ana between 2000 and 2010, and the white population grew by over 17 percent. The downtown corridor where La Calle Cuatro resides is now filled with new artist spaces and cutting-edge, or "hipster," bars and restaurants, while

---

3   Romero, interview.

working-class Latin@s have been priced out of new developments by young professionals with higher incomes. These shifts cut across both housing and businesses, and the city of Santa Ana worked with private property owners to establish a Property Based Improvement District (PBID) in the downtown corridor that tripled taxes on businesses in and around La Calle Cuatro. The Transit District neighborhoods surrounding the downtown corridor and rising prices were also forcing people out of their homes (Gonzalez and Guaiana 2013, 539).

Activists again began to mobilize, this time against what they perceived as using space to cater to economic interests of investors through property development and by raising taxes in the community. Latin@ businesses in the downtown area were failing at record rates due to the slow economy coupled with the tripled tax assessments placed on merchants as the battle waged for contested space. Perceptions of residents about what was happening downtown became conflicted, further devastating the market for Latin@ goods since Latin@s began to leave and buy their goods from big-box establishments rather than small businesses in the downtown corridor. This change in buying patterns assisted in accelerating the process of gentrification and the changes occurring in La Calle Cuatro, which for decades before had served as a metropolis for immigrants. These patterns of gentrification along the downtown corridor have sparked not only fear of displacement among residents and business owners but also anxiety over the erasure of cultural history and social memory.

What sparked the first major critique of the new development project was the introduction of the city's proposed Renaissance Plan, or what was described in the plan as "New Urbanism," in 2007 with the passage of the Sunshine Ordinance—one of the most progressive transparency laws in the nation. According to the architect,

> Santa Ana's historic center is being transformed, rectifying the urban renewal-based practices of the past 40 years that have scarred Orange County's premier city. A new Specific Plan with regulatory status was developed for the 457-acre, 135-block area that includes two Districts (Civic Center and Downtown), three Neighborhoods, and an industrial area adjacent to the most important train station between San Diego and Los Angeles. The Plan leverages the area's historic and cultural character, reaffirming Santa Ana's identity and promoting renewed private and public investments in this important Southern California center.
> MOULE & POLIZOIDES, n.d.

Within this New Urbanism, city planners strategized to implement the streetcar line (due to be in place by 2019) but without any substantial input from the approximately 330,000 residents who live in the city. The reason for the transit system, as stated by city officials, is to boost the economy, bring in new business development and tourism, and build up the otherwise "blighted" areas throughout Santa Ana. Due to disinvestment in the poorest neighborhoods of Santa Ana, where Chinese and Mexican immigrants had originally settled because of zoning laws and redlining practices, the corridor through which the transit system will run is currently filled with abandoned homes and buildings, and vacant lots.

The reference to the "scars" (or atrophy) of Santa Ana (as cited in the Renaissance Plan) is an indictment not of the population living in the city but of the city's lack of investment in an area where the demographics are largely poor, Latin@ immigrants who lack significant political influence in the city's decision making regarding the use of urban space. In fact, they have been and still are the subjects of what several authors have pointed to as processes of sorting, racing, segregation, and now gentrification (Powell 2009; Shepard and Charles-Guzmán 2009; Chashin 2009; see also Fullilove 2013). A pivotal example is shown in one of the immigrant communities that is in the direct line of the station district. This community contains over 6,000 residents, of whom 5,246 are Latin@, many of them first-generation immigrants, and the annual household median income in this community ranges from 26,125 dollars to 34,244 dollars (Kennedy Commission 2015).

An additional concern of local residents is that the streetcar does not directly serve them. For example, for purposes of going to work the line does not serve those who commute north and south from Santa Ana. It only serves government and city officials and the potential new business owners who will invest in this corridor. They travel east and west from the train station to their offices, and then have access to new public transportation to go downtown to high-end restaurants for lunch, dinner, and other leisure activities. Activists, business owners, and residents call the new transit line the "streetcar to nowhere" as it only loops around a small area of the community and is being developed at the expense of neglecting the local, low-income immigrant population that depends on the bus system for transportation to get to work (most buses that run north and south).

Representing a voice from the local area, community organizer Claudia Ramirez summarizes the situation this way: "They keep saying that the transit system is a 'game changer,' and this is true." But she states that current changes and future plans are "not favorable to the population that currently lives in the City of Santa Ana." She continues: "For example, in 2016 OCTA [Orange County Transport Authority] wants to eliminate seventeen bus routes and cut sixteen others. In a city where thousands ride buses we have serious problems."[4]

---

4   Claudia Ramirez, interview by Madeleine Spencer, December 16, 2015.

The key persistent question underlying the streetcar project is: whose interests do these recent "development" plans serve—the local community or only developers and investors.

The Relationship between the Streetcar, Gentrification, and Gang Injunctions

Critics further agree that Renaissance Plan initiatives, under the pretense of urban development, are expanding to control certain spaces, such as the Townsend neighborhood, located in central Santa Ana and one of the prime stops on the transit line. Foucault's conceptualization of "biopower"—how authorities find tools to control urban spaces and, in particular, certain segments of the population by creating and enforcing new forms of disciplinary power—is useful for understanding this problem. He argued that this is part and parcel of the microphysics of biopower by establishing, through the use of coercion and surveillance, ever-novel techniques of discipline and domination. These, Foucault asserted, are operationalized through institutions of law, governments, and politicians to normalize behavior of groups deemed as threatening to the status quo (1976, 138).

In the case of Santa Ana, as gang injunctions were designed, the city, assisted by law enforcement, set up a "safety zone," which prohibits *assumed* gang members from associating with each other. This includes standing, sitting, walking, driving, bicycling, gathering, or appearing anywhere in public view with any other defendant named in the injunction, or with any other known gang member (O'Deane 2011). Thus, gang injunctions criminalize activities that are typically legal in other jurisdictions. They indirectly serve as a form of gentrification because individuals and family members who are placed on a gang injunction are likely to move from these neighborhoods so that they can publicly associate with family members for outdoor activities—deemed illegal and subject to criminal penalties in their current neighborhood. Although research into the relationship between gang injunctions and gentrification is relatively new, researcher Aris Polanco (2009) and historian Frank Barajas (2009) have found that gang injunctions are often implemented in areas undergoing gentrification, or what Barajas refers to as "privileged adjacent" areas rather than in areas that only have a serious crime problem (395).

Another community organizer, Dylan Thompson, describes gang injunctions as communities having "an outdoor prison in their own neighborhood."[5]

---

5   Dylan Thompson, interview by Madeleine Spencer, December 8, 2015.

In addition to serving as a mechanism of biopower as delineated by Foucault, to control behavior, these police methods also create fear and threaten the mere visibility of certain groups and behaviors outside of the normative and disciplined venue of proper, normalized civic behavior.

Another part of the Renaissance Plan and streetcar project, also connected to the relationship between gang injunctions and gentrification, is the revitalization of a historical golf course called Willowick located in the Santa Anita neighborhood. It is currently a public golf course that is used by low-income Latin@s. The newest plans intend to transform the golf course into "something similar to Central Park" in New York City in order to change its reputation (Elmanhrek 2015). In other words, a space used previously by low-income Latin@s will shift to one that will provide entertainment and services for mostly white middle- and upper-class tourists or other visitors from outside of the immediate neighborhood. The streetcar conveniently runs beside the Willowick Golf Course, which makes its loop at Harbor Boulevard and connects back to the downtown corridor at La Calle Cuatro, and thus offers opportunities for tourists to play golf and enjoy recreational activities, such as fine dining, at the other newly gentrified end of the streetcar locality.

A gang injunction has for many years, beginning in the 1980s, been placed on the Santa Anita neighborhood, another example that Foucault (2004) would refer to as the manipulation of power through the use of space. While Santa Ana does have a serious problem with gang activity and violence, local resident activists along with the American Civil Liberties Union are beginning to build up case studies questioning the constitutional basis of gang injunctions, and their function. Are gang injunctions truly an attempt to reduce violence or to make certain segments of the population invisible?

Conclusion: Regaining a Voice

Redevelopment and zoning policies intended to accommodate the streetcar project and those who will benefit from it are affecting low-income and racially segregated areas in a similar way as the highway planning projects did in the 1950s. Frustrated by city officials' lack of transparency and not having their voices heard, the Latin@ community—people who have been subject to urban blight and the reproduction of power relations through urban reorganization—continue to organize at the grassroots level in order to halt the plans for the streetcar project and the gentrification processes that will be accelerated by the transit line and the newly established Townsend gang injunction (see map 2.4).

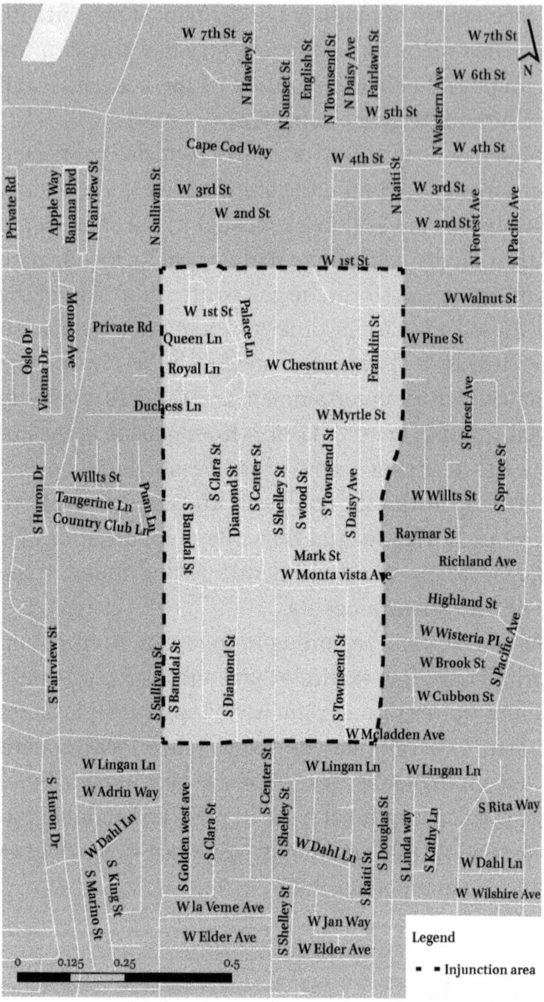

Source: Human Impact Partners

MAP 2.4   *Townsend Street gang injunction safety zone.*
SOURCE: DARÍO MACIEL AND SOPHIA SIMON-ORTIZ,
DIGNIFIED & JUST POLICING: HEALTH IMPACT ASSESS-
MENT OF THE TOWNSEND STREET GANG INJUNCTION
IN SANTA ANA, CALIFORNIA (OAKLAND, CA: HUMAN
IMPACT PARTNERS, SEPTEMBER 2015), FIGURE A1, 10,
HTTP://WWW.HUMANIMPACT. ORG/WP-CONTENT/
UPLOADS/DIGNIFIED-JUST-POLICING-HIA-2015-09-29.
PDF (ACCESSED MARCH 30, 2016).

Community activists and organizers are working to increase community awareness and provide opportunities for constructive resident engagement and community input about these three long-standing interconnected issues. Additionally, long-time business owners located in La Calle Cuatro have sent to city officials hundreds of letters opposing the transit plan, claiming that this is a marker of sorting. These kinds of planning policies at the city level have discretely sustained segregation, racing, and sorting as they reproduce the spatio-political reproduction of power relations and further marginalize poor and immigrant communities. This is done through the microphysics of power which is very discreet and has been continuously carried out through formal institutions of government.

Foucault's theory of biopower and the microphysics of power (2003) accompanied by Fullilove's (2013) and others' research on contemporary processes of racing and sorting are useful in understanding the case study of Santa Ana and its urban renewal strategy (Powell 2009; Shepard and Charles-Guzmán 2009; Chashin 2009). Control, discipline, surveillance, and fear are tools that are profitable for the city and for investors and developers but have a devastating impact on communities.

Yet, throughout the last several decades, new forms of control and disciplinary power have necessitated resistance. The fight of residents (who later created the broader community group SANO) to change the zoning laws in the Logan neighborhood, shifting the status from industrial to residential, is similar to the way that local community groups are currently challenging new forms of disciplinary and discriminatory government policies. These government efforts shape and develop the urban environment in a manner that reproduces old power relations, which continue to create even more segregated communities, while development plans are continually disguised in planning language that falsely heralds what for residents cannot be considered an urban "Renaissance."

Bibliography

Barajas, Frank. 2009. An invading army: A civil gang injunction in a Southern California Chicana/o community. *Latino Studies* 5, no. 4:393–417.

Burawoy, Michael. 2005. For public sociology. *American Sociological Review* 70, no. 1:4–28.

Chashin, Sheryll. 2009. Race, class, and real estate. In Pavel 2009, 59–66.

Elmanhrek, Adam. 2015. Now it's Santa Ana's turn to dream of great park. *Voice of OC*, October 16. http://voiceofoc.org/2015/10/santa-ana-wants-to-turn-willowick-golf-course-into-big-park/.

Foucault, Michel. 1976. *The history of sexuality*. New York, NY: Penguin.

Foucault, Michel. 1977. *Discipline and punish: The birth of the prison*. London: Penguin.

Foucault, Michel. 2003 *"Society must be defended": Lectures at the Collège de France 1975–1976*. Trans. David Macey. New York, NY: Picador.

Foucault, Michel. 2004. *Security, territory, population: Lectures at the Collège de France 1977–1978*. Trans. Graham Burchell. New York, NY: Palgrave Macmillan.

Freire, Paulo. 1998. *Pedagogy of freedom*. Lanham, MD: Rowman and Littlefield.

Fullilove, Mindy Thompson. 2013. *Urban alchemy: Restoring joy in America's sorted-out cities*. New York, NY: New Village Press.

Gonzalez, Erualdo Romero, and Lorena Guaiana. 2013. Culture-led downtown regeneration or cultural gentrification. In *The Routledge companion to urban regeneration*, ed. Michael E. Leary and John McCarthy, 536–47. New York, NY: Routledge.

Gould, Steven. 1995. *The burning of Santa Ana's Chinatown and the murder of Anaheim's Mock Law Fat*. Hollywood, CA: Sundance Press.

Haas, Mary Elizabeth. 1985. The barrios of Santa Ana: Community, class, and urbanization, 1850–1947. PhD diss., University of California, Irvine.

Johnson, Robert A., and Charlene M. Riggens. 2009. *A different shade of Orange: Voices of Orange County, California, black pioneers*. Fullerton, CA: Center for Oral and Public History.

Kennedy Commission. 2015. Kennedy Commission report. Unpublished report. Irvine, CA.

Mohl, Raymond A. 2002. The interstates and the cities: Highways, housing, and the freeway revolt. Research report. Poverty and Race Research Action Council. http://www.prrac.org/pdf/mohl.pdf.

Moule & Polizoides, Architects and Urbanists. n.d. Santa Ana renaissance specific plan. http://www.mparchitects.com/site/projects/santa-ana-renaissance-specific-plan.

O'Deane, Matthew D. 2011. *Gang injunctions and abatement: Using civil remedies to curb gang related crimes*. Boca Raton, FL: CRC Press.

Palen, J. John, and Bruce London. 1984. *Gentrification, displacement, and neighborhood revitalization*. Albany, NY: State University of New York Press.

Pavel, M. Paloma, ed. 2009. *Breakthrough communities: Sustainability and justice in the next American metropolis*. Cambridge, MA: MIT Press.

Polanco, Aris. 2009. Spatial analysis of the relationship between gang injunctions and gentrification in San Francisco. Unpublished study.

Powell, John A. 2009. Reinterpreting metropolitan space as a strategy for social justice. In Pavel 2009, 23–32.

Sagawa, Shirley, and Eli Segal. 1999. *Common interest, common good: Creating value through business and social sector partnerships*. Boston, MA: Harvard Business Press.

Shepard, Peggy M., and Kizzy Charles-Guzmán. 2009. The roots of environmental justice. In Pavel 2009, 35–48.

CHAPTER 3

The Politics of Immigration and a Catholic Counternarrative: A Perspective from the United States

Kristin E. Heyer

I begin with a testimony from a recent graduate of my previous university, Santa Clara University, José Arreola, who spoke out courageously on National Public Radio a few summers ago in a series called *My Life Is True*.

> We had to decide whether we were going north or south to get into California. My friend decided it was best to go south, to avoid a big snow-storm up north. But south would take us through Arizona. I really, really didn't want to go through Arizona.
>
> I got more and more nervous. I felt paralyzed. My friend kept asking me what my problem was. Finally, I told him: I'm undocumented. I came to the United States when I was three with my family. And Arizona had just passed a law that gave police officers the authority to check people's immigration status. If we got stopped in Arizona, I could be detained and deported.
>
> My friend is white. He comes from a really privileged, upper-class background. He attended a private high school, then Santa Clara University, with me. I went on scholarship. Politically, he sees things a little differently than I do. We've had our disagreements.
>
> He was quiet for a while.
>
> Then, he barraged me with questions. I answered the best that I could. Silence again.
>
> Then he told me about his grandfather, how he hadn't been able to find work in Ireland, so he decided to hop on a fishing boat, and get off in New York. He worked as a janitor, without citizenship. Now his son, my friend's father, is a high-ranking bank executive.
>
> The whole time, through Arizona, my friend drove, like, 50 miles an hour. He didn't even wanna change lanes. He told me he wasn't gonna lose his best friend. He wasn't gonna let that happen.
>
> The immigration debate became real to my friend in the car that day. We had a very different conversation than the one politicians are having

right now. The minute actual undocumented immigrants are included, the conversation changes.

Now, I'm completely open about my status. I'm still afraid. Conversations don't always go well. And it's always a risk. But as long as I remain in the shadows, I will never really get to know you, and you will never really know me.

ARREOLA 2011

José's courage, together with the resilience of so many others, points to enduring hope. Taking the migrant's side as our own changes our perception, with implications for political discourse, policy reforms, and ecclesial practices. Experiences wherein questions of citizenship and enforcement tactics take on flesh and blood have shaped my reflections about the Christian narrative in light of migration and globalization.

The path of migrants en route to the United States, from Mexico and Central America in particular, remains paved by suffering and death, despite unprecedented fortification and search-and-rescue operations. The death toll of migrants crossing the deserts of Arizona has steadily mounted even as crossings decline. Since 1998, there have been more than six thousand confirmed deaths and those working in the desert estimate that the number is five to ten times higher (Brian and Laczko 2014, 24). Amid the pervasive scripts and misinformation that cloud the exploitation of immigrants, a Catholic ethic of kinship across borders offers guideposts along the journey from exclusion to solidarity. The realities shaping the "choice" to flee one's country highlight the shortcomings of individualistic paradigms, of absolutist categories, and of approaches that flatly criminalize irregular migrants (as in, "what part of illegal don't you understand?"). Talking points that emphasize scarce resources, scheming lawbreakers, or demographic threats fail to register the social contexts that compel migration and its harmful consequences: ruptured family lives and border deaths.

In this chapter, I use both theological and sociological lenses to present current issues surrounding the immigration debate. Public sociology (Burawoy 2005) allows for such a venue of dialogue because it lends itself to a holistic and interdisciplinary approach to societal concerns, creating partnerships between scholars and community activists and citizens to work toward social justice. At the heart of this is political theorist Antonio Gramsci's idea of the "organic intellectual" (1971), engaged in both academics and the community. As sociologist Patricia Hill Collins confirms (2013, 36), this kind of engagement is critical to a genuine understanding of the social reality as lived by others, and by embracing empathy and compassion, it allows for a radical departure from the neutrality so often prioritized within the ivory tower. In essence, this new approach favors a common understanding and purpose.

Sociologist Michael Burawoy (2005, 12) also espouses the importance of counternarratives that challenge what we hear from mainstream media and political pundits, while simultaneously rejecting the often self-imposed political and social indifference among many scholars. Critical theorist Edward Said stated:

> You do not want to appear too political; you are afraid of seeming controversial;... you want to keep a reputation for being balanced, objective, moderate.... For an intellectual these habits of mind are corrupting *par excellence*. (1994, 100–101)

I also employ sociologist C. Wright Mills's "sociological imagination" perspective (1959): understanding personal troubles as political issues, which is helped by hearing voices from the victims.

In the spirit of Gramsci, Collins, Burawoy, Said, and Mills, this essay gives a human face to immigration struggles so often overlooked by scholars and policymakers. I argue that to truly understand immigration complexities we need informed and intelligent debate rooted in empirical research, which can integrate theory and praxis.

Immigration from a Faith-Based Lens

The regional juxtaposition of relative luxury and misery while basic needs go unmet challenges basic notions of distributive justice. The nearly two-thousand-mile U.S.–Mexico border, spanning six Mexican and four U.S. states, bisects the sharpest divide in average income on the planet. The impact of free trade agreements and utterly outmoded visa policies impede rather than empower persons' active participation in societal life (social justice). A Christian ethic of immigration demands basic, unmet responsibilities in justice, particularly given the role the United States has played in shaping conditions that directly contribute to irregular migration (Hoeffner and Pistone 2009, 74).[1] In short, justice for immigrants will not be achieved by pursuing market or security concerns alone.

Once people do immigrate, the Catholic tradition profoundly critiques patterns wherein stable receiving countries accept the labor of millions without

---

1   For an excellent discussion of such connections, see O'Neill (2009).

offering legal protections. Such "shadow" societies risk the creation of a permanent underclass, harming both human dignity and the common good. From Pope Leo XIII's 1891 warnings against employers' exploitation through Pope Francis's condemnations of harmful global economic practices, the protection of human dignity has remained the central criterion of economic justice. The tradition makes clear that "every economic decision and institution must be judged in light of whether it protects or undermines [human dignity] realized in community with others" (National Conference of Catholic Bishops 1986a, nos. 1, 14). Pope John Paul II condemned the exploitation of migrant workers based on the principle that capital should be at the service of labor and not labor at the service of capital. This idea that the economy should serve the person raises serious concerns not only about the freedom of markets compared to people but also about the significant financial stakes in the broken immigration system—detained immigrants fill beds, deportations fill private buses.

So we also inherit a counternarrative of economic ethics critiquing global dynamics that allow capital, goods, and information, but not laborers, to flow freely across borders as well as critiquing the concrete treatment of undocumented laborers. Pope Francis (2013a) has been outspoken about the dictatorship of faceless economies that remain distant from humane goals; his image of humans as commodities in a throwaway culture particularly resonates with vulnerable migrant workers' experiences. The Southern Poverty Law Center recently interviewed 150 undocumented women across various sectors of the food industry, and respondents overwhelmingly reported "feeling like they were seen by their employers as disposable workers with no lasting value, to be squeezed of every last drop of sweat and labor before being cast aside" (2010, 23). Hence the Catholic social tradition explicitly protects the basic human rights of undocumented migrants in host countries in light of longstanding teachings on human and workers' rights, which do not depend on citizenship status.

Furthermore, with more than 60 percent of undocumented immigrants in the United States having lived here for over ten years and two million undocumented students in primary and secondary schools across the country, a "double society" increasingly threatens the common good, "one visible with rights and one invisible without rights—a voiceless underground of undocumented persons" (National Conference of Catholic Bishops, 1986b, 10). Obstructing viable paths to legalization for the majority of immigrants welcomed in the marketplace but not the voting booth, college campus, Department of Motor Vehicles, or stable workplace risks making permanent this underclass of disenfranchised persons, undermining not only Christian commitments but also significant civic values and interests. Ultimately an approach rooted in human rights championed by Catholic commitments must both reduce the need to migrate and protect those who find themselves compelled to do so as a last resort.

Patterns of migration across scripture do not readily resolve complex modern dilemmas but contributions from scripture and the Catholic social tradition do offer a counternarrative of civic kinship that challenges dominant, instrumentalist frameworks as scripture shapes moral perception. By engaging the voice of scripture in a manner that dislocates dominant frameworks of interpretation, we become attuned to how our perspective affects our moral response and how scripture might enhance our perceptive imagination. For example, flowing from its scriptural "optic nerve" of compassion (Spohn 2000, 87), the Catholic social tradition champions robust rights for immigrants in its documents, outreach, witness, and advocacy. For example, 2013 marked the tenth anniversary of the Mexican and U.S. bishops' joint pastoral "Strangers No Longer: Together on the Journey of Hope." The joint bishops' conferences called for the United States and Mexico to address root causes of and legal avenues for migration and to safeguard family unity; by contrast, border enforcement has remained the primary focus in the U.S. context. The consequent deportation-by-attrition practices and removal quotas have nevertheless failed to resolve the problem of a significant undocumented presence.

Recent History and Backlash against Migrants Masked under the "Rule of Law"

Over the past forty years, the number of international migrants worldwide more than doubled, and the United States remains the world's leading destination for immigrants. U.S. residents are increasingly confronted with newcomers. Across the United States, some reactions reflect the nation's historic openness to immigrants, and others reflect its deep ambivalence about "outsiders." The number of agents stationed at the border has quintupled over the past two decades and spending on enforcement has increased fifteen-fold since 1986 (the last time Congress overhauled U.S. immigration policy) with the United States spending more today on immigration enforcement than all other enforcement activities of the federal government combined (American Immigration Lawyers Association 2007). Even with bipartisan signals toward reform in the past year, legitimate concerns regarding disproportionate burdens on local services and the need to set workable limits understandably persist. At the same time, mounting threats to human dignity indicate the urgency of overhauling the system.

Despite significantly beefed up fortification, the recent increase in arrivals of unaccompanied minors and family units from Honduras, El Salvador, and Guatemala rekindled fears of a "border out of control." For example, "less than 48 hours after the nation collectively chanted 'USA!' for the national soccer team in the World Cup [in July 2014], a much smaller group of Americans in Murrieta, California," coupled the same rally cry with chants of "Return to Sender," "Save Our Children from Diseases," and "Bus Illegal Children to White House." The protesters employed the slogan to turn back busloads of Central American youth destined for a new detention center in their community. Chants of "USA" evoke noble and ignoble sides of American patriotism (Garcia 2014).

This immigrant nation's "celebratory narrative" underscores ideas like hospitality, liberty, and democracy, exhibited in Emma Lazarus's poignant words in "The New Colossus," "give me your tired, your poor, your huddled masses yearning to breathe free." Yet legislative debates about immigration have historically centered on issues of national security, economic instrumentalism, and social costs rather than human rights. Today policy debates remain framed by a law-and-order lens, which casts unauthorized immigrants as willful lawbreakers, posing national security threats. A criminal rhetorical frame facilitates scapegoating immigrants as threats to the rule of law, without evoking skepticism about outdated policies, such as the considerable mismatch between labor needs and legal avenues for pursuing work. For example, in 2009, the Council on Foreign Relations' task force on U.S. immigration policy noted that over the first decade of the twenty-first century approximately eight hundred thousand undocumented immigrants arrived per year with the large majority finding employment, which indicates that the legal migration system "has not remotely reflected market demand" (2009, 50).

The rule of law rightly occupies a privileged place in our country, yet I was struck during my visit to an Operation Streamline hearing in Tucson, Arizona, by the sharp contrast between our law-and-order rhetoric on the one hand, and the lack of accountability or transparency in border patrol procedures on the other, as well as a lack of due process afforded immigrant detainees. Operation Streamline operates on the basis of fast-track prosecutions and group hearings, sometimes over one hundred per day, and many sentencings being ordered in one day without due process. I watched young men and women shackled at the wrist, midsection, and ankles collectively herded through the legal process, lacking sufficient time with an attorney to comprehend what was happening and several lacking adequate translation. One of the ironies is that migrants from Honduras flee a home with the world's highest number of homicides per capita where gang members murder with impunity—the threat driving many such migrants is precisely the breakdown of the rule of law at home (Overseas Security Advisory Council 2015).

Immigration "Threats": Myths or Reality?

Another common paradigm deems newcomers economic threats, whether as a net burden on the tax base or as competitors for finite social resources and low-wage work opportunities, a perception heightened in times of economic downturn. Studies consistently show that immigrant laborers provide a net benefit to the U.S. economy. In addition, the detention industry profits off of irregular migrants and confounds the "economic threat" frame. At a press event in the midst of congressional reform debates in June 2013, for instance, Congressman Randy Weber from Texas insisted that "you don't get to come here and be 'takers,'" even in the face of the Congressional Budget Office study that week which found that the reform package would reduce the federal debt by 197 billion dollars in the next decade and 700 billion dollars in the following decade and estimated that "newly legalized immigrants would generate more tax revenue than they expend in federal benefits" (Narea 2013). Moreover, elements of the "immigration industrial complex" have become a transnational, multibillion dollar affair.[2] Share prices of leading private corrections management provider Corrections Corporation of America spiked sharply in the summer of 2014, with the influx of migrant children crossing the border in light of improved occupancy across their federal "real estate portfolios" (Flatow 2014).

A related lens is the perceived threat newcomers pose to a nation's identity, as evident in the face of resurgent nationalistic responses across diverse regions. In the United States, anti-immigrant sentiment rooted in this construal of a fixed national identity over and above an "outsider" has led to the demonization of populations of color through increasingly mainstream outlets—the United States saw a 40 percent increase in anti-Hispanic hate crimes between 2003 and 2007 (Hsu 2009). A political science study in 2008 tracked significant differences in white voter anxiety over news stories featuring immigrants José Sanchez and Nikolai Vandinsky (Brader, Valentino, and Suhay 2008). The politics of exclusion continue to play out in the ongoing debates about executive

---

2   See Golash-Boza (2009) for a genealogy of this idea, which alludes to the conflation of national security with immigration law enforcement and "the confluence of public and private sector interests in the criminalization of undocumented migration, immigration law enforcement, and the promotion of 'anti-illegal' rhetoric" (295).

action following the 2016 presidential election. On the whole, these frameworks reflect legitimate concerns regarding the current status of immigration, but employed on their own, they serve to distort and eclipse fundamental features of the whole picture.

There emerged great hope and expectation that these frameworks would dramatically change after the initial election of President Barack Obama, hailed by many in immigrant rights communities as nearly messianic. However, he backed off promises to overhaul immigration reform once elected to address the recession and health-care reform. He built a mixed record on immigration during his two terms in office. Whereas the Obama administration's approach replaced the large-scale employee-targeted ambushes with company audits, his deportations exceeded any administration's in history.[3] Although the Obama administration's moves to provide prosecutorial discretion and deferred action for certain childhood arrivals had been lauded by immigrant rights communities, its Secure Communities program "use[d] the fingerprints of people in custody for other reasons to identify deportable immigrants" (Slevin 2010).

Whereas the number of unaccompanied youth arrivals has decreased for now (their arrival to the United States thwarted by aggressive efforts by the Mexican government to close the southern Mexico border and by raids of trains by Mexican immigration authorities—the primary means that immigrants were using to reach the United States), recent polls show diminishing trust in the Obama administration's handling of immigration (Chishti and Hipsman 2014). With both the Republican and Democratic parties distancing themselves from the administration on the issue where contested 2014 midterm races factored, nativist rhetoric returned to the scene playing on familiar fears. The Tea Party Patriots launched a major new campaign that warns:

> An unprecedented wave of illegal immigration is washing over America today, threatening the very fabric of our nation. The Obama Administration refuses to enforce our immigration laws, resulting in tens of thousands of people illegally entering the US. Rather than securing our border, President Obama leaves it wide open, and instead of returning illegal immigrants to their home nation, our government is

---

3   The pace of company audits roughly quadrupled since President George W. Bush's final year in office. The Obama administration moved away from using work-site raids to target employers. In August 2011, the administration introduced new guidelines for the use of prosecutorial discretion in deportation case review, potentially suspending deportation proceedings against those who pose little threat to national security or public safety.

sending them to our hometowns. This isn't just a crisis for citizens who live in southern border states. Today, we all live in a border state. (Tea Party Patriots, n.d.)

As this essay goes to press, fears of an influx of immigrants and refugees have only intensified in the wake of global developments, with early signals from the Trump administration reflecting similar concerns about threats to security and the need to refuse entry to keep Americans safe.

Family Issues: Women and Children as Exceptionally Vulnerable

As unaccompanied women undertake the journey in increasing numbers (about half of migrants worldwide are female), they face unique threats, from sexual assault by smugglers and officials to harassment on the job and manipulation in detention facilities. Additionally, in terms of the recent "surge" of migration, El Salvador and Guatemala rank in the top three for highest homicides against women and girls in the world (Geneva Declaration Secretariat 2015, cited in United Nations High Commissioner for Refugees [UNHCR] 2015, 2). Less likely to qualify for employment-based immigration than men, migrant women overwhelmingly work in unregulated jobs in the informal sector. Undocumented women are often perceived by predators as "perfect victims" of sexual assault: they remain isolated, are uninformed about their rights, and are presumed to lack credibility. Beyond well-founded fears that reporting abuses will risk job loss and family separation via deportation, such women lack access to legal resources and face language barriers and cultural pressures (Capps et al. 2003, 42).

Returning to the issue of "choices" regarding leaving one's home country and going to an unknown locality and culture, migrant women frequently cite family reunification as their primary motive for migrating. Today 16.5 million people in the United States live in "mixed-status families." Last year, United States Immigration and Customs Enforcement (ICE) removed 72,410 immigrants who reported they had U.S.-born children (Foley 2014). In the aftermath of detention or deportation, families face major economic instability, and affected children suffer poor health and behavioral outcomes. Such foreseeable consequences violate fundamental norms regarding human dignity and care for the vulnerable. Escalating enforcement mechanisms continue to dismantle trust between immigrant and law enforcement communities, risking unreported crimes. Consider also the unique conditions facing women and children as they cross the border. Nearly half of unaccompanied minors entering the United States report experiencing violence or threats by gangs, drug cartels, or state actors (UNHCR 2014, 6). As a result, from 2011 to 2014, the number of unaccompanied children crossing the U.S. border has doubled annually (UNHCR 2015, 2). Smuggling networks profit from these lower-risk passengers who frequently turn themselves in upon crossing.

Families comprise our most intimate relationships such that protracted separation threatens our very human subjectivity. Policies that undermine family unity frustrate this core relationally. Theologian Ada María Isasi-Díaz characterizes *la familia* as the central institution in Latin@ culture, noting it functions as a duty, a support system, and a primary identity marker (2010, 181). Hence for those migrant women whose agency is caught up in motherhood, the inability to provide for or reunite with children can fracture integrity in profound ways.

A Humanistic Perspective: Lens from Faith-Based Groups as Counternarrative

As noted earlier, operative lenses shaping the immigration debate can mask realities and can become surrogates for other cultural and political concerns. The voices of reluctant or desperate migrants rarely register in national debates about border-control policy or visa quotas or scrutinize dominant rhetoric and shed light on the interests and values that principally drive immigration policy. So if the conventional politics of immigration are driven in large part by instrumental values, what might a "scriptural" politics of immigration prioritize in shaping a Catholic counternarrative? If fear and profit largely hold sway, dehumanizing newcomers, according to these dominant scripts, I suggest the Catholic tradition's commitments shape a different story, a (counter)narrative of our common humanity, our kinship, with implications for a just immigration ethic. Christian understandings of what it means to be human radically critique pervasive exploitation and prevailing immigration paradigms.

Hebrew and Christian scriptures are replete with examples of displaced families, revealing a pattern not unlike what we encounter today:

> Families are forced to uproot themselves, leaving behind their homes, their relatives and friends, the security of their lands and their provisions, the familiarity of their language and support of their communities.
>
> SANCHEZ 1981, 19–20

A Christian family ethic offers significant resources for reorienting the immigration paradigm in several constructive ways: its profoundly relational anthropology, the family as "domestic church" and mediator of covenantal love, and the family's social mission.

Catholic social thought integrates a family's intimate communion with its charge to mutually engage the broader social good. If families serve as basic cells of civil society—"schools of deeper humanity"—social conditions must protect their participation in the demands and benefits of the common good. Deprivation of dignified labor opportunities and traumatic enforcement mechanisms signify hostile social forces impeding immigrant families' access to social goods.

Despite intermittent family values rhetoric on U.S. political and religious scenes, a relational anthropology confronts a culture with a primarily individualistic ethos that does not value caregiving labor. The credo in *el Norte* (the North) that we pull up our bootstraps and make our own fate is as entrenched as it is incompatible with a solidaristic idea that we share each other's fate. A Christian understanding of humans as interdependent critiques migrant exploitation at personal, policy, and cultural levels.

Certainly the story of the Jewish and Christian pilgrim communities is one of migration, diaspora, and the call to live accordingly. Indeed, after the commandment to worship one God, no moral imperative is repeated more frequently in the Hebrew scriptures than the command to care for the stranger.[4] Despite convenient amnesia in our own nation of immigrants,

> it was Israel's own bitter experience of displacement that undergirded its ethic of just compassion toward outsiders: "You shall not wrong or oppress a resident alien, for you were aliens in the land of Egypt" (Ex 22:21).
> MYERS and COLWELL 2012, 15

When Joseph, Mary, and Jesus flee to Egypt, the émigré holy family becomes the archetype for every refugee family (Pope Pius XII 1952b, introduction). In Matthew's Gospel,

> Jesus begins his early journey as a migrant and a displaced person—Jesus who in this same gospel would radically identify with the "least" and make hospitality to the stranger a criterion of judgment (Mt 25:35).
> SENIOR 2008, 23

Hebrew and Christian scriptures are replete not only with injunctions regarding hospitality to strangers but also with examples of families uprooted and

---

4 See, for example, O'Neill (2007, 113). O'Neill cites Plaut (1996, esp. 20–21). For a comprehensive discussion of New Testament themes related to migration, see Senior (2008).

migrating: Abraham is called forth from his homeland to establish a great nation of peoples in the Promised Land; Jacob's family migrates from Israel to Egypt due to the great famine; Moses leads the Israelites' exodus from Egypt in search of religious and political freedom; and Mary and Joseph flee their home in Palestine into Egypt, seeking asylum from religious and political oppression.

One of the most persistently recurrent themes in scripture is justice and compassion for the vulnerable (Spohn 2000, 76). The prophets repeatedly connect bringing justice for the poor to experiencing God ("He judged the cause of the poor and needy.... Is not this to know me? says the Lord" [Jer 22:16]). Concern for the economically vulnerable echoes throughout the New Testament as well, particularly in the Gospel of Luke, which depicts Jesus being born in a stable among mere shepherds and as inaugurating his public ministry in terms that emphasize his mission to bring good news to the poor and release the oppressed. New Testament scholar Donald Senior notes that in

> the overall landscape of the gospel stories, the rich and powerful are often "in place"—reclining at table, calculating their harvest, standing comfortably in the front of the sanctuary, or seated on the judgment seat passing judgment on the crimes of others. The poor, on the other hand, are often mobile or rootless: the sick coming from the four corners of the compass seeking healing; the crowds desperate to hear Jesus, roaming lost and hungry; the leper crouched outside the door. (2000, 27–28)

Senior suggests that the mobility and experiences of migrant people "reveal a profound dimension of all human experience" and "challenge the false ideologies of unlimited resources ... of unconditional national sovereignty, and the absolute claim to individual satisfaction that," in his words, "plague our contemporary world and choke its spiritual capacity" (29).

Although the scriptures do not provide detailed solutions to current economic and social challenges posed by immigration, "for people who turn to the Scriptures for guidance on how to live and what sort of people to become, it is clear they should show a deep concern for poor" and marginalized persons (Vogt 2012, 253). A concern for biblical justice (Donahue 2005, 15), which demands active concern for the vulnerable and prophetic critique of structures of injustice, challenges approaches to immigration driven by market or security concerns alone. A key contribution a scriptural imagination offers, then, is to bring perspectives of the most vulnerable and often silenced into the equation.

In the parable of the Good Samaritan, Jesus identifies neighbor, love, and just living with care for the vulnerable stranger among us. Recall that Jesus reverses the lawyer's expectations with the story of a perceived enemy's loving response to one in need lying in the ditch. Jewish audiences would have been shocked to hear of a discredited priest and a Samaritan exemplar. In the parable, the priest and the Levite notice the wounded man yet "keep their distance to avoid any contact that might defile them." Unlike the Samaritan who sees the man as a fellow human being in distress, the others do not allow themselves to be affected by his plight. By sharp contrast, the Samaritan "apprehends the situation as the man in the ditch experiences it." Typical of Jesus's parables where the "extraordinary keeps breaking out of the ordinary," the Samaritan "surpasses the care that would be appropriate for a fellow countryman to aid this stranger, who might belong to his ethnic group's worst enemies." Hence as moral theologian William C. Spohn notes, "Jesus stretches the limits of vision and compassion precisely where fear, enmity and inconvenience want to constrict them" (2000, 90, 91).

How might this parable where Jesus exposes the lawyer's categories as "too cramped" shape imagination about immigration? Posing the lawyer's very question of "who is my neighbor?" erects boundaries between members and outsiders. We quickly remove ourselves from the scene to balance (abstract) duties and obligations. Perceptions of immigrants as threats alone significantly influence immigration analyses. This prior question of perception shapes our assessment: Whom do we see as the immigrant? Freeloaders who take advantage of American generosity while taking jobs from U.S. citizens? Threats to the neighborhood? Outsiders overcrowding our kids' schools? The student whose narrative I recounted?

If we "see" the face of immigration as "illegal," anchor babies and forever foreigners, or if we "see" separated mothers, displaced third-generation small family farmers, taxpayers, or honest workers, we pursue different avenues of analysis. In other words, utilizing Mills's conceptualization of the sociological imagination (1959), seeing immigrants' humanity as primary does not resolve conflicting claims over stretched resources or absolve cases of immigrant crime. Yet it does foreclose on death-dealing and profiteering practices and invite us away from simplistic scapegoating, toward lasting solutions. To get at root causes and complex motives, like the Samaritan, we must identify with and become neighbor to the immigrant (Spohn 2000, 91).

Compassion as a Platform for Social Justice

Jesus repeatedly serves as both host and guest across gospel narratives. He "preaches a radical hospitality to those in need, and ... commands the same of anyone hoping to sit down at the messianic banquet" (McCormick 2004, 47). Gospel hospitality is unqualified in nature, and its issuance converts lives, including the lives of a despised tax collector, an estranged Samaritan woman, or the exiled blind, even as it provokes animosity and criticism (Schaab 2008, 192–93). Taking the victim's side as our own enjoins not only compassion but also liberation. Just as the Good Samaritan promises additional recompense to the innkeeper, Christians are called to enter the world of the neighbor and "leave it in such a way that the neighbor is given freedom along with the very help that is offered" (Donahue 1988, 133).[5] The "unfreedom" of present and would-be migrants pointedly illustrates the urgency of this responsibility. The radical hospitality that informs our vision does not reduce the immigration paradigm to charity or largesse, or move it out of the inclusive civic conversation; it requires justice. An ethic marked by compassion interprets situations from the perspective of those who suffer, inviting solidarity instead of exclusion.

In July 2013, Pope Francis modeled a gospel of hospitality that counters immigrant injustice. During his first official trip outside of Rome since his election in March, the pope celebrated mass on Lampedusa, an island in the southern Mediterranean that has become a safe haven for African migrants seeking passage to Europe. There he commemorated in ritual and word the estimated twenty thousand African immigrants who have died over the past twenty-five years trying to reach a new life in Europe. Pope Francis's homily noted the pervasive idolatry that facilitates migrants' deaths and robs us of the ability to weep. In vestments of penitential violet, the pope celebrated mass within sight of the "graveyard of wrecks" (Hooper 2013). Amid his admission that even he remains "disoriented," and his plea for the grace to weep, he did not merely condemn "the world" for this indifference and its consequences, but repented: "Forgive us Lord!" whether for being closed in on our own well-being in a way that leads to anesthesia of the heart or for making global decisions creating situations that lead to these tragedies (Pope Francis 2013b). Pope Francis's reflections and symbolism underscore the need for ecclesial and civic repentance from complicity in injustice.

Hence, attitudes and policies that compel and then punish irregular migration are profoundly at odds with Christian commitments. In particular, the Christian tradition's understanding of human rights and the political community squarely challenges the fact that the vast majority of contributing

---

5 I am indebted to Christopher Vogt's work for this reference.

and vulnerable migrants remain excluded from a viable, timely path to citizenship and its protections (Pope Pius XII 1952a; Pope John XXIII 1963; Pope Paul VI 1967; Second Vatican Council 1965, nos. 69, 71; see also *Catechism of the Catholic Church* 2000, no. 2402). Returning to the U.S. context, the "unfreedom" immigrants experience fundamentally stems from their exclusion from membership in society. Undocumented immigrants remain deprived of the primary good of membership, or, in political theorist Hannah Arendt's terms, "right to have rights" (Arendt 1966, Chap. 9).

Conclusion

A Christian immigration ethic is grounded in its vision of the person as inherently sacred and made for community. All persons are created in the image of God and therefore worthy of inherent dignity and respect. Whereas this vision does not compromise autonomy, it understands humans as profoundly interdependent. Therefore human rights are claims to goods necessary for each to participate with dignity in community life (Himes and Himes 1993, 46). Catholic principles of economic and migration ethics protect not only civil and political rights but also more robust social and economic rights and responsibilities. These establish persons' rights *not to migrate* (fulfill human rights in their homeland) and *to migrate* (if they cannot support themselves or their families in their country of origin) (Pope John XXIII 1963, no. 106; see also United States Conference of Catholic Bishops 2003, nos. 34–35). Once people do immigrate, the Catholic tradition profoundly critiques patterns wherein stable receiving countries accept the labor of millions without offering legal protections. Such "shadow" societies risk the creation of a permanent underclass, harming both human dignity and the common good.

An operative value hierarchy prioritizing capital to persons diametrically opposes Christian values and is as subtly formative as it is harmful to families. From Pope Paul VI's concern for the survival of children and well-being of families in light of international development, through Pope Francis's lament that we have forgotten how to weep for young men and women migrating to support family members who meet death en route, Catholic social teaching decries systems that deny basic goods to families in the name of economic instrumentalism (Pope Paul VI 1967, no. 80; Kington 2013). Beyond a critique of economic idolatry, the sanctity and social mission of the family developed in Christian ethics reorient immigration stakes away from deportation quotas or political calculations.

Bibliography

American Immigration Lawyers Association (AILA). 2007. AILA resource guide: Making the case for comprehensive immigration reform. AILA Doc. No. 07022172, February 27. http://www.aila.org/resourceguide.

Arendt, Hannah. 1966. *The origins of totalitarianism.* New York, NY: Harcourt, Brace & World.

Arreola, José. 2011. Get to know me. In *My life is true.* National Public Radio/KQED Radio, Friday, July 8, 7:35 a.m. http://www.kqed.org/a/perspectives/R201107080735.

Brader, Ted, Nicholas A. Valentino, and Elizabeth Suhay. 2008. What triggers public opposition to immigration? Anxiety, group cues, and immigration threat. *American Journal of Political Science* 52, no. 4:959–78.

Brian, Tara, and Frank Laczko, eds. 2014. Counting migrant deaths: An international overview. In *Fatal journeys: Tracking lives lost during migration,* ed. Tara Brian and Frank Laczko, 15–44. Geneva: International Organization for Migration.

Burawoy, Michael. 2005. For public sociology. *American Sociological Review* 70, no. 1:4–28.

Capps, Randy, Michael Fix, Jeffrey S. Passel, Jason Ost, and Dan Perez-Lopez. 2003. A profile of the low-wage immigrant workforce. Urban Institute, Brief No. 4, November.

Catechism of the Catholic Church. 2000. 2nd ed. Strathfield, NSW: St. Pauls Publications.

Chishti, Muzaffar, and Faye Hipsman. 2014. Unaccompanied minors crisis has receded from headlines but major issues remain. Migration Policy Institute. *Migration Information Source,* September 25. http://www.migrationpolicy.org/article/unaccompanied-minors-crisis-has-receded-headlines-major-issues-remain.

Collins, Patricia Hill. 2013. Truth-telling and intellectual activism. *Contexts* 12, no. 1:36–39.

Council on Foreign Relations (Jeb Bush and Thomas McLarty III, chairs, Edward Alden, project director). 2009. *U.S. immigration policy.* Independent Task Force Report no. 63. Washington, DC: Council on Foreign Relations. file:///E:/Downloads/Immigration_TFR63%20(1).pdf.

Donahue, John R., SJ. 1988. *The gospel in parable.* Philadelphia, PA: Fortress Press.

Donahue, John R., SJ. 2005. The Bible and Catholic social teaching: Will this engagement lead to marriage? In *Modern Catholic social teaching: Commentaries and interpretations,* ed. Kenneth R. Himes, 9–40. Washington, DC: Georgetown University Press.

Flatow, Nicole. 2014. Private prison companies' stocks soar as companies cash in on incarcerated immigrants. *Think Progress,* September 2. http://thinkprogress.org/justice/2014/09/02/3477866/private-prison-investors-see-profit-in-central-american-migrant-influx/.

Foley, Elise. 2014. Deportations separated thousands of U.S.-born children from parents in 2013. *Huffington Post,* June 25. http://www.huffingtonpost.com/2014/06/25/parents-deportation_n_5531552.html.

Garcia, Matt. 2014. The thousands of children fleeing Central America have nothing to do with our ongoing debate over immigration. *Zócalo Public Square*, July 10. http:// www.zocalopublicsquare.org/2014/07/10/whats-happening-at-the-border-is-a -humanitarian-crisis-not-a-political-one/ideas/nexus/.

Geneva Declaration Secretariat. 2015. *Global burdens of armed violence 2015: Every body counts.* Cambridge: Cambridge University Press.

Golash-Boza, Tanya. 2009. The immigration industrial complex: Why we enforce immigration policies destined to fail. *Sociology Compass* 3, no. 2:295–309.

Gramsci, Antonio. 1971. *Selections from the prison notebooks*, ed. Quintin Hoare and Geoffrey Nowell Smith. New York, NY: International Publishers.

Heyer, Kristin E. 2012. *Kinship across borders: A Christian ethic of immigration.* Washington, DC: Georgetown University Press.

Himes, Michael J., and Kenneth R. Himes. 1993. *Fullness of faith: The public significance of theology.* New York, NY: Paulist Press.

Hoeffner, John J., and Michele R. Pistone. 2009. But the laborers are ... many? Catholic social teaching on business, labor, and economic migration. In *And you welcomed me: Migration and Catholic social teaching*, ed. Donald Kerwin and Jill Marie Gerschutz, 55–92. Lanham, MD: Lexington.

Hooper, John. 2013. Pope Francis condemns global indifference to suffering. *The Guardian*, July 8.

Hsu, Spencer S. 2009. Hate crimes rise as immigration debate heats up. *Washington Post*, June 16.

Isasi-Díaz, Ada María. 2010. Kin-dom of God: A mujerista proposal. In *In Our Own Voices: Latino/a Renditions of Theology*, ed. Benjamín Valentín, 171–90. Maryknoll, NY: Orbis.

Kington, Tom. 2013. Pope criticizes indifference toward immigrants' plight. *Los Angeles Times*, July 8.

McCormick, Patrick T. 2004. *A banqueter's guide to the all-night soup kitchen of the Kingdom of God.* Collegeville, MN: Liturgical Press.

Mills, C. Wright. 1959. *The sociological imagination.* Oxford: Oxford University Press.

Myers, Ched, and Matthew Colwell. 2012. *Our God is undocumented.* Maryknoll, NY: Orbis.

Narea, Nicole. 2013. Latino rights groups blast Rep. Weber for calling immigrants "takers" during Capitol Hill rally. *Texas on the Potomac* (blog), June 20. http://www .zocalopublicsquare.org/2014/07/10/whats-happening-at-the-border-is-a -humanitarian-crisis-not-a-political-one/ideas/nexus/.

National Conference of Catholic Bishops. 1986a. *Economic justice for all: Pastoral letter on Catholic social teaching and the U.S. economy issued by the National Conference of Catholic Bishops.* Washington, DC: National Conference of Catholic Bishops, November 13.

National Conference of Catholic Bishops. 1986b. *Together a new people: Pastoral statement on migrants and refugees.* Washington, DC: National Conference of Catholic Bishops, November 8.

O'Brien, David J., and Thomas A. Shannon, eds. 1992. *Catholic Social Thought: The Documentary Heritage.* Maryknoll, NY: Orbis.

O'Neill, William, SJ. 2007. Rights of passage: The ethics of forced displacement. *Journal of the Society of Christian Ethics* 127, no. 1:113–35.

O'Neill, William, SJ. 2009. Anamnestic solidarity: Immigration from the perspective of restorative justice. Paper presented at the 2009 convention of the Catholic Theological Society of America, Halifax, Nova Scotia, June 5.

Overseas Security Advisory Council. 2015. Honduras 2015 crime and safety report. U.S. Department of State, Bureau of Diplomatic Security, April 21. https://www.osac .gov/pages/ContentReportDetails.aspx?cid=17494.

Plaut, W. Gunther. 1996. Jewish ethics and international migrations. *International Migration Review: Ethics, Migration and Global Stewardship* 30 (Spring): 18–36.

Pope Francis. 2013a. Address of Pope Francis to the new non-resident ambassadors to the Holy See: Kyrgyzstan, Antigua and Barbuda, Luxembourg and Botswana. Vatican City: Libreria Editrice Vaticana, May 16. http://www.vatican.va/holy_father/francesco /speeches/2013/may/documents/papa-francesco_20130516_nuovi-ambasciatori _en.html.

Pope Francis. 2013b. Pope on Lampedusa: "The Globalization of Indifference." Vatican Radio, July 8. http://www.news.va/en/news/pope-on-lampedusa-the-globalization -of-indifferenc.

Pope John XXIII. 1963. Pacem in terris: Peace on earth (April 11, 1963). In O'Brien and Shannon 1992, 129–62.

Pope Paul VI. 1967. Populorum progressio: On the development of peoples (March 26, 1967). In O'Brien and Shannon 1992, 238–62.

Pope Pius XII. 1952a. Exsul familia (On the spiritual care to migrants) (August 1, 1952). In Tessarolo 1962.

Pope Pius XII. 1952b. Exsul familia (On the spiritual care to migrants) (September 30, 1952). In Tessarolo 1962.

Said, Edward. 1994. *Representations of the intellectual.* New York, NY: Vintage.

Sanchez, Robert Fortune. 1981. Migration and the family. *Catholic Mind* 79 (February): 19–24.

Schaab, Gloria L. 2008. Which of these was neighbour? Spiritual dimensions of the US immigration question. *International Journal of Public Theology* 2, no. 2:182–202.

Second Vatican Council. 1965. Gaudium et spes: Pastoral constitution on the church in the modern world. In O'Brien and Shannon 1992, 164–237.

Senior, Donald. 2008. "Beloved aliens and exiles": New Testament perspectives on migration. In *A promised land, a perilous journey: Theological perspectives in migration,* ed. Daniel G. Groody and Gioacchino Campese, 20–34. Notre Dame, IN: University of Notre Dame Press.

Slevin, Peter. 2010. Deportation of illegal immigrants increases under Obama administration. *Washington Post*, July 26.

Southern Poverty Law Center. 2010. Injustice on our plates: Immigrant women in the U.S. food industry. Montgomery, AL: Southern Poverty Law Center, November 7. https://www.splcenter.org/20101108/injustice-our-plates.

Spohn, William C. 2000. *Go and do likewise: Jesus and ethics*. London: Continuum.

Tea Party Patriots. n.d. Home page. http://www.teapartypatriots.org/theborderstates/ (accessed September 25, 2014).

Tessarolo, Giulivo, PSSC. 1962. *The church's Magna Charta for migrants*. Staten Island, NY: St. Charles Seminary.

United Nations High Commissioner for Refugees (UNHCR). 2014. Children on the run: Unaccompanied children leaving Mexico and the need for international protection. Washington, DC: UNHCR, March 12.

United Nations High Commissioner for Refugees (UNHCR). 2015. Women on the run: First hand accounts of refugees fleeing El Salvador, Guatemala, Honduras and Mexico. Washington, DC: UNHCR, October.

United States Conference of Catholic Bishops (USCCB) and Conferencia del Episcopado Mexicano. 2003. Strangers no longer: Together on the journey of hope. Washington, DC: USCCB.

Vogt, Christopher. 2012. Liturgy, discipleship, and economic justice. In *The Almighty and the Dollar: Reflections on Economic Justice for All*, ed. Mark Alman, 242–62. Winona, MN: Anselm Academic.

CHAPTER 4

Embracing the "Other": Dreamers Navigating Higher Education

Harriett D. Romo and Raquel R. Marquez

The growth of the undocumented immigrant population over the last two decades in the United States and the decrease in circularity of migration because of tightened security has meant that more immigrants are remaining in the United States for longer periods of time. These factors have resulted in an accumulative growth of 1.5- and second-generation children whose fates are largely interlinked with their undocumented parents (Gonzales 2008b, 223). While undocumented children are confronted with numerous barriers and exclusions, they are entitled to a K–12 public school education as a result of the 1982 Supreme Court decision *Plyler v. Doe*. Hundreds of thousands of these children have gone on to receive a high school diploma. Several states have granted undocumented students in-state tuition to public colleges and universities, and some of these students have taken the opportunity to pursue postsecondary education. As a result of President Barack Obama's executive actions in 2012 and 2014, undocumented youth who meet eligibility requirements for Deferred Action for Childhood Arrivals (DACA) can receive temporary work permits, but they are still left with no route to citizenship. Many of these undocumented students participate in marches and demonstrations, work to educate others, and organize for policy changes. By engaging in civic and political action and advocating for immigration reform, they provide a critical channel for the voices of undocumented youth in public politics.

We position this research project in which we document the reflections of undocumented youth's organizing efforts in higher education as an embodiment of "public sociology" as defined by sociologist Michael Burawoy (2005). In his 2004 American Sociological Association presidential address, Burawoy challenged scholars to use the academic platform to link vital social issues, such as immigration reform, to a public platform. By presenting this research in an accessible manner, by linking social problems that are often perceived as undocumented students' personal experiences outside of cultural and political dynamics to a social movement, and by illustrating the way these students frame the undocumented student movement in everyday discourse, we hope to bring these issues to the forefront of American debate.[1]

In this essay, we draw from thirty-five in-depth interviews conducted from 2010 to 2013 in Texas with "Dreamers," youth who were brought to the United States as infants or as young children without legal immigration documents, and from ethnographic fieldwork, attending and participating in activities organized by these students. We document how Dreamers navigate higher education and how their civic engagement creates a sense of agency, collective identity, and inclusion. The Development, Relief and Education for Alien Minors (Dream) Act was first introduced in 2001 as bipartisan legislation in the U.S. House of Representatives to extend in-state tuition and provide a route to citizenship for undocumented students. The legislation has undergone numerous revisions and has not yet been enacted. In its most recent version, the Dream Act would allow undocumented students to attend public colleges and universities, allow options for such benefits as in-state tuition and financial aid, provide a legal means to work, and offer a pathway to citizenship (Olivas 2009).[2] Despite setbacks in proposed Dream Act legislation, the students we interviewed continued to be positive about their futures and continued to be civically engaged. Their involvement in the Dream Act movement gave them a sense of purpose, a way to reach out and help others, and a shared identity as Dreamers that enabled them to navigate higher education and remain optimistic despite the lack of official immigration status. The failure of the 2011 Dream Act legislation represented a major defeat for Dreamers, yet they felt a renewed sense of hope with President Obama's DACA executive actions, which authorized renewable work permits (U.S. Citizenship and Immigration Services [USCIS], I-821D, n.d.; see also USCIS, Executive actions on immigration, n.d.). Individuals who qualify for DACA status are no longer subject to deportation, but DACA does not provide a path to citizenship or to permanent residency.

The U.S. Congress has been unable to pass comprehensive immigration reform. Congress is the designated legislative arm that can grant undocumented residents a path to citizenship (Chavez 2014, 95; Olivas 1995, 464). In February 2014, President Obama announced an expansion of DACA provisions. These executive actions were quickly challenged in the courts (Taurel 2015), and as late

---

1   On the framing perspective, see Snow et al. (2014).

2   Olivas (2009) explains the recent revisions on page 410.

as August 2015, the USCIS was not accepting applications for any of the DACA expanded provisions until the legal challenges were resolved.[3]

The students in our study believed that Congress will eventually pass comprehensive immigration reform, and they were actively engaged in efforts to change national immigration policy. Walter J. Nicholls, sociologist, and Jerry Price, vice chancellor for student affairs and dean of students at Chapman University, describe similar efforts by Dreamer activists in Alabama, California, Georgia, and Texas, who have organized campaigns against restrictive financial aid policies, deportations, and the stripping of immigrant rights (Nicholls 2013; Price 2010).[4] Due to variations across the country, higher education administrators in Texas and California have pointed out that it is essential for educators to remain informed of the constantly changing immigration policies and their impact on undocumented students (Gildersleeve, Rumann, and Mondragón 2010, 5–6). Yet, despite numerous setbacks and the possibility that they may not be able to pursue the careers they have prepared for in higher education, Dreamers continue to set high personal goals for themselves.

Dreamers as a Social Movement: Collective Identity and Framing

Undocumented immigrant youth grow up and attend U.S. schools feeling very much a part of the United States as they learn the English language and are socialized to be Americans. The reality for them is that they live without any real options to participate as full American citizens. They are denied access to avenues that offer social mobility and are systematically channeled into the larger underclass of American society in a way that peers who are citizens are not (Gonzales 2008b, 224–26). Sociologists Cecilia Menjívar and Daniel Kanstroom edited a collection of essays (2014) that demonstrates how the criminalization of undocumented immigrants relegates undocumented youth and their parents to an outsider status within mainstream American culture. Menjívar (2006, 1003) has also documented the effects of this uncertain legal status on ability to travel, to seek out job prospects, and to find suitable working conditions, and has shown how the lack of legality shapes immigrants' incorporation and membership in the host society.

---

3   DAPA refers to Deferred Action for Parents of Americans and Lawful Permanent Residents. The expanded DACA created this new program for undocumented parents of U.S. citizens and green-card holders.

4   Price's edited collection (2010) addresses laws, academic experiences of undocumented students, and students' personal stories and efforts to pass Dream Act legislation.

As these young people confront the embattled definition of the phrase "undocumented immigrant," they form a strong sense of identity as a group through "humanistic dialogue," and in "coming out" as Dreamers, they call for a large-scale movement for immigration reform and unite to help others like themselves (Moon 2012, 1343). By identifying themselves as Dreamers rather than as undocumented immigrants, these youth have symbolic power (Bourdieu 1991) that they have appropriated as a group, making others see and believe that they are a part of American society. This "framing" or construction of meaning (Snow and Benford 2000, 614) is contentious in the sense that it generates interpretive frames of Dreamers that differ from conservative frames of "illegal" immigrants, and thus challenges dominant existing frames. We argue that the Dream Act movement merges power, as experienced through the ability to speak out and influence policy, and the production of meaning. Dreamers' participation in public dialogue by telling their stories to demonstrate their worthiness as Americans has created a sense of unity and has drawn additional participants to their movement. We argue that a university environment allows students such as the Dreamers to align their individual and group understandings and the construction of their grievances to a larger social and political collective action, which sociologists David A. Snow and Robert D. Benford conceptualize as "frame alignment processes" (2000, 625). These students' willingness to share their vulnerability as undocumented youth demonstrates their commitment to the Dream Act movement and to other Dreamers, which establishes a sense of unity for the activists, allowing them to frame themselves as worthy, contributing members of American society. These are essential components of a social movement.[5]

Much of the leading work by sociologists Roberto G. Gonzales (2007; 2008a; 2008b; 2010; 2011) and Leisy Janet Abrego (2006; 2008), as well as work coauthored by both (2010, 151–52), details the difficult transition of undocumented youth as they realize they do not have legal documents to allow them to apply for driver's licenses; obtain financial aid for college; or, in some states, even attend college. Abrego (2006, 223, 227) found that undocumented status depresses motivations and sensitizes undocumented youth to the reality that they cannot become full members of U.S. society. She argues that U.S. schools foster expectations and aspirations that make undocumented youth feel like Americans but do not prepare them for the illegal status that awaits them in adulthood. Gonzales (2011) uses life-course theory to look at how and when undocumented youth become aware of and come to understand their status under the law, and how they experience this shift as they move through

---

5   On the framing perspective, see Snow et al. (2014, 37–38).

adolescence and young adulthood. He shows how these youth "learn to be illegal" and points to the consequences of undocumented status on identity formation, friendships, aspirations and expectations, and the lack of opportunities for social and economic mobility. Gonzales demonstrates clearly that undocumented legal status becomes a defining feature of late adolescence and adulthood. For these youth, transition into adulthood means transition into illegality because they cannot legally work, vote, receive financial aid for higher education, or drive in most states.

Dreamers in this study show that participation in civic activism on college campuses around the Dream Act movement and immigration reform promotes a sense of incorporation into U.S. society that other undocumented youth are not able to experience.[6] Many of the "early exiters," those who did not continue with higher education, have seen older siblings blocked from participation in the workforce and excluded from a broad range of activities because they lacked a U.S. social security card. Often these youth express feelings of anger, frustration, and despair, and lose motivation as they realize the stigmatized identity of being undocumented and the possibility of legal problems or deportations. They face the same limited employment options their undocumented parents encountered with mobility blocked by legal status. The youth and their families experience constant fears of being separated by deportations or incarcerations (Dreby 2015).

The youth in this research project continued in higher education despite the many barriers they faced and were civically engaged in a social movement that gave them an additional sense of empowerment and a feeling that they were contributing to society by helping others. The segments from the interviews included in this chapter are reflections of collective efforts told through an individual perspective. There is a sense of community empowerment and protection that is liberating for those who live in the shadows of being undocumented. While the youth we interviewed attended higher education institutions in Texas, there are many examples of collective organization on the part of Dreamers documented in the media. The New Jersey Dream Act Coalition helped pass the New Jersey Dream Act in October 2013. The year and a half drive for Education Not Deportation and the Right to Dream campaigns, the strongest collective efforts in the youth movement, encouraged President Obama to enact the DACA executive action. Sociologist Alberto Melucci argues that collective actions of youth groups work best when societies "keep a space for youth voices to be heard" (1996, 13). Philosopher Peter Levine (2008)

---

6   Gonzales (2011, 604–7) also finds differences between college-going youth and those who exit
    the educational system after high school graduation or earlier.

similarly finds that civic engagement in youth's formative years leads to positive outcomes in other areas of their lives. The youth Levine studied developed strong, positive peer networks and their positive outlooks resulted in a sense of agency and enhanced self-worth. Several of the students we interviewed were originally from Arizona where undocumented immigrants have been stripped of most of their rights, yet these students felt empowered by their Dreamer activities in college and through their national-level activities.[7] As a modern social movement emphasizing cultural issues, the Dream Act movement has produced a collective identity resulting from contentious actions.[8] Civic engagement in the Dream Act movement ultimately led the participants we interviewed to feel empowered because they felt they were effecting social change.

There is a body of social science literature on social movements addressing the actors in the civil rights movement and the ways in which they secured resources to act collectively. Scholars have documented the women's rights movement and have shown how collective actors formed around issues affecting women and the more recent lesbian, gay men, bisexual, and transgender, or the LGBT, movement, and what persuaded this group to mobilize (Moon 2012; Polletta and Jasper 2001; Reagon 1983; Somers 1994). Sociologists Francesca Polletta and James M. Jasper define collective identity as "an individual's cognitive, moral, and emotional connection with a broader community" (2001, 285). According to this definition, collective identity involves a perception of a shared status and positive feelings for other members of the group. Many studies of previous social movements involve people's conceptions of who they are as collectives and as individuals as well as how they organize shared experiences into meaningful collective self-definitions and mobilize resources for political purposes (Somers 1994; see also Tilly 2004).[9]

Dreamers who are participating in the Dream Act movement are defining who "undocumented youth" really are, and, in effect, are changing the public consciousness about undocumented immigrants and the public's perception of who they are as collectives and as individuals. We also draw from French sociologist Pierre Bourdieu's position (1989, 23; 1991) that when categorizing the world and those in it, there is a level of privilege that comes with social power. Dreamers are challenging who defines the boundaries of being American and what it means to be a citizen. The students involved in the Dream Act movement are engaged actively in identity politics; they are consciously

---

7   On Dreamer activism in Arizona, see Nicholls (2013, 44–45, 85, 90).

8   Melucci (2013, 73–74) argues that collective identity is a useful analytical tool to explain social movements.

9   Tilly is considered one of the most prominent scholars on political social movements.

trying to change policy, attempting to transform people's consciousness about the stigmatized perceptions of undocumented students and their families, and defining boundaries and citizenship (Moon 2012, 1337). The Dream Act movement has allowed undocumented students to form a community within higher education that provides a safe haven in which they can share their experiences as undocumented youth and mobilize against exclusion.[10] The students' professors, student organizations, and peers act to form a supportive network that embraces them.

Methodology

As sociologists and authors, we have done previous interviews with Mexican immigrants who came to the United States on EB-5 investment visas. This form of visa allows individual conditional permanent residence to those who invest a minimum of five hundred thousand dollars and create or preserve ten or more permanent full-time jobs.[11] We have also published research on Mexican Americans and Mexican immigrants who live transnational lives, some of whom migrated to the United States without documents (Romo 2013; Marquez 2008; Romo and Marquez 2008; Romo and Mogollon-Lopez 2016).

A fundamental principle of the research we have conducted on the U.S.–Mexico border is that our research offers "voice" to those persons who entrust us with their stories. A goal of this research, which is also a goal of public sociology (Burawoy 2005), is to create public debate on pressing moral issues and to link this debate to academic theories and research. Interviews with Dreamer activists and participant observations in their organizing activities provide the framing data in this essay (Snow et al. 2014, 35–39).[12] We began this research project by becoming informed and by participating in community activities prior to engaging in interviews. We are conscious that the stories are not ours; the stories belong to the participants and to the communities in which they live.

---

10   Reagon (1983, 343–44) discusses the experiences of black youth and broader social issues that emphasize the importance of a safe haven to share experiences.

11   EB-5 allows for a range of investment options, which includes sole proprietor, partnerships, holding companies, joint ventures, corporations, and business trusts. The investor is required to create or preserve at least ten full-time jobs for U.S. workers. Spouses and unmarried children under the age of twenty-one can apply for a green card if they meet certain requirements (USCIS, EB-5 immigrant investor program, n.d.).

12   In their entire article, Snow et al. (2014) review framing approaches in qualitative research. Our framing methodology is influenced by their techniques.

We first established trust and credentials in immigrant communities through our voluntary roles in various organizations. We were also known by students as involved in immigrant rights issues on campus and in the Spanish-language media. We employed similar methods that social scientists Alice Bloch (2007), Wayne A. Cornelius (1982), Fumiko Hosokawa (2010), and Ilse Van Liempt and Veronika Bilger (2009) have used in their data collection and research strategies with vulnerable populations in their work with undocumented immigrants living in the United States. These methods include locating and gaining access to interviewees, establishing researcher credibility, and increasing the reliability and validity of responses.

We developed a semi-structured interview guide (Berg 2007, Chaps. 4–5) that drew select questions from previous immigration studies we had conducted in San Antonio, Texas.[13] This interview guide focused on undocumented students engaged in civic activities in the community, specifically students involved in the Dream Act movement. The guide contained numerous open-ended questions, which gave respondents the opportunity to "tell their story" and expand on their experiences in the movement with as little interference of the researchers as possible, keeping the interview format informal and conversational. The conversations lasted from one and a half to two hours. Hosokawa's research (2010) draws attention to the "power of story" and stresses how informal conversations can lead to stories that provide important information, such as background, intentions, family history, and a person's perception of the world they live in, the "real world."[14] Our interviews allowed Dreamers to tell their stories about their experiences as undocumented students. Hosokawa's work with vulnerable populations provided insights about the need for cultural sensitivity in our research with undocumented students.

We interviewed thirty-five students active in the Dream Act movement and transcribed or summarized all interviews. We took detailed notes during six interviews that were not tape recorded. We hand-coded the interviews based on issues identified in research literature on undocumented students and on the themes that emerged from more than one interview (Rubin and Rubin 2012;

---

13 Berg is a prominent qualitative researcher whose qualitative research methods text is widely used. We edited *Transformations of La Familia on the U.S.–Mexico Border* (2008), which includes chapters on children and families who live transnational lives in both Mexico and the United States, and Romo (with Toni Falbo) wrote *Latino High School Graduation: Defying the Odds* (1996). Marquez co-authored (with Jordana Barton, Emily Ryder Perlmeter, and Elizabeth Blum) an essay on colonias in South Texas (2014).

14 Hosokawa's book (2010) is a helpful guide on how to conduct research that provides a deep understanding of ethnic group members' perceptions of their experiences.

Hesse-Biber and Leavy 2011).[15] Table 4.1 shows that the overwhelming majority of the students originally came from Mexico, yet we did interview students from other countries. Three participants are now U.S. citizens, but they formerly lived in the United States without documents. They remain actively involved in the movement. We also interviewed four students involved in the Dream Act movement who were born in the United States and were citizens but had a sibling or parent who was undocumented. The majority was also in their early twenties, and the participants reflected a balance by gender.

Table 4.2 provides important insight about this group of Dreamers. Twenty-five were undergraduate students, six had recently graduated with a bachelor's degree, and four were enrolled in graduate programs in such fields as public administration, political science, and medicine. Others pursued degrees in

TABLE 4.1   *Origin of the participants.*

Origin		Ages	Gender	
			Males	Females
Mexico	26	19 to 31	15	11
United States	4	21 to 34	1	3
Latin America	3	20 to 22	1	2
Middle East	1	21		1
Canada	1	23		1

TABLE 4.2   *Level of education of the participants.*

Education		Ages	Gender	
			Males	Females
Undergraduate Students	25	19 to 28	13	12
Bachelor's Degree Completed	6	20 to 26	2	4
Medical Student	1	23	1	
Master's Student	1	23		1
Master's Degree Completed	1	34		1
PhD Student	1	34	1	

---

15   Books by Rubin and Rubin (2012) and Hesse-Biber and Leavy (2011) are widely used in university qualitative research methods courses.

mechanical engineering, pharmacy, nursing, biology, sociology, and psychology, all rigorous degrees.

To locate participants, we used a snowball technique (Cornelius 1982), an approach that enables access to difficult to reach populations and allows researchers to cross-check information provided by respondents. In addition to using snowball sampling, we sought out students by attending events organized by the Dream Act movement where we obtained permission from organizers to make announcements about our research project and to ask students to participate. The institutional review board (IRB) allowed us to establish an e-mail address where students could contact us anonymously to participate in interviews. We were especially concerned about safeguarding the confidentiality of respondents so the IRB allowed us to waive signed consent. A document containing all information required in a signed consent—including our contact information, the purpose of the study, procedures for guarding confidentiality, and interview procedures—was sent to any students responding to the e-mail before we set appointments for interviews and was given to participants before the interviews. We allowed students to ask questions about the study before interviews commenced. In addition, we gave code names to each participant to ensure anonymity. Initial contacts tapped into three different student organizations involved in the Dream Act movement.

Over a two-year period, our research team participated in and observed Dream Act students' hunger strikes, demonstrations and marches, press conferences, community panels on undocumented immigration in which Dreamers participated, student-organized workshops on college access for Dream Act youth, sessions to help students apply for DACA work permits, campus activities in which Dreamers participated, and graduation ceremonies and celebrations with their families. The aim of this team approach to doing ethnography was to participate with the students who were involved in the Dream Act movement. This approach allowed us to understand what they were confronting, to listen to how they delineated their interactional strategies, to analyze qualitative episodes, and to hear stories about their situations.[16]

The students interviewed represent three different universities—a major research institution, a small Catholic college, and a large Hispanic-serving university—which provided a diverse sample of Dreamers active in various ways in the Dream Act movement and immigration reform. Student leaders in campus Dream Act groups helped recruit participants. All interviews were conducted in the privacy of on-campus offices familiar to the students. Interviewers included the authors of this essay and Mexican-origin students trained in qualitative research methods. Three Dreamers read this essay and provided

---

16   On ethnographic research methodology, see Angrosino (2007, 1–27).

positive feedback and suggestions. This is consistent with strategies suggested by qualitative methodologists Colette Daiute (2014, 10–26) and Uwe Flick (2007, 33–35) for increasing validity in qualitative research by eliciting reports and having participants review the overall results of the study.[17] One Dreamer said he got "goose bumps" as he read the comments of other students, and he was reminded of why he is involved in the Dream Act movement. Another Dreamer read a draft of the essay and offered helpful comments. This methodological approach was a conscious decision by us as authors in our effort to engage in public sociology (Burawoy 2005). The inclusion of students' perspectives represented a deeper understanding of the historical and social contexts that have made them who they are.

What Motivates Dreamers to Pursue Higher Education?

Dreamer students represent a unique subset of the much larger undocumented population in this country. Most Dreamers have grown up in the United States and, most important, their educational foundation has been formed in the American educational system.[18] Beyond their schooling, these are youth who live their lives as Americans and consider themselves to be American. One can argue that the secondary educational system treats them as Americans, so one can infer that as the educational system invests in these youth, the youth are folded into the larger American community. In this sense, Dreamers are no different than other American youth and many come to recognize the value of higher education. In some cases, these values are internal and motivated by the students' academic success, and for others, as our sample indicates, the drive for higher education comes from their families. For the students interviewed, education is tied closely to the idea that they are Americans and are no different from other youth. They have internalized the important role that education plays in U.S. society, and they aspire to obtain well-paying jobs and to give back to their community.

Ramiro, for example, saw himself as an American and explained that being in college would allow him to support himself as an American. He desired better opportunities for his future.

---

17   These qualitative researchers have written about the interpretive practice of making sense of data in qualitative studies and in conducting research that is faithful to the lived experiences of those studied.

18   Andrew Stevenson (2004) traces the legal implications for undocumented youth in U.S. schools.

> You can still be a Dreamer, being an American, you know, I mean, in the end of the day we still want the same, the same thing, you know … for education, job opportunities, just the opportunity itself will give you something after you graduate.[19]

Ramiro connected his goals to those similar to other American youth, and he expressed expectations that investment in his education will provide positive work opportunities in the future. He and the other undocumented youth we interviewed recognized the limitations of their undocumented status, but they optimistically believed that legislation will be changed or something will happen that will allow them to pursue their careers. While Ramiro remained optimistic, in their California study, Abrego and Gonzales (2010) have found that legal barriers are so insurmountable that undocumented students are often unable to gain a job in their field after they graduate, and such youth must often rely on getting jobs through non-legal ways. However, students involved in the Dream Act movement had a sense of optimism and agency, spoke confidently about their futures, and saw higher education as an investment as they worked to change immigration laws.

Cristina regarded the time she had put into her education as effort that will ultimately result in jobs that are better than menial work.

> That's what I thought, that the whole point of going to school, aside from all that you know, all the learning that you do, social things, okay there's a lot of reasons to go to school, but the main one is to where I don't want to work at fast food the rest of my life, right? So I get a college education, you think, "I get a college education, I no longer have to work at fast food."[20]

Cristina trusted that completing a college education would be the key to job mobility. She did not let the struggles she experienced deter her expectation that hard work and a college education would allow her to move up economically to a more prestigious job than one in fast food or the service industry. For Ramiro and Cristina, education represented a path to a successful future. More specifically, a college education opened a path to better work opportunities. Ramiro went one step further when he linked his two identities in his statement, "You can still be a Dreamer, being an American." All of the undocumented students we interviewed felt that they were "Americans," they just lacked official papers. They also expressed a sense of self-confidence and a

---

19   Ramiro, interview by Cristina Cigarroa, August 23, 2011.
20   Cristina, interview by Cristina Cigarroa, September 2, 2011.

sense of agency that several attributed to feeling a part of a larger community and to being participants in a movement that represented a cause larger than their individual dreams.

Guadalupe graduated as a valedictorian in her high school class and was determined to continue to a university despite discouragement from teachers and even from her father because of her status as an undocumented youth. She explained her commitment to her studies and to her community.

> Being valedictorian, all those efforts, all those sleepless nights, just went down the drain and it was devastating for me to learn that I was undocumented because I worked very hard. I was committed to the community. I was committed to academics. I knew the importance of an education and I wanted to do the best that I could be and despite obstacles, despite my own teachers ... despite all the discrimination. Even my dad at one point told me, "Why do you keep trying so hard if you are undocumented?" Something in me always turned all that negativity and it pushed me harder into [being] positive.... I do not blame my father for that because he wasn't aware of the opportunities and he didn't understand that with the will power, everything is possible. So I didn't give up.... I maintained my status as valedictorian. I worked even harder within my AP [advanced placement] classes and honors classes. And I was blessed to be accepted to a university that granted me a full ride.

Guadalupe did well in college and immediately became engaged as an active leader in the Dream Act movement on her campus. She led demonstrations and fund-raisers for Dream Act students. Even after she managed to obtain legal documents through a relative, she continued to work for the movement. At one point, she was called into the dean's office because of her activism. She explained,

> I'm extremely blessed and grateful for the opportunities I have received at college but I believe what I'm doing is right and just and I will continue doing it.... I will continue doing what I have to do, because it's a cause that needs attention and help. And I'm not willing to leave these students in the shadows anymore.... That's what I told the dean of students and actually he was very disappointed in a way. He called me an aggressive grassroots activist, and I said, "Can I have that in writing?"[21]

---

21   Guadalupe, interview by Harriett D. Romo, March 11, 2013.

Guadalupe did not let the discouragement she faced from family members, teachers, and administrators stop her from achieving her goals and from participating in the movement.

Cristina was an activist who recognized her advantages as a student able to continue in higher education, and she was determined to use those advantages to give back to the United States. She saw herself as an American, just one lacking the formal recognition that citizenship would bring. In addition, she recognized that she was better off than many U.S. citizens who are poor and have not had an opportunity to pursue higher education. She desired to work and give back to her community. Cristina identified with the collective Dreamer identity as she stated, "We're already here.... We just haven't been formally accepted.... the fight for the whole, the fight for other people." She explained,

> Of course, the ideal thing would be to be able to work, not just obtain higher education because there are students who've graduated from bachelor's, master's, and doctorate degrees. To be able to work for now because citizenship will take ten years to thirteen but if it will be recognized by society, like on the legislative level, of course that would be success. To be able to give back to America, to give back to the United States, with this degree or that degree or with whatever, I think that would be the success.... I believe this is a continuation of the civil rights movement ... but success would be the Dream Act passing. It would be America actually accepting us undocumented immigrants into their society because we're already here. We just haven't been formally accepted under the law. I just don't give up, cause there's a lot of problems in our community.... It's hard, lots of people are dropping out and we have the highest pregnancy rate in the city, so all these things, like they keep me motivated and optimistic because I'm so, such a part of America that I feel it's my responsibility now to guide the people toward the right reasons. I don't know of any Dreamer that's not participating in their communities somehow, to be honest, so I think that's why we should be optimistic. There's so much to do, the fight for the whole, the fight for other people. There are a lot of poor families too, like I know I'm poor, but I can afford education and I have a place to live.[22]

Cristina wanted to work and get the most from her education, but she was aware that most Dreamers were not able to put their success in higher education into practice without legal immigration status (Gonzales and Chavez

---

22   Cristina, interview.

2012).[23] She believed that with increased education her community could improve the living conditions for its residents, and she felt a responsibility to help. She is a good example of the Dreamers who hoped to be allowed to make a difference in their communities. She recognized that the full route to citizenship is a lengthy process, so she adjusted her goals to be able to work and use her education to address the more immediate problems of teen pregnancy and high dropout rates among Latin@s in her community.

Natalia has already put these goals into practice. She viewed herself as a Dreamer activist and believed that experience allowed her to apply her education right now.

> Before participating in the organization, I would not have thought that I could have continued beyond a bachelor's degree. I thought, maybe I'll finish this degree and then go and try and find work, maybe help my parents, but now I feel like it's opened up, like the types of options I have, because I see the possibilities. And in terms of community, I definitely see myself being involved in this group [the Dream Act movement] ... for a long while just because I know there is so much need for it. To do group advocacy in the community.[24]

Natalia's plans have shifted as she transferred her personal goals into broader community engagement. As Table 4.3 demonstrates, the majority of the students we interviewed wanted to work legally in the United States. Eight

TABLE 4.3   *"American Dream" of the participants.*

American dream		Ages	Gender	
			Males	Females
Work Legally in the United States	15	19 to 25	10	5
Become Community Activists	8	21 to 34	5	3
Get a PhD, MA, or Law Degree	6	19 to 26	2	4
Avoid Deportation	3	21 to 31	1	2
Get U.S. Citizenship	3	19 to 26	1	2

23   Sociologists Gonzales and Chavez (2012) have done extensive research with undocumented youth. Their article is a study of how undocumented status constrains the lives of 1.5-generation Latin@s in Orange County, California.
24   Natalia, interview by Maricela Oliva, September 28, 2011.

Dreamers, like Natalia, identified becoming a community activist as a goal that would allow them to support other Dreamers and help residents in their communities. Participating in social justice activism created new constructions of meanings as Dreamers participated in collective identity discourse with others throughout the United States.[25]

In his research with California Dreamers, Gonzales makes the case that the civic engagement shown by immigrant youth involved in the Dream Act movement is producing a new generation of activists, which might form the base for future social justice activism in this country (Gonzales 2008b). The students we interviewed expressed a strong commitment to social justice and are part of this generation of activists. The complexity of the U.S. immigration system created space in which the Dreamers and their networks were able to identify with their own cultural interpretation of immigration and determine what immigration means in their communities. In his essay on collective identity, Melucci (2013, 73–74) explains that this form of collective action represents the ways modern social movements have been able to move from more traditional social factors, such as race and class, to efforts in collective action based on issues with a cultural emphasis. The undocumented status of the students we interviewed is the basis of their collective identity, rather than ethnicity, race, or social class.

Navigating the Educational System

The students we interviewed were innovative and resourceful about navigating the higher education system. They faced many obstacles because they lacked legal documents, but sensitive teachers, peers, adults in the community, and other Dreamers often supported them and shared helpful information. We were reminded how, as young adults, they were denied an American rite of passage when they spoke about their inability to obtain a driver's license (Gonzales 2011, 605–6).[26] But not having a driver's license implies more than simply being denied an American rite of passage. These Dreamers connected being able to drive to being able to work and to being able to live at home and get to classes. DACA and President Obama's extension of this action to include a greater number of youth has enabled those who qualify to obtain documents

---

25   On the framing perspective in the study of social movements, see Snow et al. (2014, 31).

26   Gonzales has written extensively about the developmental processes as youth realize their undocumented status.

that allow them to apply for a driver's license and work legally.[27] The cases are determined on an individual basis. Applications for DACA cost 465 dollars, require extensive documentation and paperwork, and must be renewed on a regular basis. In Paloma's words,

> I felt very fortunate that I was able to receive deferred action [DACA]. Even though I'm still considered undocumented, my undocumented experience is going to change. It is going to be completely different from that of another Dreamer who is still unable to obtain identification documents from the Texas State Department [of Motor Vehicles]. Or to be able to drive and have a driver's license and ultimately be able to work.[28]

Paloma indicated that she already experienced the impact of these changes.[29] Having DACA allows Dreamers to be lawfully present in the United States, although it does not confer lawful status and it is a temporary authorization. DACA authorization allowed Dreamers to obtain a driver's license in some states, which gave the Dreamers greater independence and reduced the fear of being apprehended and possibly facing deportation.

Some students drove without a license but were in constant fear of being stopped for a minor violation and then subjected to deportation. Others refused to risk breaking the law and rode public buses, often having to change buses several times and leave home hours early to attend classes. Still, they mastered the often irregular bus schedule and knew the important routes to get them where they needed to go. Some shared a ride in an automobile with a peer who was a citizen. Many of the students lived with their parents in areas where someone with a license was willing to offer a ride, or they shared an apartment with someone who was a citizen and had a car. In Francisco's case, he felt strongly about not breaking the law, but he saw his future so limited by not being able to drive legally that he was willing to move elsewhere.

---

27   The U.S. Department of Homeland Security memorandum (2012) authorized President Obama's Executive Order for DACA. USCIS (Consideration of Deferred Action for Childhood Arrivals, n.d.) provides information about DACA guidelines, filing process, and eligibility. USCIS (Executive actions on immigration, n.d.) provides an update of the expansion of DACA. USCIS (I-821D, n.d.) provides DACA application instructions.

28   Paloma, interview by Harriett D. Romo and Cristina Cigarroa, August 18, 2011.

29   In their article, Roberto G. Gonzales, Veronica Terriquez, and Stephen P. Ruszczyk (2014) draw data from a national sample of DACA beneficiaries to show how undocumented young adults benefit from DACA.

I wanted to continue within the greatest extent of the law where I didn't have to break it.... And a driver's license was always an issue. I don't have a license. So yeah, I explored other options as far as going to other states, talking to family I had in other states where they could get it. If not, it's moving over there, and being able to apply for a license and then get it. And then at least have a valid driver's license from another state.[30]

Francisco's solution to obtaining a driver's license illustrates the variances in context within the different states regarding undocumented immigrants and their rights. Texas, for example, denies a driver's license but allows undocumented immigrants to pay in-state tuition.

All of the students we interviewed actively participated in high school student organizations or community organizations, and in these groups, they sometimes found adult mentors who assisted them in applying to college or helped them find scholarships. Students engaged in the community while in high school continued their involvement in the Dream Act movement in college and also participated in other organized student groups, which provided large social networks of friends and adults who might help them. Students recognized sympathetic teachers, counselors, and other adults in the community who had resources to assist them. David reported,

I remember, like all my ESL [English as a Second Language] class was undocumented and we joked around all the time, and, of course, we knew we were undocumented.... We'd talk about it all the time, it was not something hush, hush, you don't talk about that. Like other students, I had heard their stories, it was mostly about that something that you had that is part of you and you just have to, you had all these people in the same situation, so it really wasn't any fear factor or anything like that.... When I got to (city in Texas), it was different 'cause it was mostly a Latin@ school.... I didn't talk to my counselor, it was my teacher, my government teacher, a U.S. history teacher. I knew that I could trust him and I talked to my college advisor at the school. He also knew, because he was helping with the scholarships and all the stuff like that. And I talked to a person from the YMCA [Young Men's Christian Association]. He was my counselor kind of. I did YMCA youth government. I don't know if that's what it's called, I don't remember. YMCA—it was government something related. And he was the one. He was like a counselor, like a big brother kind of deal.

---

30   Francisco, interview by Harriett D. Romo and Cristina Cigarroa, August 11, 2011.

David also reported being helped by an immigrant activist group. This group especially motivated him because he was being encouraged to go to college by students who were also undocumented and had succeeded in college. He was so inspired that he became determined to participate in a similar activist group in college in order to help other undocumented students. He explained his motivation,

> Dreamer students, yes and they were a group called Jovenes Inmigrantes por un Futuro Mejor [Immigrant Youth for a Better Future]. I still have their little flyer they gave me. I think that, that was kept, that will stay with me. They were the ones that helped me, that told me that information, it was students. And I think it's something that really gets me motivated. I was helped by those students. I was helped by Dream Act students, so I want to do the same and actually that's what motivated me to find an organization similar to that here.[31]

David's case is an example of the way collective identity provides a sense of agency that can make social change possible. Intergroup relationships helped construct the meaning of the movement and aligned prospective members with the movement's goals. David was resourceful throughout his educational career, finding others who were in similar situations and seeking out adults who could help him achieve educational success. He also demonstrated clearly how the Dreamers' activism empowered undocumented youth to have aspirations for college and how the movement recruited others and encouraged youth to help one another.[32]

Guadalupe was also a student activist committed to helping other Dreamers. She told us about the difficulties she faced when she qualified for prestigious scholarships, international programs, and internships but could not apply because she was not a citizen or did not have a social security number. Professors expressed disappointment that she would not apply for awards or scholarships they knew she might win or when she could not travel with a student group to an academic competition, but she felt she could not tell them about her undocumented status. Instead, she organized bake sales, T-shirt sales, and other events to raise funds to help pay for Dreamers' applications for deferred action work permits. She raised 4,650 dollars in one month, which

---

31   David, interview by Cristina Cigarroa, October 18, 2011.

32   Perez et al. (2010, esp. 259–60) surveyed 126 undocumented Mexican students and found that despite their undocumented status, they were likely to be civically engaged and to have participated in activism.

allowed ten students to submit their DACA applications. She was determined to have the money ready as soon as they had their application paperwork completed. Confiding in Dreamers in similar circumstances, learning how other Dreamers overcame obstacles, and seeing youth who had been successful in their educational pursuits despite their lack of legal status gave college Dreamers determination to pursue their dreams and provided a sense of collective identity that motivated them to help others.

Self-determination of Dreamers

As faculty, we see the excitement that comes when students are graduating from college and discussing the different opportunities they are entertaining. It is important to remember at these times that Dreamers are products of the U.S. primary and secondary educational system. Those who pursue higher education are often students who have a sense of what they want to do when they graduate from a university. The risks that Dreamers and their families have undertaken channel them into a self-awareness that leaves them very focused. For example, one of the Dreamers we interviewed declined an offer of a job in her field of study to take a position working with United We Dream, a national advocacy group. Her organizational skills were featured in the *New York Times* when the group held a demonstration at the U.S.–Mexico border.

Although Dreamers are having the same discussions about their futures as their peers who are citizens, they struggle with the complexity of creating their own path hampered by outside forces that have a negative impact on personal goals.[33] In her work on Salvadoran and Guatemalan immigrants, Menjívar (2006) has documented how Dreamers' self-determination is hampered by the liminal status of being undocumented.[34] Sophia shared critical insight, explaining that Dreamers are hindered through no fault of their own.

> For a long period of time, I was very angry because I had always worked really, really hard since I was very young. And my parents had always

---

33 Stevenson (2004) presents case studies of undocumented high school and college students and the realities they face, discusses constitutional controversies surrounding their rights to an education, and analyzes legislative barriers and solutions.

34 Menjívar (2006) documents how legal status affects identity, relationships, health risks, opportunities in the labor market, and sociocultural spheres. She argues that it is not simply undocumented status but the long-term uncertainty of legal status that is so constraining and disempowering.

pushed me to do the best. So when I was salutatorian of my class, I had very high expectations of myself. That was the biggest thing. It's something you continue to deal with, to sort of not meet your own expectations. That is still something I cope with today. I have certain goals for myself so I always speak about it to other people who are undocumented. It's just a certain look you get, like in speaking with professors or people who don't know your status, and it's like "Oh you have so much potential and I just don't understand." And you're like, "What really stops me is my undocumented status." So it's something you continue to cope with, but ... I always try to do my best if it's in my work, in my research, always try to make it more challenging for myself. That way I know that I am capable of doing great work and that it's not something on my behalf that's stopping me.[35]

Sophia understood that her skills, along with her ambitions, were sound. She also knew that it was not a lack of ambition or ability that held her back. She openly shared her status as a Dreamer in the media, in community forums, and with other students. Sophia and the other students we spoke with saw their future here in the United States, despite their undocumented status and the barriers they faced because they lacked legal documents.

Dolores emphasized the collective identity of undocumented students, even those who managed to normalize their status in some way. In her career, she aspired to use her higher education to give back to the undocumented community.

Our common ground is not having status, we don't all have papers. I have a driver's license, and a lot of them [Dreamers] don't. I have a social security number, license, and a lot of them don't. I have a job and a lot of them don't even have deferred action status. The common ground is the fact that we don't have papers. But to even say that sounds like I'm minimizing it. The fact that we don't have papers seems like a little issue but the reality is, IT IS THE ISSUE. IT'S A HUGE ISSUE.... I really want to go to law school.... I want to open a low-income immigration clinic because the amount that my parents pay is ridiculous. The reason why people can't afford it so much is because they can't afford to go to a lawyer. You don't know how to fill out the paperwork. Who's going to help you? It makes sense to use those resources available more to a population that actually needs it and can't afford it.... What made me want to give back to

---

35   Sophia, interview by Maricela Oliva, October 11, 2011.

the community is really understanding what kind of a strategic position I was in to speak on behalf of a lot of people.... It just seems like a lot of people are not as educated about the issue. And so for me I was able to immerse myself educationally in this movement. I feel like I should use that education as a platform to give back on behalf of the people who might not know as much or who might just be too afraid to talk about it, right?... I want to get my story out and I want to talk to people and I want to help them understand what it means to be undocumented.[36]

Dolores is a good example of the motivations of the Dreamers in this study to tell their stories to raise awareness of the difficulties undocumented youth face. She also recognized that as an undocumented student who had the opportunity to pursue postsecondary education she had an even greater responsibility to use her education to inform the public about the plight of undocumented youth. Despite the barriers presented by immigration status, these Dreamers excelled and aspired to professional careers that would allow them to give back to their communities. They continued to have high expectations of themselves, even when faced with situations in which their legal status prevented them from reaching their goals. The students we interviewed who qualified for DACA status continued to identify as Dreamers and found ways to advocate for others.

Hope and the Future

Despite the reality that thus far the U.S. immigration debate has not generated comprehensive Dream Act legislation or comprehensive immigration reform, which is the Dreamers' broader goal, the students in our study remained cognizant of the fact that their futures are tied to whether and when the United States passes immigration legislation that includes a route to citizenship. Paloma argued that a real future lies with the Dream Act, and not with other ideas that have been circulating or with the two- or three-year stay of deportation through DACA enacted by President Obama in 2012 and extended in 2014. Paloma explained,

The Dream Act would be the best option for undocumented students to really be able to get an education and then be incorporated legally. The

---

36   Dolores, interview by Harriett D. Romo and Raquel R. Marquez, May 22, 2013.

work visa is not incorporating them into a culture and into a society that they are already a part of.[37]

In Paloma's view, DACA and other legislative ideas do not do enough to grant undocumented students the rights that they need. In the short term, DACA reduces some of the challenges undocumented young adults face in achieving economic and social incorporation by allowing them to work and have less fear of deportation. In the long term, employers may be reluctant to hire youth with the temporary status that DACA provides, since DACA must be renewed regularly. Additionally, not all undocumented youth qualify for DACA.

Another student, Francisco, explained that DACA holds his "near future," providing him with the ability to work legally and to earn a living, but he also acknowledged that his long-term future is tied to comprehensive change that will provide a route to U.S. citizenship. Immigration reform will ultimately define where he will live and will determine his ability to fully participate in a society where he was raised. He deliberated about the future.

> I don't have any intentions of going back to Mexico. I don't consider that as my home, and I would really like to stay here and be able to work here. To be able to stay with a path toward citizenship or something like that— right now, to tell you the truth, if they didn't give me that, I'd be okay with it as long as I could be able to work here and live here. Maybe later on, when I was older, and I actually wanted my voice to be heard, and maybe if I was more politically involved, then maybe I would want to have the ability to vote and then maybe I would want to be a citizen. But right now, I think the only thing that's stopping me is not being able to work. And I know I might be thinking only short-term and not long-term.[38]

When the students talked about the future in short terms, it was because they had few long-term prospects. As young adults with the possibility of deportation to a country of origin with which many had weakened ties, their daily university experiences are their future. Their identities as college students who were actively engaged in a social movement allowed them to deal with their status on a day-to-day basis. When we asked Ramiro about his plans for the future, he explained, "I mean, just go to school. Continue to go to

---

37   Paloma, interview.
38   Francisco, interview.

school.... Hopefully, the Dream Act passes so my situation gets relieved. I don't know ... but mainly go to school, I mean, keep on going."[39]

In contrast to the short-term goals expressed by some of the younger students still in college, Dreamers who had already graduated used the skills and sense of collective identity formed during college activism to act in solidarity with other groups to change policy. Several of them spoke of goals to pursue long-term strategies on immigrant-related issues. Dolores was undertaking a major initiative engaging Dreamers and community members in an effort to make her city a sanctuary city. She explained how the Dreamers could make an impact: "once you have strengths in numbers it's really hard for a group, like a city council that's representative of what the city wants to turn away from, when you have their constituents speaking out about this."[40] Dreamers organized public meetings, vigils, rallies, and demonstrations to participate in public politics even though they lacked official citizenship. This created what sociologist Charles Tilly described as "worthiness, unity, numbers, and commitments" (2004, 12). Dreamers effectively used social media, electronic communication, and the Internet to sustain commitments and make collective claims on others, and in their protests, these students drew prospective members to their cause.

Guadalupe, who has achieved permanent U.S. resident status, shared her long-term commitment to the Dream Act movement.

> I do have my permanent residence ... from two years ago. Somebody questioned me about it. "You can't call yourself a Dreamer," and I said, "For nineteen years of my life, I have been discriminated. I have been talked down upon. I have been put through so many obstacles, and you're telling me I'm not a Dreamer! Just because a year and a half ago I received my social security number?" No, I'm still a Dreamer ... and I'm still fighting for this cause.... I'm applying for U.S. citizenship. Maybe as a citizen, I will be able to do more. And one of my long-term goals, or maybe short-term goals, is to be a public official.[41]

Guadalupe's long-term goal of becoming a public official is embedded in her previous status as an undocumented student.

Dreamers expressed hope and optimism despite the challenges most of them endured in paying for their college education and managing to navigate

---

39   Ramiro, interview.
40   Dolores, interview.
41   Guadalupe, interview.

college life without citizenship documents. They all believed that continuing their education and working for immigration reform was the best way to position themselves for the future. Sophia described what success meant to her.

> Success to me in my status would probably be being able to graduate college, actually being able to attend college. I realized that there are some states where undocumented students can't, it's not as feasible to do so. But being able to meet that goal that you planned for yourself, those expectations that you had set. So in my case, it was going to college, and I've accomplished that.... I see it in terms of I already have it and I can't do anything with it. But I know eventually if reform was to happen or some sort of way to legalization, I'd be ahead of the game. I feel that it will be of good use eventually.[42]

Ramiro also explained that he and his friends are hedging their bets for the future by getting an education. In fact, Ramiro followed his mentor's advice.

> I have a lot of friends that they're in my, in my situation ... like my coach he always tells me ... "Yeah you're undocumented ... you don't know about the future. Your future might change so just stay there, don't quit school."[43]

Sophia and Ramiro understood the fact that continuing their education was crucial for a better future.

Katalina recognized that activism in the Dream Act movement in college had enabled her to make sense of the discrimination she had faced and motivated her to change the social stigmatization of being undocumented. She was proud of the commitment of the students from her campus and their impact on their community.

> I think activism is really important to have success in college, not only for yourself but [also] for other people. A staffer called this the best activist work that I've seen since the sixties.... It really resonated with us because we knew that what we were doing was really effective activism.[44]

---

42   Sophia, interview.
43   Ramiro, interview.
44   Katalina, interview by Cristina Cigarroa, October 16, 2011.

Dreamers, such as Katalina, were well aware of the important role that student activism played in her life and on a broader community level.

Conclusion

As youth identify themselves as activist Dreamers they are challenging the boundaries of "the other." The students we interviewed explained that their efforts to find a path to citizenship gave them a sense of purpose and a shared identity as Dreamers. All of the Dreamers interviewed in this study have been civically engaged (Perez et al. 2010) through participation in student organizations and demonstrations, and through service to their communities. Similar to participants in other social movements, these Dreamers discovered that the Dream Act movement changed their lives profoundly. They realized that their own self-identification was tied to broader social issues of discrimination and unjust social arrangements.[45]

Continuing in higher education and being involved in the Dream Act movement allowed Dreamers to maintain a non-stigmatized student Dreamer status versus an undocumented status. Being a Dreamer provided a collective identity as an activist versus an individual identity as someone without legal documents. Despite specific and important limitations because of the lack of immigration papers, Dreamers in higher education continued to function much like they had in high school: gaining recognition for their academic achievements, participating in school organizations and activities, and hoping that success in education and their involvement in the Dream Act movement would bring them a better future.[46] Higher education remains an important goal for undocumented students with almost half of those who graduate from high school continuing on with higher education (Passel and Cohn 2009, 11–12, fig. 17). The Dreamer students interviewed have persevered against significant barriers to gain admission into higher education. They have proven their initiative, resilience, and dedication to their cause.

The process of meaning construction, the way that individuals involved in the Dream Act movement create social meaning of a situation, is an ongoing, dynamic process as the immigration debate continues. There are many

---

45   Moon, a sociologist with expertise in culture and power relations, explores how participation in a social movement can create a positive group identity (2012, 1337). In the Dream Act movement, students no longer have to think of themselves as undocumented youth; they become Dreamers.

46   On immigrants' civic engagement, see Levine (2008, 102).

obstacles for undocumented youth, and surmounting them requires commitment and sacrifice that many Dreamers have already made and continue to make by telling their stories publicly. We, as sociologists who value public sociology, hope that this research provides visibility to the invisible and makes the private public through the discourse the students shared in their interviews.

The Dreamers have offered opposition to the liminal status of undocumented immigrants by providing support for actions that recognize the accomplishments and contributions of undocumented youth and their families. These Dreamers constitute a unified force to be reckoned with in terms of "worthiness, unity, numbers, and commitment" (Tilly 2004, 12). The anti-immigrant political environment in the United States has influenced the evolution of the Dream Act movement, the activities of the Dreamers, and the character of the movement's goals. The movement has expanded as participants in the movement communicate with one another, exchange ideas, and adapt rhetoric and models of action. However, it is unclear what will happen to the Dream Act movement in the future. If the courts approve the expansion of DACA and legalized work status, the momentum for further inclusion may stall. Still, a shift toward internationalization with a focus on human rights of migrants globally may expand the movement to an international scale. Uncertainties remain, but the voices of the Dreamers and their activism have provided crucial channels for this group of young people to make the issues they confront visible in public politics.

Bibliography

Abrego, Leisy Janet. 2006. "I can't go to college because I don't have papers": Incorporation patterns of undocumented youth. *Latino Studies* 4:212–31.

Abrego, Leisy Janet. 2008. Legitimacy, social identity, and the mobilization of law: The effects of Assembly Bill 540 on undocumented students in California. *Law and Social Inquiry* 33:709–34.

Abrego, Leisy Janet, and Roberto G. Gonzales. 2010. Blocked paths, uncertain futures: The postsecondary education and labor market prospects of undocumented Latino youth. *Journal of Education for Students Placed at Risk* 15, nos. 1–2:144–57.

Angrosino, Michael. 2007. *Doing ethnographic and observational research*. Los Angeles, CA: SAGE Publications.

Berg, Bruce L. 2007. *Qualitative research methods for the social sciences*. 6th ed. Boston, MA: Pearson-Allyn and Bacon.

Bloch, Alice. 2007. Methodological challenges for national and multi-sited comparative survey research. *Journal of Refugee Studies* 20, no. 2:230–47.

Bourdieu, Pierre. 1989. Social space and symbolic power. *Sociological Theory* 7, no. 1:14–25.

Bourdieu, Pierre. 1991. *Language and symbolic power*. Ed. and introduced by John B. Thompson. Trans. Gino Raymond and Matthew Adamson. Cambridge, MA: Harvard University Press.

Burawoy, Michael. 2005. For public sociology. *American Sociological Review* 70, no. 1:4–28.

Chavez, Leo R. 2014. Illegality across generations. In Menjívar and Kanstroom 2014, 84–110.

Cornelius, Wayne A. 1982. Interviewing undocumented immigrants: Methodological reflections based on fieldwork in Mexico and the U.S. *International Migration Review* 16, no. 2:378–411.

Daiute, Colette. 2014. *Narrative inquiry: A dynamic approach*. Los Angeles, CA: SAGE Publications.

Dreby, Joanna. 2015. *Nervios*: On the threat of deportation. In *Everyday illegal: When policies undermine immigrant families*, 19–54. Berkeley, CA: University of California Press.

Flick, Uwe. 2007. *Managing quality in qualitative research*. Los Angeles, CA: SAGE Publications.

Gildersleeve, Ryan Evely, Corey Rumann, and Rodolfo Mondragón. 2010. Serving undocumented students: Current law and policy. In Price 2010, 5–18.

Gonzales, Roberto G. 2007. Wasted talent and broken dreams: The lost potential of undocumented students. *Immigration Policy in Focus* 5, no. 13:1–11.

Gonzales, Roberto G. 2008a. Born in the shadows: The uncertain futures of the children of unauthorized Mexican migrants. PhD diss., University of California, Irvine.

Gonzales, Roberto G. 2008b. Left out but not shut down: Political activism and the undocumented student movement. *Northwestern Journal of Law and Social Policy* 3, no. 2:219–40.

Gonzales, Roberto G. 2010. On the wrong side of the tracks: The consequences of school stratification systems for unauthorized Mexican students. *Peabody Journal of Education* 85, no. 4:469–85.

Gonzales, Roberto G. 2011. Learning to be illegal: Undocumented youth and shifting legal contexts in the transition to adulthood. *American Sociological Review* 74, no. 4:602–19.

Gonzales, Roberto G., and Leo R. Chavez. 2012. "Awakening to a nightmare": Abjectivity and illegality in the lives of undocumented 1.5–generation Latino immigrants in the United States. *Current Anthropology* 53, no. 3:255–81.

Gonzales, Roberto G., Veronica Terriquez, and Stephen P. Ruszczyk. 2014. Becoming DACAmented: Assessing the short-term benefits of Deferred Action for Childhood Arrivals (DACA). *American Behavioral Scientist* (October 1): 1–21.

Hesse-Biber, Sharlene Nagy, and Patricia Leavy. 2011. *The practice of qualitative research.* 2nd ed. Los Angeles, CA: SAGE Publications.

Hosokawa, Fumiko. 2010. *Building trust: Doing research to understand ethnic communities.* Lanham, MD: Lexington.

Levine, Peter. 2008. The civic engagement of young immigrants: Why does it matter? *Applied Development Science* 12, no. 2:102–4.

Marquez, Raquel R. 2008. Transborder interactions and transnational processes in the border community of Laredo, Texas. In Marquez and Romo 2008, 163–84.

Marquez, Raquel R., Jordana Barton, Emily Ryder Perlmeter, and Elizabeth Blum. 2014. Las colonias along the Texas–Mexico border. In *Ten-gallon economy: Sizing up economic growth in Texas,* ed. Pia M. Orrenius, Jesús Caña, and Michael Weiss, 213–29. New York, NY: Palgrave Macmillan.

Marquez, Raquel R., and Harriett D. Romo, eds. 2008. *Transformations of la familia on the U.S.–Mexico border.* Notre Dame, IN: University of Notre Dame Press.

Melucci, Alberto. 1996. Youth, time and social movements. *Young* 4, no. 2:3–14.

Melucci, Alberto. 2013. The process of collective identity. In *Social movements and culture,* ed. Hank Johnston, 72–109. Hoboken, NJ: Taylor and Francis Press.

Menjívar, Cecilia. 2006. Liminal legality: Salvadoran and Guatemalan immigrants' lives in the United States. *American Journal of Sociology* 111, no. 4:999–1037.

Menjívar, Cecilia, and Daniel Kanstroom, eds. 2014. *Constructing immigrant "illegality": Critiques, experiences and responses.* New York, NY: Cambridge University Press.

Moon, Dawne. 2012. Who am I and who are we? Conflicting narratives of collective selfhood in stigmatized groups. *American Journal of Sociology* 117, no. 5: 1336–79.

Nicholls, Walter J. 2013. *The DREAMers: How the undocumented youth movement transformed the immigrant rights debate.* Stanford, CA: Stanford University Press.

Olivas, Michael A. 1995. Dreams deferred: Deferred action, prosecutorial discretion, and the vexing case(s) of DREAM Act students. *William & Mary Bill of Rights Journal* 21, no. 2:463–547.

Olivas, Michael A. 2009. Undocumented college students, taxation, and financial aid: A technical note. *Review of Higher Education* 32, no. 3:407–16.

Passel, Jeffrey S., and D'Vera Cohn. 2009. *A portrait of unauthorized immigrants in the United States.* Washington, DC: Pew Research Center, Pew Hispanic Center, April 14. http://www.pewhispanic.org/files/reports/107.pdf.

Perez, William, Roberta Espinoza, Karina Ramos, Heidi Coronado, and Richard Cortes. 2010. Civic engagement patterns of undocumented Mexican students. *Journal of Hispanic Higher Education* 9, no. 3:245–65.

Polletta, Francesca, and James M. Jasper. 2001. Collective identity and social movements. *Annual Review of Sociology* 27:283–305.

Price, Jerry, ed. 2010. *Understanding and supporting undocumented students: New directions for student services.* Hoboken, NJ: Wiley Periodicals.

Reagon, Bernice Johnson. 1983. Coalition politics: Turning the century. In *Home girls: A black feminist anthology*, ed. Barbara Smith, 343–55. New York, NY: Kitchen Table Women of Color Press.

Romo, Harriett D. 2013. Formal and informal institutions in the construction of transnational lives. In *Immigration and the border: Politics and policy in the new Latino century*, ed. David L. Leal and José Limón, 45–85. Notre Dame, IN: University of Notre Dame Press.

Romo, Harriett D., and Toni Falbo. 1996. *Latino high school graduation: Defying the odds*. Austin, TX: University of Texas Press.

Romo, Harriett, and Raquel R. Marquez. 2008. Identity construction in transnational lives: Characteristics and complexities. In *Boundaries in depth and in motion*, ed. I. W. Zartman, 217–34. Athens, GA: University of Georgia Press.

Romo, Harriett D., and Olivia Mogollon-Lopez. 2016. *Mexican migration to the United States*. Austin, TX: University of Texas Press.

Rubin, Herbert J., and Irene S. Rubin. 2012. *Qualitative interviewing: The art of hearing data*. 3rd ed. Los Angeles, CA: SAGE Publications.

Snow, David A., and Robert D. Benford. 2000. Framing processes and social movements: An overview and assessment. *American Review of Sociology* 26, no. 1:611–39.

Snow, David A., Robert D. Benford, Holly J. McCammon, Lyndi Hewitt, and Scott Fitzgerald. 2014. The emergence, development, and future of the framing perspective: 25+ years since "frame alignment." *Mobilization: An International Quarterly* 19, no. 1:23–45.

Somers, Margaret. 1994. The narrative constitution of identity: A relational and network approach. *Theory and Society* 23, no. 5:605–49.

Stevenson, Andrew. 2004. Dreaming of an equal future for immigrant children: Federal and state initiatives to improve undocumented students' access to postsecondary education. *Arizona Law Review* 46, no. 3:551–80.

Taurel, Patrick. 2015. Why DAPA applications were not accepted by USCIS today. American Immigration Council Immigration Impact, May 19. http://immigrationimpact.com/2015/05/19/why-dapa-applications-were-not-accepted-by-uscis-today/.

Tilly, Charles. 2004. *Social movements, 1768–2004*. Boulder, CO: Paradigm Publishers.

U.S. Citizenship and Immigration Services (USCIS). n.d. Consideration of Deferred Action for Childhood Arrivals (DACA). http://www.uscis.gov/humanitarian/consideration-deferred-action-childhood-arrivals-daca (last updated January 4, 2016).

U.S. Citizenship and Immigration Services (USCIS). n.d. EB-5 immigrant investor program. http://www.uscis.gov/eb-5 (accessed March 27, 2016).

U.S. Citizenship and Immigration Services (USCIS). n.d. Executive actions on immigration. http://www.uscis.gov/immigrationaction (last updated April 15, 2015).

U.S. Citizenship and Immigration Services (USCIS). n.d. I-821D, consideration of Deferred Action for Childhood Arrivals. http://www.uscis.gov/i-821d (last updated August 19, 2015).

U.S. Department of Homeland Security. 2012. Exercising prosecutorial discretion with
    respect to individuals who came to the United States as children. Memorandum,
    June 15. http://www.dhs.gov/xlibrary/assets/s1-exercising-prosecutorial-discretion
    -individuals-who-came-to-us-as-children.pdf.
Van Liempt, Ilse, and Veronika Bilger. 2009. *The ethnics of migration research methodol-
    ogy: Dealing with vulnerable immigrants.* Portland, OR: Sussex Academic Press.

PART 2

Immigrants and Community Narratives

∴

Latin@ Immigrant Youth in the Age of Mixed Messages: A Perspective on Deferred Action and Unaccompanied Minors

Lisa D. Ramirez

The United States has long been perceived as a land of great prosperity and opportunity. For two centuries, immigrants have come to the United States primarily to seek employment opportunities; to be reunified with family members already living here; and to escape violence, poverty, and persecution. In 2014, there were about 42.4 million immigrants living in the United States (about 13.3 percent of the total U.S. population) (Zong and Batalova 2016). This includes individuals who have legalized their status and have become lawful permanent residents, who have temporary legal status, who are present unlawfully, and who are naturalized U.S. citizens. According to the Department of Homeland Security (DHS), as of January 2012, 11.4 million undocumented immigrants lived in the United States (Baker and Rytina 2013, 1). Most undocumented immigrants come from Latin America, but there are also millions of undocumented Asians, Europeans, and Canadians. Between 40 and 50 percent of undocumented immigrants entered the United States lawfully, with a nonimmigrant tourist visa, for example, but overstayed their lawful status; the rest have crossed the border without authorization, illegally (Zong and Batalova 2016; Pew Research Center 2006).

Prior to 1882, immigration to the United States was not regulated; therefore, there was no illegal immigration to the United States. From 1880 to World War I, only 1 percent of the 25 million immigrants arriving through Ellis Island were denied admission (American Immigration Council 2008). Today, however, lawful immigration is limited to the immediate relatives of U.S. citizens or lawful permanent residents (sometimes with long waiting periods of up to twenty-four years); limited numbers of employer-sponsored immigrants; a fraction of 1 percent of the world's refugees fleeing persecution (not fleeing poverty); and winners of an online lottery for nationals of historically underrepresented countries (odds are about one in two hundred).[1] Our federal immigration laws

---

1   The Immigration Act of 1990 established the Diversity Visa (DV) program, where fifty-five thousand immigrant visas would be available in an annual lottery, starting in fiscal year

have changed dramatically, making it much more difficult for individuals with no family or employment ties to the United States to migrate legally. Therefore, many who are desperate enter or attempt to enter without permission, or worse, have been brought here involuntarily by force, coercion, or under false pretenses (for example, through human trafficking).

As an immigration attorney, I have the honor and privilege to assist individuals, families, and businesses to navigate the complexities of the U.S. immigration and nationality system. Unfortunately, regardless of the experience or expertise of the practitioner, we do not determine the outcome, the access to benefits or opportunities, or who stays and who goes. In fact, all too often, our hands are tied by the current law and its application, which often results in unjust and unintended outcomes. As a result, we are left with the daunting task of attempting to effectively and sensitively explain why there is no opportunity available for an individual to legalize his or her status or to live or work in the United States.

These challenges are amplified when representing a minor or a young adult who was brought to the United States involuntarily as a child; who entered as an unaccompanied minor; or who has been abandoned, abused, or trafficked. Many of these children already have endured and overcome a great many challenges in their short lives. Yet they have hope and expectation for the opportunities available in the United States. Many of these young people have already lived a great part, if not most, of their lives in the United States and, in fact, consider themselves American. They have been educated in the American school system. They were taught to work hard and study hard, to aim high and dream big; what they were not told or prepared for was that at the end of their journey, they would have limited, if any, access to a job, opportunity for higher education, or the ability to serve in the military unlike their American-born peers with whom they grew up. As a result, they often become disillusioned and begin to question the point of their hard work and accomplishments or even the purpose of their lives. Many of these individuals lose hope and some are lured by a life of crime.

The devastation is far greater for those who believed they were born in the United States. In many cases, it isn't until they apply for a driver's license, to college, or for financial aid that they learn, for the first time, that they are not U.S. citizens. It is a shock and a life changing discovery to realize that the foundation on which they built their hopes and aspirations is gone in an instant. In California, given the proximity to our Latin American neighbors, most of

---

1995. For recent statistics, see U.S. Visas, U.S. Department of State, Bureau of Consular Affairs (2015).

the youth who find themselves in this situation are from Mexico and Central America (specifically El Salvador, Honduras, and Guatemala).

This essay will explore a number of programs and efforts that have had bittersweet results. Families continue to be broken up due to deportation, undocumented youth are often apprehended, and the future for them remains unclear. It is an unfortunate truth that we, as a nation, have sent mixed messages to these young immigrants.

Deferred Action: A Presidential Directive with Mixed Results

One area in which these young adults have received mixed messages is in the deferred action program. Deferred action protects an individual from deportation, prevents the accumulation of unlawful presence,[2] and entitles individuals to work authorization if they have a compelling reason to work (in other words, to pay for school, to become financially independent, to support a family, etc.). In June 2012, President Barack Obama, through his executive authority, expanded deferred action for young adults who arrived in the United States as children (through the directive known commonly as DACA, Deferred Action for Childhood Arrivals). Although deferred action, due to this relatively recent DACA program, has become a popular term in the mainstream media the last several years, it is not something new. And what most people do not understand is that it does not offer lawful status or amnesty, it is not a pathway to permanent residency, and it does not pardon immigration violations. Prior to this announcement, taxpayers had heavily invested in many youth through the public school system. These undocumented young adults studied hard and were eager to seek employment or enter the armed services; however, they simply were not permitted to do so. As a result, a generation was becoming

---

2 Stopping the accumulation of unlawful presence is very important to an individual who has not maintained legal status in the United States and wishes to legalize their status in the future. For example, under U.S. immigration law, if an individual has lived in the United States without lawful status for more than six months but less than one year and voluntarily departs the United States for any reason, including to attend their visa interview, they will trigger what is commonly referred to as a three-year bar. They will be prohibited from returning to the United States for three years. Those who have accumulated more than one year of unlawful presence and voluntarily depart will be prohibited from returning for a period of ten years. Therefore, because an individual does not begin to accrue unlawful presence until they reach the age of eighteen, deferred action allows many of these youth to avoid these harsh penalties.

disengaged and hopeless about their future and concerned about their inability to contribute to a society they considered home.

With this expansion of deferred action, generations have benefited. Applicants are protected from deportation, given employment authorization and the most coveted nine-digit social security number, and given access to a driver's license. Siblings who were once divided by place of birth (one having been born in the United States and afforded all the privileges and opportunities available and the other born a few years earlier abroad and brought to the United States without any legal status) now have equal opportunities to contribute to their communities and to our nation.

However, many are still left behind. They are left behind because not everyone qualifies. Two DACA requirements state that the applicant must have entered prior to reaching the age of sixteen and have demonstrated continuous physical presence in the United States since June 15, 2007. Therefore, youth, for example, who entered after this date or who were sixteen years old or older when they entered the United States cannot apply (U.S. Citizenship and Immigration Services [USCIS] 2016). As a result, families remain divided. They are left behind because youth who are protected by deferred action are still faced with a broken immigration system that deports their parents without consideration of the impact these parental deportations will have on them. These children cannot be deported; they have the right to live and work in the United States, but they potentially can lose something much greater: their parents and their families.

On November 20, 2014, the Obama administration sought to expand the DACA program to allow individuals who have been present since January 1, 2010, (versus June 15, 2007) to apply. The president also announced the Deferred Action for Parents of Americans and Lawful Permanent Residents (DAPA) program, also known as Deferred Action for Parental Accountability, which would allow undocumented immigrant parents to request deferred action from deportation and obtain employment authorization if the parent has lived in the United States since January 1, 2010, and has a U.S. citizen or lawful permanent resident child born on or before November 20, 2014, the date of the announcement.[3]

According to USCIS, it is estimated that Obama's executive actions would help approximately 4.9 million undocumented immigrants (see question 2 under "Key Questions and Answers" in USCIS, Executive actions on

---

3   For more information, see USCIS (Executive actions on immigration, n.d.).

immigration, n.d.). However, on February 16, 2015, one day before the updated DACA and DAPA guidelines were to be implemented, a temporary injunction was issued and at the time of this writing continues to remain in effect. In response to the injunction and what is perceived as an unjust political tactic, millions of people desperate to keep their families safe, secure, and intact have organized protests and hunger strikes across the country (Attanasio 2015; Cortés 2015). Only time will tell whether the courts will allow for the expansion of DACA or the creation of DAPA to eventually take place.

Setbacks and Hopes for Unaccompanied Minors

Unaccompanied minors are children who have no lawful immigration status in the United States; who have not reached eighteen years of age; and with respect to whom there is no parent or legal guardian in the United States or no parent or legal guardian in the United States is available to provide care and physical custody for them. Prior to 2012, it was estimated that approximately 8,000 migrant children entered the United States each year (Migration Policy Institute 2012). In 2014, over 90,000 such unaccompanied migrant children entered the country. It is estimated that this number will rise to 130,000 in 2015 (Migration Policy Institute 2014).

Unaccompanied minors and undocumented immigrants generally leave their home country to join family already in the United States; escape abuse, persecution, or exploitation in their home country; or seek employment or educational opportunities. The rise in street violence in places like El Salvador and Honduras, both of which vie for the unenviable distinction of having the highest homicide rates in the world, for example, has led many to flee to the United States. Today, the desire to escape violence in their home countries outweighs the desire for family reunification and job opportunities (Hiskey et al. 2016).

According to the Department of Health and Human Services, every year, the federal government apprehends thousands of unaccompanied minors. In 2002, with the passage of the Homeland Security Act, Congress transferred the care and custody of unaccompanied children from the former Immigration and Naturalization Service (INS) to the Office of Refugee Resettlement (ORR). It also instructed the ORR to develop a plan to ensure the timely appointment of legal counsel for each unaccompanied minor. Although heroic steps have been taken to provide legal counsel through nonprofit organizations or the Unaccompanied Children Pro Bono Project (UACPBP), the need for representation falls appallingly short (Commission on Immigration 2015).

The care and treatment of unaccompanied children has changed significantly over the years. Take the story of Jenny Lisette Flores, who in 1985, at the age of fifteen, was arrested and detained by INS. While Jenny was confined for two months awaiting her deportation hearing, she was kept in a jail-like juvenile detention facility where she was continually subjected to arbitrary strip searches; housed with others, some of whom may have been adults; and not provided adequate education, recreation, or medical attention (on this case, see Gamboa 2014). As a result of her experience, in 1997 a settlement agreement was reached in *Flores v. Reno,* which established the first uniform standard of care and treatment of immigrant and refugee minors in INS custody.[4] These standards are now part of the United States Immigration and Customs Enforcement (ICE) and the ORR. Today we see group home facilities and facilities that are better suited to house immigrant children. Children are able to attend school and receive medical attention, and it is far easier to reunite them with family than it once was.

Although in criminal prosecutions, under the Sixth Amendment to the U.S. Constitution, the accused is entitled to "have the Assistance of Counsel for his defence," a defendant does not have a Sixth Amendment right to counsel in any civil proceeding, including a deportation hearing (even though deportability is often a collateral consequence of a criminal conviction).[5] Therefore, although individuals in removal proceedings, including unaccompanied children, have a statutory right to legal counsel pursuant to Section 292 of the Immigration and Nationality Act (INA), they do not have a right to legal counsel at government expense. This means that people in removal proceedings have three options: hire a legal representative through their own means, obtain pro bono legal assistance, or proceed pro se.

Some unaccompanied minors are fortunate enough to encounter nonprofit organizations or pro bono networks that provide free legal representation; however, almost half of all minors who appear before an immigration judge

---

4   See the Flores Settlement Agreement, Case No. CV 85-4544-RJK(Px), http://web.centerforhu manrights.net:8080/centerforhumanrights/children/Document.2004-06-18.8124043749. Some of the agreement's terms have been codified at 8 CFR §§236.3, 1236.3. For cases culminating in the settlement agreement, see *Flores v. Meese,* No. 85-4544-RJK(Px)(CD Cal. November 30, 1987); *Flores v. Meese,* No. 85-4544-RJK(Px)(CD Cal. May 25, 1988); *Flores v. Meese,* 934 F.2d 991 (1990); *Flores v. Meese,* 942 F.2d 1352 (1992); and *Flores v. Reno,* 507 U.S. 292 (1993).

5   See *INS v. Lopez-Mendoza,* 468 U.S. 1032 (1984); and *Bridges v. Wixon,* 326 U.S. 135 (1945).

are unrepresented by legal counsel. According to the U.S. Department of Justice Executive Office for Immigration Review (EOIR) statistical yearbook for 2015 (2016, F1), 42 percent of all individuals, referred to as "respondents," were unrepresented. Many of these are children who may be eligible to remain in the United States based on their past experiences or fear of future persecution. Yet, without the advice or representation of a lawyer, children have very little chance of fighting government efforts to deport them. This is particularly troubling given that many of these children return to countries where they risk mistreatment, abuse, and even death.

These children need legal assistance. In one case, a Guatemalan teenager "was supposed to ask the judge for a continuance so his uncle," who lived in another state and who was a U.S. citizen, "could arrange for his transfer." "Rattled at being in a courtroom, he agreed to be deported, even though he was eligible for voluntary departure" (American Immigration Lawyers Association, n.d.). Having access to legal counsel would have availed him of his right to a continuance and enabled him to assert a defense or access an appropriate remedy. Accepting voluntary departure does not affect future applications for entry to the United States. A person who is deported must wait a decade before returning to this country or face a possible federal prison term.

Most recently, Jack H. Weil, a longtime immigration judge who is responsible for training other judges, made the assertion in a deposition in federal court that three-year-olds could defend themselves in court. He was ridiculed on a variety of social media platforms with many immigration lawyers taking videos of their own toddlers on the stand as if they were in court to demonstrate the absurdity of his statements. His comments nonetheless effectively highlighted the plight of thousands of juveniles who are forced to defend themselves each year in immigration court (Markon 2016).

The future for an unaccompanied minor is unpredictable at best and bleak at worst. After overcoming the many hurdles and challenges of traveling to the United States—fleeing danger, abuse, abandonment, or extreme poverty—they are offered little in terms of a safe, secure future. Instead they arrive to face a complex bureaucracy that is impossible for them to navigate alone. Without professional guidance or assistance, they do not have much of a fighting chance.

The good news is that due to the recent increased influx of unaccompanied minors traveling to the United States, we are beginning to see some compassionate policy changes. For example, on December 1, 2014, the U.S. State Department announced the official launch of the Central American Minors (CAM) Refugee/Parole Program, an in-country refugee/parole program in El Salvador, Guatemala, and Honduras. This program allows certain parents who are legally present in the United States to apply for their children to immigrate safely and legally, thereby providing an alternative to the dangerous journey that some children undertake to come to the United States.[6]

In addition, on August 21, 2015, a federal court judge in California ordered the government to release immigrant children from family detention centers, with their mothers when possible, and found that in detaining these children, the government was in violation of the *Flores v. Reno* settlement agreement. At the time of the ruling, the *Los Angeles Times* reported that there were 1,400 parents and children being held at three centers: one in Karnes City, Texas; one in Dilley, Texas; and one in Berks County, Pennsylvania (Hennessey-Fiske 2015). Further, in California, through the signing of SB-873, Governor Jerry Brown made available three million dollars to nonprofit groups that provide legal assistance to unaccompanied minors.[7] Unfortunately, in the wake of the recent deadly terrorist attacks in Paris, France, many states—such as Texas, Michigan, and Alabama—are refusing to permit refugees from Iraq or Syria to be resettled in their state, and the House of Representatives passed a bill halting the resettlement of Iraqi and Syrian refugees. Therefore, the future of how we are going to treat immigrant children fleeing danger remains unclear.

Conclusion

The manner in which our government handles immigrants, even lawful immigrants, is a conundrum. On the one hand, we graciously open our schools (for an enhanced fee) to foreign students, educate them, and give them opportunities for optional practical training, and, on the other hand, we make it difficult for them to remain in the United States legally to put to use the education they received. We invest heavily in educating undocumented youth and then give them no opportunity to continue their education, to work, or to contribute by other means. We have harsh restrictions on employers hiring unauthorized workers, but make it extremely simple for undocumented workers to pay taxes. We offer protection from deportation to immigrants who are otherwise not permitted to remain in the United States, while giving them no legal status or a pathway to legal status. By way of DACA, we have extended protection

---

6   For more information on the CAM Refugee/Parole Program, see USCIS (In-country refugee/ parole processing for minors, n.d.).

7   On SB-873, see Immigrant Legal Resource Center (n.d.).

to the young adults who arrived to the United States as children but deport their parents with unprecedented fervor. We provide a special court system for immigrants not fluent in our language and ignorant of our laws to have a fair hearing but provide no legal representation. These mixed messages only add to the inefficient and ineffectual patchwork of federal immigration laws—laws that are outdated, are out of sync, and result in unintended consequences.

In November 2014, President Obama announced that his administration would extend deferred action to the parents of U.S. citizens and lawful permanent residents. As stated above, this effort is currently being challenged in court and is pending before the U.S. Supreme Court. However, even if the highest court of the land agrees to side with the attorney general in this case, our country needs significant reform of our immigration laws. Otherwise, families will continue to live in the shadows, and many of our Latin@ immigrant youth will continue living in limbo.

Bibliography

American Immigration Council. 2008. De-romanticizing our immigrant past: Why claiming "my family came legally" is often a myth. American Immigration Council, November 25. http://www.immigrationpolicy.org/just-facts/de-romanticizing-our-immigrant-past-why-claiming-my-family-came-legally-often-myth.

American Immigration Lawyers Association. n.d. Protecting unaccompanied children. Issue packet. http://www.google.com/url?sa=t&rct=j&q=&esrc=s&source=web&cd=1&cad=rja&uact=8&ved=0ahUKEwjX1eHokPLMAhVIPiYKHfrNB7oQFggdMAA&url=http%3A%2F%2Fwww.aila.org%2FFile%2FDownloadEmbeddedFile%2F40608&usg=AFQjCNF768VoxMFnjFVCZd1-xZxsfOzM3A (accessed June 1, 2016).

Attanasio, Cedar. 2015. Immigration reform news: Following 9-day fast in front of 5th Circuit, hunger striker focused on 2016 presidential election. Latin Times, October 23. http://www.latintimes.com/immigration-reform-news-following-9-day-fast-front-5th-circuit-hunger-striker-focused-349435.

Baker, Bryan, and Nancy Rytina. 2013. Estimates of the unauthorized immigrant population residing in the United States: January 2012. Homeland Security, Office of Immigration Statistics. https://www.dhs.gov/sites/default/files/publications/ois_ill_pe_2012_2.pdf.

Commission on Immigration. 2015. A humanitarian call to action: Unaccompanied children in removal proceedings present a critical need for legal representation. American Bar Association, June 3. http://www.americanbar.org/content/dam/aba/administrative/immigration/UACSstatement.authcheckdam.pdf.

Cortés, Zaira. 2015. Hunger strike and protests for DAPA and DACA. *Voices of New York*, October 21. https://voicesofny.org/2015/10/hunger-strike-and-protests-for-dapa-and -daca/.

Gamboa, Suzanne. 2014. When migrant children were detained among adults, strip searched. *NBC News*, July 24. http://www.nbcnews.com/storyline/immigration -border-crisis/when-migrant-children-were-detained-among-adults-strip-searched -n161956.

Hennessey-Fiske, Molly. 2015. Ex-worker at Karnes Immigrant Detention Center says she saw unethical behavior. *Los Angeles Times*, July 27.

Hiskey, Jonathan T., Abby Córdova, Diana Orcés, and Mary Fran Malone. 2016. Understanding the Central American refugee crisis: Why they are flee- ing. Special report, American Immigration Council, February 18. http://www .immigrationpolicy.org/special-reports/understanding-central-american-refugee -crisis-why-they-are-fleeing.

Immigrant Legal Resource Center. n.d. How California's new law SB 873 benefits unac- companied minors. http://www.ilrc.org/files/documents/sb_873_ilrc_final_pdf.pdf (accessed May 12, 2016).

Markon, Jerry. 2016. Can a 3-year old represent herself in immigration court? This judge thinks so. *Washington Post*, March 5.

Migration Policy Institute. 2012. Top 10 of 2012—issue #10: As migration of unaccom- panied minors endures, and in some cases rises, governments seek to respond. Migration Policy Institute, December 1. http://www.migrationpolicy.org/article/ top-10-2012-issue-10-migration-unaccompanied-minors-endures-and-some-cases -rises-governments.

Migration Policy Institute. 2014. Unaccompanied minors: A crisis with deep roots and no simple solutions. Migration Policy Institute, June 25. http://www.migrationpolicy.org/ multimedia/unaccompanied-minors-crisis-deep-roots-and-no-simple-solutions.

Pew Research Center. 2006. Modes of entry for the unauthorized migrant population: Fact sheet. Pew Research Center: Hispanic Trends, May 22. http://www.pewhispan- ic.org/2006/05/22/modes-of-entry-for-the-unauthorized-migrant-population/.

U.S. Citizenship and Immigration Services (USCIS). 2016. Consideration of Deferred Action for Childhood Arrivals (DACA). http://www.uscis.gov/humanitarian /consideration-deferred-action-childhood-arrivals-daca (last updated January 4, 2016).

U.S. Citizenship and Immigration Services (USCIS). n.d. Executive actions on immigra- tion. https://www.uscis.gov/immigrationaction (last updated April 15, 2015).

U.S. Citizenship and Immigration Services (USCIS). n.d. In-country refugee/parole processing for minors in Honduras, El Salvador and Guatemala (Central American Minors—CAM). https://www.uscis.gov/CAM (last updated June 1, 2015).

U.S. Department of Justice, Executive Office for Immigration Review (EOIR). 2016. FY 2015 statistical yearbook. April 15. https://www.justice.gov/eoir/page/file/fysb15/download.

U.S. Visas, U.S. Department of State, Bureau of Consular Affairs. 2015. DV 2015— Selected entrants. https://travel.state.gov/content/visas/en/immigrate/diversity-visa/dv-2015-selected-entrants.html.

Zong, Jie, and Jeanne Batalova. 2016. Frequently requested statistics on immigrants and immigration in the United States. Migration Policy Institute, April 14. http://www.migrationpolicy.org/article/frequently-requested-statistics-immigrants-and-immigration-united-states (last updated April 27, 2016).

CHAPTER 6

America's Love/Hate Relationship with Immigrants and OC Human Relations' Voice for Understanding

Rusty Kennedy

The United States sends contradictory messages about its immigrant population. On the one hand, Americans recall with national pride, and sometimes even with tears, the welcome to immigrants from the sonnet on our iconic Statue of Liberty:

> Give me your tired, your poor,
> Your huddled masses yearning to breathe free,
> The wretched refuse of your teeming shore.
> Send these, the homeless, tempest-tossed to me,
> I lift my lamp beside the golden door!
> EMMA LAZARUS, "The New Colossus"

On the other hand, immigrants are vilified daily and are viewed as the cause of all bad things in our community from economic woes to terrorist plots. Donald Trump's presidential campaign serves as a perfect example. Consider this quote from one of his first campaign speeches in which he noted that Mexican immigrants are "beating us, economically." "'When Mexico sends its people, they're not sending their best.... They're sending people that have lots of problems.'" He added: "'They're bringing drugs, they're bringing crime, they're rapists—and some, I assume, are good people'" (Sanneh 2015). A few weeks later, Trump called for the building of a huge wall at our southern border, which he boasted he would make Mexico pay for; suggested that the United States should revoke the birthright citizenship embedded in the Fourteenth Amendment to the U.S. Constitution; and claimed that he would, if elected, immediately deport all eleven million undocumented residents in the United States. Perhaps the most remarkable part of Trump's comments is not that he elevated the debate on immigrants to newfound levels of national abasement but rather that his xenophobic messages did not hurt his presidential campaign. In November 2016, he was elected as the forty-fifth U.S. president.

Amid these contradictory positions on immigration, I find exceptional irony in our amnesia, or perhaps it is simply denial that we are a nation made strong by the diverse fabric of our polyglot society. The United States is a nation of immigrants and sons and daughters of immigrants. In this essay, I focus on this irony and our conflicting attitude toward immigration in the United States by sharing my experience in Orange County, California, where about one in three residents was born outside the United States. Orange County serves as the bellwether for our nation's disposition toward immigrants.

For forty years, I have worked for the governmental Orange County (OC) Human Relations Commission or its nonprofit partner, OC Human Relations. Initially I worked as a community organizer, then as the commission's executive director, and finally as the founder and CEO of the nonprofit organization OC Human Relations. The commission, a public entity, was founded in 1971 by the Orange County Board of Supervisors "to promote measures to eliminate prejudice, intolerance, and discrimination against any individual or group." In 1991, we founded the nonprofit OC Human Relations to partner with the commission and to expand proactive programs in schools and communities. With its mission "to foster mutual understanding among residents and eliminate prejudice, intolerance and discrimination in order to make Orange County a better place for ALL people to live, work and do business," OC Human Relations has become a leader in establishing model programs, such as the BRIDGES School Program, Police Community Reconciliation Program, and Dispute Resolution Program, as well as informative listening sessions among diverse groups; leadership development opportunities; advocacy work; and an annual awards event honoring individuals, programs, and organizations that foster positive human relations.[1]

In my work with the organization, I have had the privilege to see and share in the life experience of waves of existing and recently arrived immigrant communities of numerous nationalities. I have also witnessed the appreciation of as well as resistance to these immigrants. I offer stories of people and situations I have known and dealt with locally in Orange County that—I believe—dramatically illustrate our nation's love/hate relationship with immigration and the resilience of the immigrant community.

---

1   On the mission of the public OC Human Relations Commission, see http://www.ochuman-relations.org/about/oc-human-relations-commission/. On the mission of the nonprofit OC Human Relations, see http://www.ochumanrelations.org/about/mission/. For more information on both, see www.ochumanrelations.org.

History of Backlash against Immigrants in Orange County

Orange County grew rapidly in the 1940s and 1950s as the postwar baby boom got underway and middle-class, predominantly white residents fled cities, creating segregated suburbs where blacks were systematically excluded. With a history of agriculture dependent on immigrant farm laborers, Orange County was home to Latin@ families but they were confined to barrios and segregated schools and churches. By the 1960s, the county was known as the white suburban home of the John Birch Society, a radical right and anti-Communist movement focused on limited government, and home to anti–civil rights elected officials, such as Congressmen James Utt, John Schmitz, and Robert Dornan as well as anti-gay crusader and California state senator John Briggs.

This legacy of activists fighting against fair housing and civil rights became the launching pad for anti-immigrant movements, such as the California Coalition for Immigration Reform, led by Orange County Congressman Dana Rohrbacher and anti-immigration activist Barbara Coe, which sponsored Proposition 187, the so-called Save Our State initiative. This 1994 ballot measure aimed to establish a state-run citizenship screening system and prohibit undocumented immigrants from using health care, public education, and other services in the state of California (Prop. 187 approved in California 1994). In 2004, the Minuteman Project was founded by Jim Gilchrist and Chris Simcox. Gilchrist, who later unsuccessfully ran for Congress in Orange County, led this vigilante group. The group, now largely disbanded, was similar to an armed neighborhood watch group made up of hundreds of volunteers; they patrolled the twenty-three-mile space of the border separating Arizona and Mexico to prevent illegal immigration. Their stated concerns were the inability of the federal government to control the border, the heightened fear of terrorists entering the country illegally post-9/11, and the flourishing drug trade that exists across the Mexico/Arizona border. Their presence was a media spectacle more than anything else, and the group never formalized into a sustained social movement (Medrano 2014).

Despite anti-immigrant activism, the positive economic benefits of immigration were underscored by President Ronald Reagan's Council of Economic Advisers. In their report, they articulated the national consensus among economists in the mid-1980s just before the passage of the Immigration Reform and Control Act of 1986 (IRCA). The report indicated that

> Market principles suggest that immigration in a competitive economy increases output and improves productivity.... The net effect of an increase in labor supply due to immigration is to increase the aggregate income

of the native born population. The economic benefits of immigration are spread throughout the economy. These include increased job opportunities and higher wages for some workers as well as the widely diffused benefits of lower product prices and higher profits. (Council of Economic Advisers 1986, 221–22)

IRCA created the Amnesty Program, which allowed a path to citizenship for applicants who paid back taxes and a fine. Most of the applicants were long-time U.S. residents. To qualify for amnesty, under IRCA, immigrants also were required to have seven years of continuous residency; proof that they were not guilty of any crime; and minimal knowledge of U.S. history, U.S. government, and the English language via a citizen test.

IRCA also required employers to check immigration status of all employees and outlawed the hiring of undocumented workers. This created a huge market for fake documents as immigrants became desperate for social security numbers to gain employment and led to an explosion of "con" lawyers who assured vulnerable immigrants that they would handle their legal cases to expedite the process to citizenship. Immigrants could readily and cheaply secure a fake social security number, but this would change with the passage of E-verify in 2004 (which evolved from the Basic Pilot Program that was implemented in 1997), which made the task of finding work much more difficult as the government had a stored database to check the authenticity of social security numbers (Hass 2013; Rosenblum and Hoyt 2011).

While IRCA granted amnesty to a large number of undocumented immigrants (though simultaneously creating difficulties to obtain work), it also incited the fears of anti-immigrant activists. One of the consequences was a concern that newly legal residents would become a more potent political force. While many appreciated the labor immigrants provided, they also feared immigrants' growing power if they were granted legal status. This fear of losing power to emerging immigrants, or the "browning" or "Latinization" of Southern California, provided fertile ground for growth of anti-immigrant movements and anti-immigrant sentiments in general.

Love/Hate Exemplified in Orange County

In my work with the commission and OC Human Relations, over the years I have come across many cases, some subtle and some explicit, of America's love/hate sentiments toward immigrants. For example, in 1984, I was at a management retreat with colleagues and I was telling my roommate that the commission was helping day laborers collect wages for work they had completed. Their employers refused to pay them. I explained how we had worked with day laborers to move the location where they lined up at 6:00 a.m. several times to accommodate complaints from neighbors. My colleague then told me that he had seen day laborers lined up along Chapman Avenue in the neighborhood El Modena, and he said, "As much as I hate them, I have learned to use them."

Nowhere had I heard such an explicit expression of Orange County's love/hate relationship with immigrants. He was not directly affected by these men seeking low-paid, often dirty, and dangerous work, yet he "hated them." His negativity arose from their mere presence. And, in fact, the surprising reality was that my colleague actually benefited from day workers, because he often engaged their services. He sought their assistance with his yard work yet did not consider the reality of their harsh and challenging situation. He did not respect that these men worked long hours for low wages and often engaged in dangerous work without any professional security or health insurance in case of injury, only to be left dirty and sometimes cheated out of their meager wages. He did not appreciate that they offered him—and many others—a valuable service that he had actively solicited, yet he "hated them." He saw them as a "necessary evil."

While the politics of immigration reform have divided our community into pro- and anti-immigration factions, businesses, individuals, and the overall economy benefit from the supply of low-wage laborers. At the very least, they keep the prices of goods and services low through their occupations in low-wage labor work—such as day laborers, farmers, gardeners, construction workers, and restaurant workers—and help keep many businesses afloat. An exclamation point on this case was the crackdown on undocumented workers in Georgia in 2011. Excessive work and home raids received significant media attention, and hundreds of undocumented immigrants either fled voluntarily or were deported, which resulted in a labor shortage. Consequently, farms lay idle as there was no one to harvest the crops (which dispels the myth that immigrants steal jobs from Americans); farmers and their buyers lost huge sums of money; and the price of what they managed to sell rose significantly, which hurt consumers. Certainly, legal residents were not lining up to help with the labor shortage. After witnessing this debacle, other states, such as Alabama, that were considering similar tactics of increasing raids to create fear in immigrant communities thought twice and refrained from implementing similar practices (Powell 2012).

On average, immigrants contribute almost 120,000 dollars more in taxes than they consume in public benefits. Undocumented immigrants, according to the

Social Security Administration, as a whole pay about 13 billion dollars into Social Security on a yearly basis yet only receive about 1 billion dollars in benefits. In sum, undocumented workers, over the past ten years, have paid more than 100 billion dollars into the system (American Immigration Council 2015).

Also, despite stereotypes that undocumented persons are a drain on social services, they are precluded from any type of services other than emergency health care and K–12 public education. They cannot apply for other social services, such as food stamps or subsidized housing. Furthermore, in many states, undocumented students pursuing higher education are not eligible for in-state tuition and federal grants or loans.

In sum, Orange County residents love the low cost of day laborers, farmworkers, nursery workers, gardeners, janitors, nannies, maids, busboys, and construction workers, but they hate the immigration system and call it "broken." Many who vilify immigrants and call for securing the border, deporting "illegal aliens," and outlawing employment of undocumented workers also love the low prices sustained by these same individuals. In fact, as we contract out for services we often turn a blind eye toward the employment practices of those lowest bidders who might rely on low-paid undocumented workers. For me, this is a prime example of our love/hate relationship with immigrants.

I also think it is ironic that we speak of a "broken" immigration system, pointing the finger here or there, yet this "broken" system of immigration with large numbers of undocumented workers surviving in low-paid, dangerous, and undesirable jobs is part of the economic engine that makes our economy strong. In fact, the most substantially "broken" part of our immigration system is the poor way we treat these taxpaying individuals and families who are a vital part of our community and economy. We contemplate keeping them forever in second-class status without a path to citizenship, without a voice in the decision-making process of the communities where they live, without representation, and without a vote.

The system is "broken" for the vulnerable but works perfectly for those who benefit from their labor as well as for government and private contractors who militarize the border and build new prisons and detention centers to warehouse those escaping crushing poverty, crime, and drug violence rampant throughout many parts of Mexico and especially border regions. Indeed, the system works brilliantly for those who benefit from the profit-driven exploitation of the most vulnerable. This is akin to Michelle Alexander's book *The New Jim Crow* (2010) in which she argues that historically white society has found ways to guarantee black Americans second-class status. She contends that with the abolition of slavery and later Jim Crow laws and in the contemporary era, it is the criminal justice system that finds creative ways to criminalize, dehumanize, punish, and instill fear among threatening (in other words, primarily black and Latin@ youth) populations.

The Commission Responds to Backlash and Fears

In Orange County, the commission has been responding to this backlash against undocumented immigrants for many years. As we have seen, some immigrants have been welcomed to the United States but at the same time they have been resented. When the Vietnam War ended in 1975, for example, the United States welcomed tens of thousands of Southeast Asian refugees in waves that reached a population of over 1.7 million in 2010 according to the U.S. Census Bureau (2012). The United States provided welfare and special refugee resettlement benefits to help these allies acclimate to their new country. Yet when Vietnamese refugees organized a day to honor their veterans with a parade in Westminster, Orange County, in 1989, Frank Fry, a council member, rejected a request for a parade permit and stated "'If you want to be South Vietnamese, go back to South Vietnam'" (quoted in Aguilar-San Juan 2009, 79). As much as these refugees who were our allies in the Vietnam War were welcomed, they were also resented for their differences. Some, like Fry, felt that these immigrants should give up their traditions and be assimilated into the American culture.

The commission, on the other hand, advocated for respect of these differences and for understanding of the hard path of refugees who lose their homes, families, and countries. We focused on teaching compassion and appreciation of the culture and traditions of Vietnamese refugees. For example, in the early 1980s, we collaborated with the police force and refugee agencies to create the Task Force on Police Asian Relations (TOPAR), whose mission was to create police cultural awareness training materials. In 1990, we produced *With Respect*, a police training video focused on teaching about the Vietnamese culture. In the midst of the backlash against refugees that Fry and others have shown, the commission responded with compassion and understanding.

Immigrants became targets of hate crime in the six weeks after 9/11 as well. Our neighbors who were assumed to be Muslims or Arabs were especially targeted across the United States. In Orange County, the commission documented ten times the number of hate crimes targeting those perceived to be Arab or Muslim in those weeks than in any previous year (OC Human Relations Commission 2001, 7). Ironically, Sikhs were the first victims of 9/11 backlash even though they are neither Arab nor Muslim. The commission organized "Listening Sessions" in which commissioners went to Sikh gurdwaras and

Islamic mosques to meet with representatives following their weekly religious services.

At these sessions, Sikh children shared stories of being bullied due to their faith garb and stated that they don't tell their parents for fear that their turbaned fathers would come to school and make things even worse for them. In the West Anaheim neighborhood along the Brookhurst corridor, Arab and Muslim immigrants congregated in a small business community. Unfortunately, to many, these new immigrants looked like the terrorists who blew up the World Trade Center and Pentagon on 9/11. The commission organized police/ community dialogue to build understanding and positive relations among the Arab business owners, older white residents, young Latin@ residents, and police. The commission facilitated these small round-table discussions, which were designed to build awareness of the common interests of the community's diverse elements.

In 2000, the commission held a public forum to hear the stories of janitors, many of whom were immigrants. The purpose of the forum was to bring the struggle of janitors into the limelight at a time when they were seeking union contracts with the large companies for which they worked. Many offices are cleaned overnight by janitors who work for cleaning companies; they get paid much less than the Orange County public employees who used to clean them. Orange County employees got fair wages and health benefits, and if they worked long enough, they could earn retirement benefits. In our public forum, we learned that 80 percent of the janitorial companies that cleaned county buildings paid minimum wages and offered no health benefits to their workers.[2] In this forum, we heard the story of a young couple who brought their children with them when they cleaned offices even though they worked late into the night, because they could not afford childcare. We learned of their fear of getting sick since they were not offered any paid sick leave and they had no savings to get them through such difficult times.

One janitor described the garage that he and his family shared with another family because they were unable to afford better housing. Since there was no bathroom in the garage, they relieved themselves in a bucket, and when they had access to the house, they dumped the contents there. He worked long hours but received minimum wages, which were barely enough to pay rent on the garage and feed his family. Ultimately these janitors were successful in getting higher wages and benefits due to their organizing and the publicity garnered by such efforts as the commission's.

---

2   The commission also obtained copies of contracts between Orange County and janitorial services providers and examined them to see the wages and benefits offered.

In 2003, the commission also stepped in when immigrants had been swindled while trying to go through what they thought was the legal system. La Guadalupana Immigration Services, located in Santa Ana, California, was a mass immigration fraud scheme that played on the lack of awareness of this vulnerable immigrant population. La Guadalupana recruited thousands of immigrants who paid their life savings to a *notario* who promised them legalization.[3] According to the Orange County district attorney (OCDA) who successfully prosecuted the case, these unsuspecting immigrants gave their original identification papers, receipts, proof of residency, etc., to La Guadalupana only to find their cases for legalization were never filed.

When the OCDA's office called the commission in 2003 after their successful prosecution of the owners, they asked if we would take custody of boxes of large files on the three thousand immigrants defrauded by La Guadalupana. The OCDA indicated that we would need to remove truckloads of original paperwork from the La Guadalupana office over Memorial Day weekend or they would be discarded, because control of the office was being turned back to the landlord. For five months, Catholic Charities, the Orange County Congregation Community Organization (OCCCO), the Mexican Consulate, and the commission worked together to find and return 1,100 critical original documents to immigrants robbed in this fraud scheme.

The work of the commission has sought to give voice to a disenfranchised portion of our community. Undocumented immigrants are often made silent by their fears of compromising their immigration status or even of potentially being deported. Whether educating the larger community about the humanity of these families, advocating public policy to protect their rights, or standing with them against abuses they have suffered, the commission has always supported immigrants.

Mobilization Efforts and Experiences of Immigrants in Orange County

As a community organizer and an executive director of the commission, I have come across many Orange County immigrants who have shown resilience in the face of such backlash and fear. For example, Zoila worked in a small restaurant in Garden Grove owned by an immigrant family. In 1991, she came to the commission to seek wages she was owed but not paid. She told me of working

---

3   A *notario* is a notary public, understood in the United States to have no legal authority before the courts but in Mexico serves more like an attorney.

twelve-hour days, six days a week, with no overtime, at a sub-minimum wage, earning only two dollars per hour. She said that she never left the restaurant even during her meals because they needed her to be "on hand." When I called the owner into my office to address this illegal theft of wages, she said she treated Zoila as a member of the family, and directly and pleadingly implored Zoila, "Zoila, how can you do this to us? We are like family." The love ended when reality settled in and I told her she would have to pay Zoila all of her wages, including back wages for overtime, or face legal action.

Officer Jose Vargas told me that he illegally crossed the U.S. border and was deported a dozen times before he landed his job as a trash collector in the city of Stanton, located in Orange County; earned his citizenship; and ended up a beloved police officer in Santa Ana where I met and worked with him in the 1970s and 1980s. Officer Vargas always remembered his journey and sought to help others. When the parents of a young boy came to him and reported that their son, a minor, had been arrested and deported because he had no identification, he went to the Immigration and Naturalization Service (INS) to figure out what happened to the boy. Vargas learned that the boy had been dumped in Tijuana along with adult deportees. Vargas contacted the Tijuana police and asked them to look for the boy; they subsequently found him unharmed and picked him up. The boy still had no ID and no way to cross the border because he was a minor, so Vargas drove to Tijuana and as an officer of the law was able to cross the U.S.–Mexico border and bring the boy home to his parents. As an immigrant himself, Vargas understood their predicament and showed compassion for this boy and his family. He went beyond his call of duty as a police officer to assist them in their difficult situation.

The Bravo family was honored by OC Human Relations in 2015 for their courage in seeking immigration reform. As president of the faith-based Orange County Congregation Community Organization (OCCCO), Enrique Bravo works long hours as he has for over a decade in the county. His youngest child was born in the United States and was therefore a citizen, but he and his wife and four other children crossed into the country without papers in search of a better life. Enrique and his family are devout Catholics and volunteer in their church and community for the betterment of all people. So it was natural when their daughter Jessica joined an OCCCO delegation to Congressman Rohrbacher that asked him to support immigration reform.

Jessica explained that when Rohrbacher learned that she entered the United States illegally as a child, he was outraged and threatened to call INS and have her deported. Jessica and the Bravo family were not intimidated but redoubled their activism to seek immigration reform. The family marched over two hundred miles to Sacramento to bring attention to the plight of immigrants. They fasted for a week in front of the offices of Congressman Ed Royce to ask him to support a pathway to citizenship in immigration reform and participated in voter registration, education, and Get Out the Vote initiatives. Despite the setbacks the Bravo family was subject to by government officials, such as Rohrbacher, they continued in their fight for legislation that would secure basic rights for immigrants.

In 2007, the Orange County Dream Team was honored by the OC Human Relations. The Dream Team (or Dreamers), named after the Dream Act (Development, Relief, and Education for Alien Minors), are courageous activists who were children when they were brought to the United States by their parents. First introduced in 2001, the Dream Act is a bill that seeks to give young undocumented immigrants legal immigration status in the United States. We learned of their oft-repeated story of how they did not realize they were different from their peers until they applied for a job or admission to a public college in California. These young people committed no crime in crossing the border since they cannot be held culpable for their parents' actions, yet they were being denied in-state tuition, financial aid, and other scholarships due to the fact that they were undocumented.

The Dreamers shared their stories in public forums, even when faced with the threat of deportation. In part due to their advocacy, the California legislature gave them legal status to attend public colleges and to qualify for financial aid. Furthermore, in 2012, President Barack Obama initiated the Deferred Action for Childhood Arrivals (DACA) immigration policy, which allows some young undocumented immigrants who came to the United States as children to work legally and stay in the country without fear of deportation for two-year renewable periods. Two years later, Obama proposed a new policy, DAPA (Deferred Action for Parents of Americans and Lawful Permanent Residents), which would allow parents of citizens or permanent residents to work legally for three-year renewable periods and to remain in the United States without fear of deportation.[4]

However, soon thereafter, the governor of Texas filed a lawsuit claiming that Obama's executive order overextended his rights as president, and twenty-five other states joined in the struggle opposing the legislation. The U.S. Supreme Court ruled in June 2016 upholding the injunction against the president's expansion of DAPA and DACA. Yet this political discussion overshadows the humanity of the reality that the decision will have for millions of people and

---

4   On the Dream Act, DACA, and DAPA, see American Immigration Council, https://www
    .americanimmigrationcouncil.org/topics/daca-dapa (accessed March 8, 2017).

the consequences of the continuous breaking up of families, especially house-holds that are of mixed status.

Conclusion

The OC Human Relations has heard many similar stories over the years and works to show the human face of immigrants as a deterrent to anti-immigrant action. Especially during times of economic downturn and political cam-paigns, efforts to use immigrants as scapegoats increase. It is at times like these that the OC Human Relations' work becomes even more crucial. Through our work we realize that it is all too easy to give into the harsh rhetoric that vilifies immigrants during difficult economic times and draws our attention away from other factors that might actually be causing economic hardship. We also realize it is equally easy for us to close our eyes to the reality of the very low-income immigrant worker whose cheap labor brings us great profits in our businesses and low prices in our big-box stores. Our immediate short-term self-interest is served when we do not pay decent wages to our gardeners, busboys, janitors, maids, nannies, and factory workers. We love a good bargain and close our eyes to the consequences.

We are coming to a crossroads. If we choose the road of short-term immedi-ate self-interest, which leads us to a growing underclass of workers who cannot vote, do not have decent wages, lack safe working conditions, and are without health care or adequate shelter, what will be our future? If we listen to the self-serving voices of politicians who vilify the very people whose labor we all benefit from, what will we stand for?

I hope we choose the enlightened self-interest of caring about all people as if they were our brothers and sisters, our children and parents. We need to think about who picks, prepares, and serves our food; remember the hard work of immigrants who bring so much to our community and nation; and love them even when times are difficult. We must create a future where the politics of hate are scorned and the promise of this country is enjoyed by all. The OC Human Relations promotes this vision of immigrants as a positive and essential element of our diverse community.

Bibliography

Aguilar-San Juan, Karin. 2009. *Little Saigons: Staying Vietnamese in America*. Minne-apolis, MN: University of Minnesota Press.

Alexander, Michelle. 2010. *The new Jim Crow: Mass incarceration in the age of colorblindness*. New York, NY: The New Press.

American Immigration Council. 2015. Giving the facts a fighting chance: Addressing common questions on immigration. Special report, American Immigration Council, December. https://www.americanimmigrationcouncil.org/research/addressing -common-questions-immigration.

Council of Economic Advisers. 1986. Economic report of the president. Washington DC: United States Printing Office, February. http://www.presidency.ucsb.edu/ economic_reports/1986.pdf.

Hass, Douglas A. 2013. Employment and immigration law: Be careful who you hire— and who you don't. *Illinois Bar Journal* 101, no. 7. https://www.isba.org/ibj/2013/07/ employersandimmigrationlawbecareful.

Medrano, Lourdes, 2014. What happened to Minuteman Project? It's still roiling immigration reform. *The Christian Science Monitor*, April 30. http://www.csmonitor .com/USA/2014/0430/What-happened-to-Minuteman-Project-It-s-still-roiling -immigration-reform.

OC Human Relations Commission. 2001. *Report on hate crimes and incidents*. Santa Ana, CA: OC Human Relations Commission.

Powell, Benjamin. 2012. The law of unintended consequences: Georgia's immigration law backfires. *Forbes*, May 17.

Prop. 187 approved in California. 1994. *Migration News* 1, no. 11 (December). https:// migration.ucdavis.edu/mn/more.php?id=492.

Rosenblum, Mark, and Lang Hoyt. 2011. The basics of E-Verify, the U.S. employer verification system. Migration Policy Institute, July 13. http://www.migrationpolicy.org/ article/basics-e-verify-us-employer-verification-system.

Sanneh, Kelefa. 2015. A serious immigration debate, thanks to Donald Trump. *The New Yorker*, August 19.

U.S. Census Bureau. 2012. Race reporting for the Asian population by selected categories: 2010. American Fact Finder, January. http://factfinder.census.gov/faces/table services/jsf/pages/productview.xhtml?src=bkmk.

CHAPTER 7

Public Sociology in Action: The Struggle to Assist Undocumented Latin@ Youth

Eileen McNerney, CSJ

Something there is that doesn't love a wall, / That wants it down.
Poet ROBERT FROST, "Mending Wall"

• • •

I thank God for still having me alive, because if it wasn't for him I would be dead. After eight years of gang life, drugs, and alcohol, I'm still alive. People said I wouldn't make it. People said I would die.
Taller San Jose Hope Builders participant DAVID FLORES

• •
•

In this essay, I address issues of injustice that Latin@ immigrant youth are subject to by employing sociologist C. Wright Mills's introduction of the sociological imagination, or perspective, accompanied by a Freirean understanding of the world and our societies and the people that inhabit them as a living classroom (Mills 1959; Freire 1998). I was raised on a gospel that proclaims that every life is precious from conception until death. I believe the same more strongly each day. I don't know why I was called upon to care about these particular young men and women in Santa Ana, California, those caught in the deluge of poverty and instability, but I do care about them deeply. They are young, most in their late teens and early twenties. They didn't ask for the challenge of being caught between two cultures or the snare of crushing poverty, and they have fallen between the cracks too soon while struggling to find a foothold in life. Some of their brothers, cousins, and friends have already been gunned down in gang fights; some have begun to walk a path that will lead to perpetual imprisonment; still others are just scared, lost, and stuck, sitting on couches in crowded apartments waiting for life to happen.

Our broken and discarded youth need the assistance of their communities, people who acknowledge their humanity, especially given the unrealistic burdens that they carry at a young age, emotionally and socially. And they need to see a way through the stereotypes if they are to become who they were created to be. Whatever the challenges and arguments are about this current wave of immigration and its effects on American society, I've seen too much now. It is no longer possible for me to turn away from the young people who inhabit my day-to-day world, for I know that if I shut them out of my waking hours, they will surely visit me in my dreams. They don't deserve to live in darkness. I believe that we fail ourselves and our society if we label our young "dropouts," "mess-ups," and "felons"; let them lie in the gutter of life; and turn our faces away as we pass by. Their stories and their struggles are forever tattooed upon my heart.

In 2014, an estimated 11.3 million undocumented immigrants lived in the United States (Krogstad and Passel 2015). As of mid-2014, Latin@s have outnumbered whites in California, and it is predicted that by 2060 Latin@s will make up 49 percent of the total population in the state (Lopez and Krogstad 2015). The state economy is heavily affected by the burden of providing medical care, education, police protection, and a prison system to house undocumented residents. Every day, local newspapers carry stories and letters to the editor about the dilemmas and conflicts of absorbing a large illegal immigrant population. Both pro and con arguments are posited on the subject in a schizophrenic fashion, with the vast majority opposed to the massive influx of people from south of the border even though many believe that the U.S. economy probably benefits from immigration.

In other words, California has a love/hate relationship with Mexico and Mexicans who live in the Southwest. We've learned to make guacamole and tacos, blend a mean Margarita, and hire mariachis for our weddings, and piñatas often replace pin-the-tail-on-the-donkey at children's birthday parties. Our economy depends on a continuous stream of cheap labor from south of the border, whether legal or illegal. Mexicans and Mexican Americans (with or without proper papers) are the gardeners, the busboys/busgirls, the dishwashers, the cleaning ladies and men, and the nannies that make comfort and convenience affordable. It would be unthinkable to abolish this vast, largely unskilled labor force. In reality, the underclass makes the upper class possible.

Still, a number of Californians would like the Mexicans to go home, and sometimes they show little distinction between who should go home—those born in Mexico, those born in the United States to immigrants from Mexico, or those born in the United States a generation ago. And where exactly should they go and when? "Down on brown" is an attitude that floats freely throughout California and often there is little differentiation upon whom it lands. It's hardly an invitation to successful acculturation.

The Fear of the Browning of California

Throughout California one now hears Spanish spoken in supermarkets, shopping malls, banks, theaters, and restaurants. Spanish advertisements paper the billboards and cover the sides of buses. Spanish-language television and radio continue to expand and they gobble up an ever-increasing share of the media market. The population growth of Mexican Americans and Mexican nationals in California is accompanied by prejudice against the brown-skinned population. Almost daily, newspaper articles decry the preferential treatment given to the undocumented and call for the deportation of Mexicans.

The first time I heard the word "beaner," it took me a beat or two to process the sting of its meaning and message. The loaded epithet came with the donation of a second-hand refrigerator to the convent. It had been a struggle to get the giant refrigerator in our front door. The donor had to take the door off its hinges, and with the help of a dolly he awkwardly maneuvered the refrigerator into the kitchen. Sweating and winded, he put the front door back in place, and when he was finished he headed for his truck. As he departed, I thanked him for his thoughtfulness, his time, and his trouble. "Better you have it than some beaner," he quipped as he rolled up the car window and stepped on the gas. "Beaner?" I'd never heard the word before, but it altogether sounded like "nigger" the way he had said it. I wanted to chase after him and push the refrigerator back upon him, but it was too late; he was already around the corner and long gone. We were stuck with the cursed refrigerator for two years, and sometimes when I least expected, his biting words—"better you ... than some beaner"—cried out within me as I opened the door and reached for the milk.

I wonder how long you have to live in California before you are no longer considered a "beaner." It is clear to me that first- and second-generation immigrants are tagged "beaners." But what if it was your grandparents who came from Mexico or your great-grandparents, or as was the case in my family, what if the border moved south and cut off one group of "beaners" from another over 150 years ago?

Migration Flows: Border Divisions between People in the Midst of the Free Flow of Goods, Commerce, and Trade

Many present-day Americans who have roots in western Europe proudly share stories of how and why their ancestors came, in time of trouble, war, or famine. Their separation from their country of origin, their culture, and their families was not an option. It was the forced choice of economic survival. They wanted to live and to give life to their children. These immigrants of the nineteenth and early twentieth centuries hit the land hard and determined. Some ran, some fell, and others stumbled along the way. Now we point with pride to their photos and share the scraps of their lives while we stand on their shoulders and cling to the American dream. History invites nostalgia.

Yet today's immigrant experience is quite different from that of a century ago. There is not as much land, water, or resources for health care and education. Even parking spaces are harder to come by. There are more guns, gangs, and drugs to contend with, and the streets of our cities are meaner. Violence is more widespread, frequent, and unpredictable. In the midst of a world war on terrorism that we can barely name and that we prayed would never come, we demand the right to control our borders and to determine who is friend and who is foe. There are decisions to be made. So who goes and who stays and in whom do we invest for the future?

I view myself as a realist informed by the gospel. I don't know how to solve the complexities of the immigration crisis or the chaos of desperation that emerges when the poverty of Mexico butts up against the affluence of the United States. I do know that when day after day people from Mexico and Central America risk their lives on journeys through cold mountain passes, through the blistering heat of deserts, or in the back of unventilated trucks, they are not seeking "the good life" for they have never seen it. They are desperately clinging to a hope that they may have life at all and that one day they might help their children rise out of poverty.

Mis antepasados vinieron en ese viaje—My ancestors came on that trip. That's how my family got here from Mexico. They crossed a border that never existed and that has never really closed. My grandmother spoke Spanish. I had to half-learn it the hard way. But my people—they weren't Spaniards. "Don't forget you're Mexican," my father would say to us. *No creo que parezca mucha a una Mexicana*—I don't think I look much like a Mexican woman, but I've never forgotten my roots.

I've crossed a number of international borders in my life, but I've never crossed one that's the equal of the border between Tijuana, Mexico, and San Ysidro, California. The border there is a mean-looking fence with high barbed wire that's angled southward at the top. It extends a good ways out into the ocean, daring the best of swimmers to challenge rough waters and uncertain tides. As the high foreboding blockade merges out from the land and into the sea, it resembles the exterior of a colossal maximum security prison.

Nearly forty million people cross the San Ysidro border each year in cars, in buses, and on foot. There's a free flow of traffic driving south from California and crossing into Mexico, but the return trip into the United States is tedious and can try frayed nerves. It's a long bumper-to-bumper wait behind long lines of cars as you inch your way toward the checkpoint. Twenty-four lanes mysteriously merge to eighteen at the crossing. Some drivers, convinced that fate condemns them to the slow lane, forge their way from one lane to the next, using their vehicles like tanks and winning their modest victories by millimeters.

At the checkpoint, border patrol officers talk to each passenger in every vehicle, verifying citizenship, asking the purpose of their visit, surveying their claimed purchases—all the while checking for drugs or contraband or for the possibility that a Mexican national might be hiding under a blanket on the floor of a vehicle or in the trunk of a car. The only distraction during the tedious wait time is the stream of vendors who walk between the lines of cars and hawk everything from pink, glitter-framed replicas of Leonardo da Vinci's *Last Supper* to bubble gum.

The real drama, though, is the sharp contrast in lifestyle, zoning, flora, and fauna between one country and the other. North of the border, in California, a mix of palm, pine, and eucalyptus trees line the wide freeways. Lush carpets of fuchsia ice plants flow down the terraced hillsides. Shopping malls and clean bright restaurants promise travelers comfort, cleanliness, and choice. To the south, Tijuana is grimy and noisy. Dented and damaged older-model used cars are the norm on the crowded streets. If there are flowers or trees, they are all but hidden by the preponderance of concrete and the spikes of rebar jutting out of failed building projects. On the Mexican side of the border, young men perch on high ground where they can see above and beyond the tall spiked, steel wall that separates the two countries. In solitary vigil, they ponder what might await them on the other side.

It is true that there is enormous poverty in Mexico. There aren't many jobs at wages that permit people to support a family. But not everyone in Mexico is poor. There is industry, education, and opportunity in Mexico, and quite a number of Mexican citizens have either been able to live comfortably there and advance their economic position or at least to survive without great want. But Mexico's economy does not support the burgeoning population and poverty has reached a historic level. It is the poor and the hungry, not the middle-class, Mexican who sneaks across the border in the dark of night, risking his or her life and all of his or her life savings to do so. Across history and in geographies throughout the world, people have dug tunnels, skirted fences, and navigated rivers to cross a border if they believe that the key to their survival was on the other side.

Decades ago in California, legal sanctions imposing fines and other penalties were enacted against employers for hiring undocumented workers. Relying chiefly on voluntary compliance, these employer sanctions have failed.

Meanwhile the rapid expansion of service and fast food industries, along with competition of global industries, has created demand for more and more low-income workers. Hardly anyone agrees that maintaining a large, permanent, illegal population is good for the United States or even for the individuals themselves. Undocumented immigrants can be easily victimized by employers and landlords. Even a fellow countryman from Mexico can take advantage of the new immigrant, sometimes setting up scams and charging the unwary exorbitant fees while not delivering promised services (such as green cards or other documents to secure resident status).

Three thousand companies (mostly American, Chinese, and Korean) have factories—*maquiladoras* (foreign-owned factories located on the Mexican side of the border)—taking advantage of the multitude of low-wage workers available. Jobs in the *maquiladora* sector and potential employment in the United States help attract continuing waves of migrants from central and southern Mexico, assuring the rapid growth of both Tijuana and its surrounding urban sprawl. When you fly between the United States and Baja California, you can look down and see that the border is just an imaginary line, a human invention that separates the two disparate economies. Yet the line has the power to change lives in dramatic ways.

In fact, most borders are arbitrary boundaries meant to define political realities. Sometimes it's a river or a mountain range that separates one country from another. Then there are barriers like the Berlin Wall, built as a hostile reminder of the unfinished business of war, or the much-visited Great Wall of China, which serves as a giant, cultural fence. Whatever their purpose or history, barriers and borders are meant to keep people in or keep people out. Although they are meant to establish geographical clarity and to control the behavior of human transit, borders do not have much power over people's hearts—not if people want what is on the other side.

For example, a few years ago, a young woman, Marta, crossed from Tijuana to San Diego to have her second baby.[1] Marta and her husband, Guillermo, are upper-middle-class Mexicans. They both teach at a local university in Tijuana. Although they are proud to be Mexican, they want their children to have the benefit of American citizenship and a future with broad economic choices. And so Marta sought prenatal care in San Diego. She and her husband prepaid for her medical costs in cash. The weekend before her delivery, the couple registered at a motel in San Diego and visited the local movie theater where they viewed a marathon of films until her labor pains began. When the time between her contractions shortened, they drove to the preselected hospital

---

1   All names are pseudonyms.

where the physician in charge of her care attended the birth of their child. The next day, with a new American citizen in tow, they drove home, south across the border into Tijuana.

In Santa Ana, Miguel had an entirely different philosophy stemming from his machismo, nationalistic pride. He wanted his children to be born in Mexico, and so when his wife, Xochil, was nearing the time of her delivery, he drove her across the border to his sister's house. There, with no prenatal care and no physician in attendance, she gave birth to each of their six children. They then returned home to Santa Ana, where Miguel did landscaping work and Xochil cared for her children and those of her extended family in their small, rented house. The Martinez children faced a major hurdle when they came of age. Although they had been raised in California since infancy, none were American citizens. They could not get legal employment or obtain a driver's license, and if they wanted to attend the local university, they had to pay out-of-state tuition fees. These two cases are a testament to both class and cultural issues that confront immigrants so close to the U.S.–Mexico border.

Thousands of Mexican immigrants cross each year and young children either inside or outside of Mexico grow up in a state of flux between two cultures, often losing their way, and get into trouble in ways that have lifelong consequences. Taller San Jose Hope Builders (formerly Taller San Jose) was established to try to remedy some of these effects.[2]

Taller San Jose Hope Builders: Faith-Based Activism at the Grassroots Level

In 1995, the Sisters of St. Joseph of Orange began a program in Santa Ana called Taller San Jose, which is designed for young men and women who, because of poverty and hardship, get in trouble too early in life. Many had dropped out of school, used and sold drugs, procreated children that they could not afford to raise, joined gangs, got arrested, and/or spent time in prison. Ninety-four percent of those who come to Taller San Jose Hope Builders are immigrants or the children of immigrants from Mexico and Central America. With the support of my religious congregation of sisters, I rallied civic officials and local employers to address these issues. In Spanish, a *taller* is a shop, a place to fix broken things. Young people who knock on the door of Taller San Jose Hope Builders are searching for a way to fix their broken lives. San Jose is Spanish for St. Joseph, the patron of workers. I invited young men and women whose lives

---

2 For more information on Taller San Jose Hope Builders, see http://tsjhopebuilders.org/.

had been broken too early in life to walk through the doors of Hope Builders and to form communities of learning where they could heal and grow.

The real activism emerged after I, with three other sisters, moved into a barrio neighborhood in Santa Ana in 1992. That's where my eyes were first opened to the plight of immigrants—encapsulating Mills's conceptualization of the sociological imagination (1959)—walking in other people's shoes and a reality so distinct from my own as I previously lived in the comfort of the motherhouse a mile or two away. From the window over our kitchen sink, I saw every day the family who lived in the garage next door: a father, a mother, and three children. There was electricity in that garage but no heat when it was cold and certainly no air-conditioning. There was no water either, except for a trough outside. A toilet that looked like an outhouse was attached to the front of the house.

In a Freirean sense, that neighborhood became my teacher and I learned a new pedagogy that I would later embrace and put into practice. I walked the streets a lot and when I passed the century-old craftsman-style homes I always looked for the garage in the back; eventually, I learned who lived there. One day there was a sign on the house behind ours. It read: "*Una recamara: Tres hombres or tres mujeres. $300*"—One bedroom: Three men or three women. $300. I began to understand the circumstances under which those without papers, the undocumented, lived.

After observing the extreme poverty and substandard living conditions to which these immigrants were exposed, and the indignity and injustice that accompanied them, I became aware of the violence rooted in this poverty, which was being facilitated by gang activity. My initial awakening moment was in 1993 when a young man was shot and killed behind the home I shared with three other sisters. Carlos was seventeen years old. His nineteen-year-old brother had been killed by the gang the year before. On a beastly hot August night, the windows of all homes and apartments were open and the family's apartment was not more than one hundred feet from my bedroom window. I heard the mother wailing and screaming for nearly two hours and I lay awake all night horrified by what I had seen and heard. This tragic incident created a passion within me to find an alternative for troubled young people in barrio neighborhoods who were putting their lives at great risk, giving up on life before they'd had a chance to live it.

From the young people who have come to Taller San Jose Hope Builders I have learned more over the years: what it was like to always take the lowest job, to be afraid to be noticed at all in the workplace, always to be in hiding, to hope one's *suecos* (fake papers) would pass, to borrow a cousin's ID, or to drive without a license. One young woman had a job at a convenience store. She desperately needed the job but was treated poorly. She never got a break, even for lunch. The owner made her crouch down behind the counter to eat. She didn't protest—to whom could she complain? She was undocumented. She needed the job.

An acquaintance of mine hired one of our students—an undocumented young man. The employer was rich, powerful, and well connected. He told me that he could talk to his congressman and find a way for this young man to achieve legal residence. After several fruitless months, the employer called me, disheartened. "There's nothing I can do to help him, is there?" he asked. Whatever power, money, or influence this man had, he hit a brick wall, a solid brick wall that is well known to those who have come up against it.

Things continued to get worse for many youth at Taller San Jose Hope Builders despite their hard work and commitment to play by the rules and adapt to mainstream society's values and work ethic. Six years after we opened Taller San Jose, and by that time I had learned plenty about the struggles of immigrants, the terrorist events of 9/11 happened. I watched the news unfold that morning—watched the first tower fall and then the second before I went to work. I was horrified by what I saw, but I had another kind of knot in my stomach. I began to imagine how this disaster—the fact that terrorists from another country could have caused such death and destruction within our borders—would have an impact on any progress toward immigration reform.

When I told each class at Taller San Jose Hope Builders about the destruction of the World Trade Center that day, what I thought, but did not say aloud, was

> You're screwed now—those of you sitting on the fence waiting for your application for a green card to be processed. You're screwed! Another kind of door has slammed in your face. Now the borders will tighten. Now bigger and longer fences will be built. Now the flow of any pipeline toward seeking legal residence will be reduced to a tiny and very slow trickle.

My fears immediately following 9/11 were well founded.

The hopeful eighteen year olds whom I met twenty years ago when I founded Taller San Jose are now approaching forty. Many are still hiding, still taking the lowest jobs, still living in circumstances that most of us would not tolerate. They are trying to create a better future for themselves and their families. Many are married and have children of their own.

Upward, Backward, Sideways, Onward: Some Theological Perspectives

Before I began to walk with the immigrant and the poor, I never put my face into the face of poverty for a sustained period of time. My journey with these young people is changing me. I am conscious that I now carry within me the story of many people oppressed by poverty. These are not the people who are half a world away—those whose bodies are more bone than flesh and whose sunken eyes are hauntingly captured on magazine covers, those for whom we pray with compassion while filled with gratitude for our own deliverance. The people who dwell in my heart live here in my own country. They are my neighbors. They shop at Walmart. While many view immigrants and their children as intruders, I have come to understand them as victims of economic displacement, a phenomenon that defies borders. While they may not appear half-starved, their lives are often so painfully poor that it is sometimes easier not to look in their direction.

I don't know what lies ahead for the young people who have shared their stories with me, but I am privileged to know them and like the best of parents, I want to give them both roots and wings. I often think about the most troubled young people whom I meet as the lost sheep, the ones whom Jesus talked about in the scriptures. These are the sheep that stray from the flock as it moves ahead, the ones who get caught in the brambles and thorns and then become easy prey for the ever-present wolves.

When I picture Jesus, the Good Shepherd, I imagine him walking calmly amid the bramble bushes, staff in hand, freeing the lambs from their entrapment and carrying them back to the flock, one at a time, across his broad capable shoulders. I don't know how far he had to walk to rescue his errant lambs or what the rest of the flock was doing in his absence. Maybe the Good Shepherd was frantic at times, worried about both the wayward lambs and the safety of the larger flock left under the protection of the sheep dogs. I myself am more of a sheep dog than a shepherd. I have only seen these energetic border collies in the movies. I remember them leaping about, running ahead, circling the flock, and holding off potential strays with their intense gaze. Surely these worker dogs are exhausted by nightfall. They lie at the feet of their master, every fiber of their being spent in his service, yet ready to leap into action again at his ready signal.

Sometimes at Taller San Jose Hope Builders I have felt overwhelmed by the poverty that I see before me—the too-close living, the financial fear and insecurity, the hopelessness, the drug culture, and the crime-ridden neighborhoods. I have had to learn to keep my face in the face of human suffering, to stay focused, and not to turn away when I have felt powerless to help. In his book, *Sabbath: Restoring the Sacred Rhythm of Rest*, Wayne Muller describes a conversation with an emergency room physician in a busy metropolis. The doctor hypothesizes that people at the frontlines of medicine rush and hurry, because of the

> fear of the terrible things that they will feel in the quiet. They are so close to so much suffering and loss, they are afraid that if they stop, even for a moment, the sheer enormity of sorrow will suffocate and overwhelm them. (1999, 52)

I think that is how it has been for me.

I have often been horrified by the painful lives of the young people with whom I work. They, on the one hand, are caught in survival mode and cannot take the time to name their pain for fear it would paralyze them. I, on the other hand, absorb their pain and store their memories deep within me. Every day I keep these young people in my prayers. I want to surround them with the power and goodness of God—with courage, hope, perseverance, and the healing power of forgiveness. I know that tomorrow more young people will walk in the door, sharing new stories and laying out their brokenness and their needs. It is uncomfortable to be able to do so little in the face of so much human suffering.

I have wondered at times if I will tire of walking with these broken young people as they fumble their way between two cultures. Forward, backward, sideways, onward—they never take the route that I would choose for them. I suppose that every parent could say the same of their own children and that God could say the same of all his creatures. God could say the same of me. I cannot make their lives as carefree and privileged as mine has been, though I hope they have more strength and dignity because of Taller San Jose Hope Builders. I believe that they have the ability to make a better life for their children. In this brief point of contact, if I try to soften their lives and shield them from life's challenges, I take away their ability to build the strength that they will need for their journey.

Bibliography

Freire, Paulo. 1998. *Pedagogy of freedom*. Lanham, MD: Rowman and Littlefield.

Krogstad, Jens Manuel, and Jeffrey S. Passel. 2015. 5 facts about illegal immigration in the U.S. Pew Research Center, November 19. http://www.pewresearch.org/fact-tank/2015/11/19/5-facts-about-illegal-immigration-in-the-u-s/.

Lopez, Mark Hugo, and Jens Manuel Krogstad. 2015. Will California ever become a majority-Latino state? Maybe not. Pew Research Center, June 4. http://www .pewresearch.org/fact-tank/2015/06/04/will-california-ever-become-a-majority -latino-state-maybe-not/.

Mills, C. Wright. 1959. *The sociological imagination.* Oxford: Oxford University Press.

Muller, Wayne. 1999. *Sabbath: Restoring the sacred rhythm of rest.* New York, NY: Random House.

CHAPTER 8

Revolution of the Heart: Assisting Migrants in Their Quest for Dignity

Patrick Murphy, CS

Imagine your name is Juan and one day you are on your way home after a long hard day of working construction. At this point all you are thinking about is dinner and being with your wife and kids. As your thoughts drift off, all of a sudden you get pulled over by a policeman for a busted taillight. Next thing you know, you are being asked for your driver's license, and your response is "I don't have one." With that simple statement your life changes in a matter of seconds. A few hours later, you are on a bus being deported from Los Angeles, California, to Tijuana, Mexico, a country you have not visited in over thirty years, because your parents brought you across the border to the United States when you were just six months old.

This story is not a new soon-to-be-released movie by a Hollywood studio nor is it an exaggeration. It is the story of the Casa del Migrante (House of the Migrant), a story we see every day, 7 days a week, 365 days a year.[1] Our official name is the Scalabrinians, Missionaries of St. Charles. We are a religious community founded by Blessed John Baptist Scalabrini in November 1887 with the original goal of serving Italian immigrants in the Americas. However, our work in the Catholic Church has grown and today we are called to be missionaries for migrants. The Scalabrinians are found in thirty-three different countries ministering to migrants in a variety of settings. For example, we currently have a network of about twenty-five Casas del Migrante functioning under an entity called Scalabrini International Migration Network (SIMN).[2]

The story of our mission has been a journey of over twenty-eight years; during that time, we have served over 240,000 people. In the early years of the Casa, we served primarily a group of men who were desperately trying to go to *el Norte* (the North, the United States) because they could not survive in their hometowns in Mexico. They left everything behind for one simple reason: to work and support their families. Their American dream was not to stay in the

---

1 For more information about the Casa del Migrante, see www.migrante.com.mx.
2 For more information on our mission, see www.scalabrinimigration.org.

United States but to go there for a few years and then return home to be with their families.

However, about eight to nine years ago things changed dramatically for both the migrants and for our mission. Crossing the border in the area of Tijuana became next to impossible as people were asked to pay smugglers exorbitant fees of up to ten thousand dollars to assist them in illegally crossing the border. People became victims of extortion and kidnapping on a regular basis, and in the process some died in their attempts to cross the border. Around the same time, the demand for workers in the United States diminished and the U.S. government increased controls and militarized the border in the San Diego–Tijuana region.

The result is that we went from being a Casa del Migrante (House of the Migrant) to a Casa de los Deportados (House for Deportees). For example, in 2014, we had 6,539 guests at the Casa in Tijuana; 87 percent were deportees and many had stories similar to Juan's. To be honest, some were deported because they were hardened criminals but many were deported for driving with busted taillights or for not having a driver's license or, my favorite one, for fishing without a license. This is how overwhelming immigration policy has become across the U.S.–Mexico border.

The Insane Immigration Policy on the U.S.–Mexico Border

Some say the definition of "insanity" is doing the same thing over and over again and expecting different results. Not only is the current immigration system broken but it is also the definition of pure insanity.

After two years as the director of Casa del Migrante in Tijuana, I began to wonder if anyone at the institutional government level really cares, given decades of political stalemate. If the Republican Party cared, there would have been immigration reform a long time ago. If the Democratic Party cared, President Barack Obama would not have waited until 2014 to present an executive order. If the Mexican government cared, leaders would have been active in controlling extortions and kidnappings of migrants. They still have no comprehensive plan to welcome home the *pasianos* (countrymen) who are deported on a daily basis. In the meantime, some states, like Arizona, Georgia, Alabama, and Texas, have begun to legislate their own immigration laws. It has become the latest trend among some states so fed up with a lack of any federal immigration reform to take matters into their own hands and legislate statewide laws in an effort to establish law and order. The result is more chaos as laws vary from state to state and the federal government has lost even more control over the immigration system. The latest example of this is the decision in the state of Texas to not give birth certificates to children of undocumented parents. Just when you think immigration insanity cannot get any worse, it is being taken to a new level by Texas legislators who are attempting to redefine the concept of U.S. citizenship.

Another unintended result is that immigrants flee states that have become hostile toward them. Before you know it, at harvest time, there are no more people to pick crops, which literally rot on the vine. The result is economic devastation to a state's economy. I would hope that this tendency has run its course after some states have failed to enforce immigration laws. However, in the meantime, we are right back to a frustrating reality of a broken immigration system that does not work for anyone.

It is time for a new model, a new way of doing things. We need to stop the insanity and start searching for real solutions that treat people as human beings and not just as statistics. Perhaps in an effort to seek out some wisdom, it would be good to call to mind what Jesus commands us to do on Holy Thursday after washing his disciples' feet when he offers us a new model: "I, therefore, the master and teacher, have washed your feet, you ought to wash one another's feet. I have given you a new model to follow" (John 13:14–15). We should strive to "wash one another's feet" especially by helping those in need.

From where I stand here at the Casa del Migrante, I think there are some key issues that desperately need attention. To be quite honest, my generation has messed things up in terms of the immigration challenge. I hope that the younger generation can offer better solutions to these ongoing challenges.

The first challenge is the tragic impact that separation has on families, as well as the hidden crisis of child and youth immigration. In the summer of 2014, we heard a lot about the humanitarian crisis of children from Central America, particularly youth attempting to cross the Mexican border in an effort to eventually arrive in the United States. We called it the "crisis of unaccompanied minors." This was a terrible situation, but I think there is another crisis that no one seems to be speaking about; I like to call it "the crisis of the minors left behind." What happens to the minors left behind when mom and dad get deported? How many thousands of youth are left without parental support? About 2.6 million Mexicans were deported in a ten-year period (2003–2013), so there must be thousands of children of deportees living unaccompanied. In addition, there is another aspect to this crisis that demands attention. The Mexican government now states that there are over 500,000 U.S.-born children living in Mexico.[3] These statistics leave us with some important questions:

---

3 This information was presented at a panel discussion, "Repatriación: Necesidades y retos para su atención," held at the Conferencia Regional de Migración, organized by the Secretaría de Asuntos Externos de Gobierno de Mexico, in Mexico City on July 15, 2015.

Who is caring for this lost generation? How are unaccompanied kids affected psychologically? What kind of needs do U.S.-born children living in Mexico possess?

The second immigration challenge is what I call "the securing our borders first pipedream." A real insanity is involved in the process of building more fences, increasing technology, and putting more agents along the border in an effort to secure our borders before doing anything else. Some have said that we are paying about twenty-eight billion dollars per year to secure our borders. I wonder, is it worth the investment? Is this the best we can do? Is this real American exceptionalism in action? I think not and I know we can do better. All is for naught unless we attack the root of the problems of immigration in our region. It is poverty and violence that force people to leave. They have no realistic opportunities if they stay at home. Immigrants only want to do what is the best for them and their families; who can blame them?

The third challenge is south of the border and it happens when the Mexican government utters insanities like "do not leave, things are getting better." I realistically say: *"¿Donde?"*—Where? *"¿Para quien?"*—For whom? Certainly not for the people fleeing from places like Michoacán or Guerrero whose lives are threatened daily by the presence of narcos who say "We need your house so move out or you will die." Organized crime in Mexico, or what we may call the narco-drug trade, is highly sophisticated, well organized, and economically advantageous to many people. It is not just a few drug cartels running wild in the Mexican badlands; it is organized more like a multinational organization with a highly developed business plan. There is a lot of money involved in this illegal drug corporation and it is more than just buying and selling drugs. The long arms of the business cartels also feature a variety of other services that include migrant smuggling, extortion, kidnapping, collection of unofficial taxes, money laundering, and bribery of police and politicians. Confronted by a lack of opportunities and lack of trust in one's government, what else can one do but immigrate to another country; staying home may result in one's death. In the meantime, the U.S. government likes to keep things simple by more or less saying: "Please stay at home because we cannot allow everyone in who wants to come into the USA." Who can argue with that logical line of thinking?— only those who have to choose between crossing the border or dying.

Although the people who support our mission give me great hope, I must be honest and say that it is an uphill battle given the current political environment in parts of Mexico. The situation is not improving and people continue to struggle to survive day to day. In the meantime, I am inspired by people like Marisol, a thirty-nine-year-old woman who worked at our Casa del Migrante in Nuevo Laredo as a Scalabrini lay volunteer. Marisol, a reporter by trade, was a dedicated single mom with polio who also adopted her sister's kids. One day about three years ago, Marisol disappeared. A few days later, her decapitated head was found in a flower vase by the entrance to the city of Nuevo Laredo with a note that said something like: "This is what happens to people who talk too much." She continues to live on in the hearts of all of us who serve here at the Casa—a reminder that washing migrants' feet can be a risky venture for all.

Some Signs of Hope in Breaking Down the Borders

Faced with a constant wave of migrants (6,500 people arrived at our Casa in Tijuana in 2014 alone), I can see some signs of hope in this immigration dialogue. However, the question remains, how do we use these signposts of hope to break down the borders that fence us in as human beings?

One sign of hope comes from Pope Francis who calls us to be people of mercy and compassion. One of my favorite images that he has offered is when he said "I see the church as a field hospital after a battle," a place where you have to "heal the wounds" (Spadaro 2013). The immigration mess has created a lot of wounds in need of healing and so as a church and society we must give people hope by first healing wounds and restoring people's dignity. For the occasion of World Day of Migrants in 2014, Pope Francis elaborated on this theme by saying:

> Our hearts do desire something "more" ... they want to "be" more.... Migrants and refugees are not pawns on the chessboard of humanity. They are children, women and men who leave or who are forced to leave their homes for various reasons, who share a legitimate desire for knowing and having, but above all for being more. (2013)

On the occasion of World Youth Day in the summer of 2013 from a soccer field in Brazil, Pope Francis called the world to learn from the poor when he said to them and to us:

> The culture of selfishness and individualism ... is not what builds up and leads to a more habitable world: it is the culture of solidarity that does so, seeing others not as rivals or statistics, but brothers and sisters.
> Pope Francis calls for solidarity and dialogue 2013

Pope Francis repeatedly gives hope to the unfortunate of the world in both his actions and his statements and calls on others to assist those in need.

After two years of serving as the director at this mission in Tijuana, I can definitely say that the Casa is a field hospital on the frontlines of immigration battles. It is a place of healing where people find an oasis of hope in the desert of deportation. It is in giving hope that we save people's lives. It is a place where dignity is restored when one stops being referred to as a deportee and once again becomes a human being.

I also see the migrants and deportees as teachers of hope. The people I meet at the Casa continue to amaze me daily. Their spirit fills me with hope. Their dreams have been shattered and in many cases, their lives have been destroyed, but many continue to live on with an attitude that simply says: "*Si se puede*"—Yes, I can. "*Si Dios quiere manaña puede ser major*"—God willing tomorrow will be better. They show me daily that lives can be raised from the dead. Here at the Casa I see Lazarus coming out of the tomb every day ready to give life another shot. They are my teachers about hope and life and they have a lot to share with anyone who is blessed to cross paths with them.

In reflecting on the reality that confronts us daily, I cannot help but think about how here at the Casa we are experiencing in a real way what Paulo Freire refers to as "dialogical learning" (2000), a process in which we are continuously in dialogue with others and consequently in this process we create and recreate ourselves. In the Casa del Migrante, we are always in this process of forming new relationships that promote critical learning, which often reveals the truth of interacting with others and the world. Perhaps most of the time we do not even realize this is happening, but my experience demonstrates that there is a lot of mutual learning taking place in our encounters with the guests at the Casa. In the end, everyone blessed enough to participate in the process can be changed forever.

A Counternarrative: A Revolution Embedded in Compassion and Mercy

Many good people are doing a lot of good work for migrants in our midst: for example, people who live and practice the Casa logo of Matthew 25:35, "I was a stranger and you welcomed me." However, what we do is not enough. We need to do more to stop the insanity of the broken immigration system. Consequently, we are in the process of launching one of our newest projects, Casa de Transición (House of Transition). Our brothers in Christ need more time to transition back to their country of origin. They need help in getting documents and finding jobs. They need assistance in adapting to this new world called Mexico even if it is the country where they were born. At the core, they need help in coming home. The challenges of deportation are not about to stop anytime soon and so we need a plan of action. To put this plan into action, we are committed to change the mission of the Casa and to expand our tent on the battlefields of the border and work in conjunction with the Mexican government to restore dignity to those who are being repatriated.

In 2015, we began a three-year project at Casa del Migrante that will focus on about fifty people each year in an effort to save some lives. In addition to helping people get jobs, we are committed to assisting them with rent for up to three months, as well as providing ongoing workshops to support them in their adjustment back home. We hope that by successfully carrying out a pilot project we may someday convince the Mexican government that one way of stopping the immigration/deportation insanity is to invest in its people and organize a national program for helping migrants in their transition. Let's face it, after so many years of sending millions of dollars of remittances back home, it is about time that migrants receive some financial support in their time of need. Many have given for so long and now it is time for them to receive something back.

Furthermore, if we are to successfully break down the borders and become invested in a more fruitful dialogue, we need to start a revolution; it is time to do so because nothing else is working. Many would agree with me that just sitting back and waiting for Congress to move forward is no longer a viable option for the millions of immigrants who continue to wait and to suffer daily. We can no longer trust our political system to do the right thing. We need to take personal responsibility and do more to allow the revolution of the heart to begin with each one of us as active participants.

Let me share with you some inspiring words of two religious leaders that should motivate us to take part in this revolution of the heart. In the 1930s, Dorothy Day, a champion of radical hospitality who lived during the time of the Great Depression, stated: "The greatest challenge of our day is this: How to bring about a revolution of the heart, a revolution which has to start with each one of us" (1963, 210). Blessed John Baptist Scalabrini in 1887 also spoke in a similar vein when he referred to the lamentable situation of Italian immigrants, uttering the prophetic words:

> Those who would like to put a stop or limit to emigration for patriotic or economic reasons and those who, because of a mistaken idea of freedom, want emigration to be left to itself, without direction or guidance, are either not using their heads or, in my opinion, are reasoning as selfish and insensitive persons. (1987, 380)

Day's and Scalabrini's statements resonate with today's immigration situation in the United States. The challenge is clear—our hearts must desire to do something more. In fact, that is why I boldly suggest we must start a revolution of the heart. We cannot afford to wait, the time is now and all our migrant brothers and sisters are placing their hopes on us.

The popular TV program *Star Trek* began each episode with the bold proclamation: *Space the Final Frontier*. I believe that we need to reframe the concept and say "the human heart is and will always be the final frontier." For that reason, we need to do some serious reflecting about what I call "the borders of the heart."

In the summer of 2014, we had a group of eighteen pastors visit the Casa from the Midwest. During one of the sharing sessions, one pastor asked, "Father Pat how do you define borders and why do they exist?" A great question, to which I replied with one of my stock responses: "Well borders exist to control the ebb and flow of people and products between two countries. These borders tighten and loosen depending on economic conditions, as well as the need for cheap labor."

I have recently been thinking that there also exist other types of borders that are even more difficult to define and more challenging to cross: "borders of the heart." In essence, these borders exist in every part of every country and in every place that human beings live. In fact, I think it is here where we need to have the desire to do more. It is here where the revolution must happen so that attitudes may be changed and some form of comprehensive immigration reform might one day become a reality. If this revolution of the heart is to happen, all of us need to accept the responsibility to do more for our immigrant brothers and sisters and work at changing hearts, our own included, one at a time.

Conclusion

I am hopeful that this can be done. I conclude with a few suggestions to do something more and get the revolution started. First, we need to help people cross the borders of their heart by humanizing immigrants; they are not aliens nor can they be reduced to mere statistics. Immigrants are human beings and demand our respect, so let us work at changing the conversation and putting a human face on every immigrant. Second, we need to help people cross the borders of their heart by providing them with the truth. We need to be more diligent in getting the facts out or else people's hearts will be filled with the garbage of the twenty-four-hour news cycle that seeks out sensationalism over humanization. Let's try to become part of the conversation and change people's hearts with factual and useful information. Third, we need to help people cross the borders of their heart by preaching the social teaching of the church without hesitation and with courage. True conversion can only happen if the heart is shaped by the sound teaching of what Jesus has taught. It is time to become familiar with the church's teaching and proclaim it from the rooftops in an effort to change the conversation and mold people's hearts in a new way.

Blessed John Baptist Scalabrini in the 1880s called the world to change attitudes about Italian immigrants when he boldly proclaimed: "Where people are working and suffering there is the church" (1987, 394). May the prophetic words of these spiritual giants inspire us and help us all to unlock the door to new possibilities and take the risk to cross the borders of our hearts! Let the revolution begin.

Bibliography

Day, Dorothy. 1963. *Loaves and fishes*. New York, NY: Harper and Row.

Freire, Paulo. 2000. *Pedagogy of the oppressed*. Trans. Myra Bergman Ramos. 30th Anniversary ed. New York, NY: Bloomsbury.

Pope Francis. 2013. Message of His Holiness Pope Francis for the World Day of Migrants and Refugees (2014). Vatican City: Libreria Editrice Vaticana, August 5. http://w2.vatican.va/content/francesco/en/messages/migration/documents/papa-francesco_20130805_world-migrants-day.html.

Pope Francis calls for solidarity and dialogue. 2013. *America: The National Catholic Review*, August 12–19. http://americamagazine.org/issue/pope-francis-calls-solidarity-and-dialogue.

Scalabrini, Giovanni Battista. 1987. *Bishop John Baptist Scalabrini: A living voice: Excerpts from his writings*. New York, NY: The Missionary of St. Charles Scalabrinians.

Spadaro, Antonio, SJ. 2013. A big heart open to God: The exclusive interview with Pope Francis. *America: The National Catholic Review*, September 30. http://americamagazine.org/pope-interview.

CHAPTER 9

A Life's Pursuit: The Journey to Higher Education of an Undocumented Student

Oliver Lopez

My family's reasons for coming to the United States differ from the typical stories that are shown in the news, social media, and films.[1] In Mexico, my parents, Pilar and Ricardo, were successful entrepreneurs. First, together they managed a business in the food industry; they sold breakfast milk shakes, *liquados*, with a cinnamon powder topping on the milky froth. Later in the retail industry, they provided women with the latest in fashion.

Our little family consisted of my parents, my older brother Ricardo born in early 1980, and me, Oliver, born three years later in mid-1983. We lived very comfortably. In recent conversations with my parents about our *journey-story*, my father told us of his master plan for Ricardo and me. He concocted the plan before my older brother and I were old enough to be in school. He thought it would be a great idea for his sons to live in the United States long enough to learn English, and then go back to Mexico and study in the best universities and become successful entrepreneurs. The pursuit of economic success and academic glory, not economic hardships or rampant crime, is what led our family to the United States.

In the late 1980s, my father put in motion the first phase of his plan. He equipped his family with a tourist family visa to the United States, and we made the trek to Anaheim, California, where my mother's side of the family had already established roots. They were in the process of applying for the Reagan administration's amnesty initiative, the Immigration Reform and Control Act of 1986. The details and drama of the actual day Mexico became visible only through a rearview mirror are part of another story. But like the stories of my family's adventures, the day we left Mexico is freckled with miracles both big and small and with many people my mother calls our *angelit@s* (angels).

Surprisingly, my brother Ricardo bears a majority of the responsibility for why we overstayed our visa. Before kindergarten back in Mexico, his favorite game was playing "going to school." My parents cherish a picture of Ricardo

---

1 I purposefully omit specific details in this essay to protect the identity of my loved ones and the kind people who helped me along the way.

holding my grandfather's suitcase pretending to take the subway to get to school. Ricardo had completely bought into going to school in the United States, learning English, and making American friends. Once here, he thrived, managed to learn English in months, and made the friends he once imagined.

After many months, motivated by nostalgia and longing to see his parents, my father decided it was time to take his family back to Mexico. My brother responded to my father's order with a "NO!" Ricardo's desire was to live out the many dreams of pursuing an education in the United States. My mother also did not want to go back to Mexico. She wanted to escape the unhealthy lifestyle she and my father had while in Mexico. When my parents look back at the difference in their lifestyle between Mexico and the United States, they admit overstaying saved their lives. Half-jokingly they say, "If we would have gone back, our marriage would have ended." I believe our entire family would be battling diabetes and maybe alcoholism if my father had taken us back to Mexico. My brother's youthful defiance ultimately melted our father's resolve to move back. Ricardo hijacked my father's master plan and we stayed in the United States.

Looking back we all agree this was for the best. My father made the ultimate sacrifice for his family to stay in the United States. He was not able to visit his family for over two decades since going back to Mexico without the proper documentation to come back to the United States would have left him in a situation where he would need to decide between crossing a treacherous desert on his own or paying a coyote thousands of dollars for help across the border—an option that provides no more guarantee of safe passage than doing it alone. While my father was in this golden cage of exile, my paternal grandfather succumbed to cancer due to complications of diabetes. My father was consoled via phone conversations with his family members since he was not able to be there in person. Regardless of what our lives would have been like if my father's demand to go back would have prevailed, we always had a choice. The power of choice is something a majority of immigrants do not have since for many going to *el Norte* (the North) is a life or death decision.

How did my parents survive in the United States without a valid social security number and proper identification? The only jobs available to them did not require proficiency in the English language nor a valid social security card. My mother had a sixth grade education. Her first job was washing dishes at a convalescent home. My father had a high school equivalent. His first job was doing odd jobs through an employment agency. Many jobs followed for both of them. Each new job was an improvement in pay and working conditions from the last. From simple beginnings, my parents have much to be proud of. They went from scrubbing toilets and washing blood-stained hospital bed linens to mastering the English language (Lucy and Ricky Ricardo were my mom's first teachers) and obtaining employment where the minimum education requirement was a bachelor's degree. They later honed their business acumen and pursued business ventures in the food and cosmetics industries. Just over ten years after arriving to the United States, the birth of my brother Joshua signaled another miracle for our family. Joshua's birth and my parents' purchase of a home established our roots here in the United States.

There were many positive moments and goals my older brother achieved. I am eternally grateful Ricardo made positive choices, with school as his passion. Had Ricardo chosen to be a gang member, I would have followed his path. I would have made my life's pursuit to become a tougher, meaner, more effective gang member than him. Ricardo's passion for education inspired our parents and me to achieve positive things. Our family has overcome seemingly insurmountable challenges because we dream as a family. Ricardo's stubbornness and dedication helped him overcome obstacles in a time before California legislation made it possible for undocumented students to pay in-state tuition (AB 540) and receive private and state financial aid (California Dream Act), and federal legislation made it possible to work and have any deportation action deferred indefinitely (Deferred Action for Childhood Arrivals, DACA). Before those laws were in place, people who were undocumented had no proof of California residency and paid out-of-state tuition rates, which were more than triple in-state fees. It was a time when the entire state of California believed that families like ours did not belong, as shown by the overwhelming support of Proposition 187, dubbed the "Save Our State" (SOS) initiative, which denied undocumented persons from using nonemergency health care, public education, and other services in the state of California (even though this was passed and signed by then Governor Pete Wilson, it was later deemed unconstitutional and repealed). Through it all, Ricardo earned a bachelor's degree from the prestigious University of California and later a master's degree from the reputable California State University, Fullerton. He did all of this while undocumented.

The moments that taught me the biggest lessons were Ricardo's times of despair related to pursuing a dream while facing the reality of being undocumented. Upon graduating from high school, Ricardo was accepted to many prestigious public universities. He dreamed of one day becoming a medical doctor. I remember the day he adorned the family dining table with his many acceptance letters, as well as awards he had earned. He pleaded with my parents to let him go, to help pay for the inflated tuition. He begged them to do something. Anything! Our parents tearfully replied, *"no podemos hijo"*— we can't son. Over triple the rate of in-state tuition did not cripple Ricardo's dreams; his dreams were only put on hold. This experience shook us all awake. Ricardo doubled down on his resolve to pursue his academic career. Motivated by Ricardo's tears and supplications to go to college, our mother established a fruitful business with Mary Kay Cosmetics. My father gladly swallowed his pride and supported my mother's business, the primary source of income for the family. My reaction was dark and confused. Why would a California school consider my brother a foreigner? Not understanding the complexity of the issue, I only applied to one school, a private school. I did not want my parents to endure another heartbreaking conversation about school. I naïvely believed private educational institutions did not care about an applicant's immigration status.

I unknowingly gambled my education on a lie. I put myself in a precarious situation because of my ignorance and idealism. I failed to realize how much my application to the university would stand out missing a social security number. An extreme act of kindness by a stranger, one of my *angelit@s*, rescued me from myself. She allowed my application to go through the system with a fictitious social security number. I was accepted and even earned a university scholarship that paid for most of my education. My mother and her hard work and entrepreneurial savviness, coupled with my father's unwavering support, financed Ricardo's and my education. The actual process of achieving our first degrees was far from romantic and the academic institutions we went to did little to help; they did not know how to help undocumented youth. Being undocumented was like keeping a sacred secret and fearing that others would discover it. Because of this I felt I led a double life. In private I embraced this secret and allowed it to fuel me to persevere, while in public I perpetuated lies about myself to stay "safe," like being able to vote (only U.S. citizens can vote); having a driver's license (since the late 1990s the Department of Motor Vehicles in California verified that social security numbers matched the persons applying for any service); and even being able to travel, among many other nuances.

Four years later, in May 2005, my family and I graduated from college for the second time (my brother had graduated two years before me). I earned a double bachelor's degree in mathematics and computer science. I was excited for the opportunities to come: a job and financial stability, and in my wildest daydreams I believed my education would earn me residency and eventually citizenship. But to my dismay, the prospect of a job within the fields I studied remained elusive because I lacked a valid social security number. In that moment of turmoil, I became aware of the tremendous gift a high school mentor and her long-time friend, two of my *angelit@s*, gave me in 2002, three years before I graduated. A friendly request on their part for me to help their children overcome their struggles in mathematics became my sole source of income for over ten years.

In the year after graduation, I expanded my little tutoring service into an operation that funded the rest of my academic pursuits. It was a simple operation. I would arrive at my client's home, knock on their door equipped with a smile and a little white board with markers. Over the course of an hour, I helped my students with the subject they struggled in and helped them prepare for their week. Many times I played the role of therapist and mentor. Although I was helping many students, I felt stuck and unfulfilled. I looked to the only person I could for guidance and an example of what could be done without those fleeting nine digits. Ricardo's example led me to an extended education program at a local state university. What better way to wait for legislation to change or for the Dream Act (Development, Relief, and Education for Alien Minors would grant a pathway to citizenship for a younger generation of undocumented youth) to pass than to be in school? I eventually enrolled in a full-time program to earn a master's degree in applied mathematics. By May 2008, with my course work completed, I was making final preparations for my graduation and salivated at the prospect of a career and stability.

For the second time, as graduation approached, I thought "maybe now with a master's I would be noticed by someone, anyone, and finally earn my residency." Some students with the same degree went on to work at Boeing or Raytheon as engineers. Others earned a promotion from their current position. The very fortunate ones, I thought, were students whose current employer paid for their degree. "When would it be my turn?" I wondered.

Now, I realize that the process of pursuing an education was also running away from fear of the unknown. As much as I wanted my status to change, I was circumspect of the process of change. After graduation, I chose to stay in the environment I knew well. Academia always provided me with opportunities to feel success and achievement. Pursuing even higher education meant professional school or a doctorate degree. I knew little about what a PhD was. The lure of acquiring fancy new letters in front of my name was romantic. The sad truth is I had no clue what pursuing a PhD entailed. Again, I only applied to one school. Again, I chose a private school.

As the application deadline approached, I scheduled an appointment with the chair of the biostatistics division at the University of Southern California. I wore a suit to the meeting and I shakily carried my resume and cover letter in a purple file folder. During the first meeting with him, I purposefully did not mention my undocumented status. Instead, I focused on making him my ally. He explained the many opportunities of work, stipends, tuition remission, and health insurance plan for students enrolled in the program. Toward the end of the meeting he encouraged me to apply. He felt I was a strong candidate. As I walked back to my car after the meeting, I felt like everything went in slow motion. I felt like my education was finally opening doors to greater possibilities.

But my elation eroded to guilt because I had not been forthright with the chair of the program. Even as a child my father warned us not to disclose our status to anyone because of the risk to our family's unity. Only in extreme and special circumstances did I acquiesce to a bigger purpose and reveal my secret. I decided to schedule a follow-up meeting with the chair. In this meeting I disclosed my status. As I nervously confessed my family's secret, he looked confused. His head slanted about fifteen degrees to one side, his eyes squinted with what I thought was judgment, and his silence intimidated me. As I went deeper into my story he slowly shook his head. Once I finished speaking, the room filled with silence.

After what seemed like minutes he said, "I have no idea what you just told me,... but you seem like a very nice guy. Make sure to apply and I will make sure to put in a good word with the committee for you." I felt like I got away with committing a crime. My feeling of enormous relief was mediated by my overwhelming guilt. I felt blessed for having an opportunity to continue my education. The feeling of guilt stemmed from knowing I was only one of many undocumented students with this opportunity. I took his advice and submitted my application in January 2009. In March, I received in the mail a large package adorned with cardinal letters, "USC." I was accepted to the University of Southern California as a doctoral student in the biostatistics program!

I later realized that being accepted to this renowned institution was not the most amazing part of my story. The program chair was not the first person to make me the beneficiary of a small miracle, nor the last. The truth is many *angelit@s* bravely stood with me and made accessible to me resources and contacts they earned, cultivated, and maintained through their own hard work. These individuals risked their positions and reputation to pay it forward. I am awed by the diversity of *angelit@s* who crossed my path: *angelit@s* of different shapes, sizes, colors, nationalities, ideologies, and political affiliations.

My resilience and creativity were challenged during the first four years at USC. I was notified a month before I began taking courses that, due to my status, I was not eligible for the benefits the program chair explained to me in my first meeting with him. Not able to receive tuition remission, I paid 1,500 dollars per unit for eight to ten units each semester. Tutoring provided relief funding in this educational endeavor. The chair and I came to an agreement about teaching and partial funding. The arrangement consisted of me fulfilling the duties of a teaching assistant in exchange for a partial scholarship.

As simple as that sounds, it required the participation and political maneuvering of important administrators. Even with the support of my program I struggled.

On June 15, President Barack Obama announced DACA, an executive action that effectively altered the lives of many undocumented individuals. DACA granted undocumented persons, subject to eligibility criteria, a work permit, a social security number for work purposes, and deferred deportation indefinitely (DACA is neither an amnesty program nor a pathway to citizenship).[2] I delayed applying for DACA until I confirmed the first wave of applicants was not deported. I suspected the federal government used DACA as a ploy to draw us out of the shadows, to find out where we live and where we work, to have our fingerprints in a database, and then to find us and deport us. I submitted my paperwork for DACA in October 2012. The following month, I asked for a personal loan from a close friend to cover the cost of the semester's tuition. My financial situation became unsustainable and I considered dropping out of the program. I arduously waited for a response from the Department of Homeland Security. I was overcome with fear. What if my application was lost or my eligibility questioned?

On February 2013, I received a work permit and the permission to apply for a social security number. I immediately began the process to be officially employed by the university. In the weeks that followed, I took advantage of my newly obtained health insurance coverage. It had been over ten years since my last physical and dental examinations. The president's executive order breathed life into my educational pursuits. In the months that followed, my life transitioned from one of wants and desires to one of privilege.

In the past two years, I have been more productive than ever before. I have made tremendous progress in my research. My research interests are in cancer clinical trials. My dissertation focuses on finding an efficient method of data collection so that interim and final trial analyses can provide valid and meaningful results. In the winter of 2014, I began teaching statistics courses at a local college. Teaching feeds my desire to help and inspire students. It is one of many opportunities available to me now to give to others what my *angelit@s* provided for me. For the past year, I have been a member of a special board for an eminent southern California health care agency. My contributions to that board ensure the safety of participants of clinical research. The concern of deportation no longer consumes my thoughts. The safety and unity of my family is no longer in peril.

---

2   For more information about DACA guidelines, see http://www.uscis.gov/humanitarian/consideration-deferred-action-childhood-arrivals-daca.

I was the last person in my immediate family to obtain legal status to be in this country. Ricardo became a U.S. citizen in 2012. He sponsored our parents immediately and six months later they became U.S. residents. Ricardo is a disease management program educator for a reputable entity providing quality and cost-efficient healthcare services through the many partners in their network. He has been married for almost ten years and is blessed to have a four-year-old son. Joshua, after graduating from high school, enrolled in a local state university and is pursuing a degree in business. He is the embodiment our family's collective struggles and victories while in pursuit of our dreams. My parents are home owners in the beautiful city we have called home for almost thirty years. They still enjoy success in their business. As for me, I always thought my level of education would rescue me from potentially being deported without warning. In the end, it was the power of love that provided me legal status. My wonderful partner and I were married in May 2016 and she sponsored me to become a legal permanent U.S. resident. Also in May 2016, I successfully defended my dissertation and earned a doctorate in biostatistics. I am currently an assistant professor of mathematics at Chapman University and am involved in clinical research for an array of health outcomes.

Lastly, I make an appeal to all to try to understand the plight of the undocumented no matter where we come from. Many lose their lives during the journey. The danger and horrific acts of violence immigrants endure on their journey north is only the beginning of a life of fear and exclusion for the few who make their destination. I share my story to debunk myths, rumors, and misinformation about the people from my community. My hope is that my testimony gives perspective to the diversity of our stories, reasons, and places we come from. I urge all to consider the human aspect of these immigration issues and to do what you can do to be someone's *angelit@*.

CHAPTER 10

At the Partnership Table: Bridging Academia and Community through Horizontal Dialoguing

Suzanne SooHoo and Patricia Huerta

Although this story is penned by an academic, it was authored by both a community member and a university professor. This essay captures our conversations and reflections, cumulative over a five-year period about the relationship that anchored our community/university partnership. This partnership was housed specifically within Chapman University's Paulo Freire Democratic Project (PFDP) in the College of Educational Studies, which alongside the Paulo Freire Critical Pedagogy Archives, located in the Leatherby Libraries, recognizes and promotes the scholarship of philosopher Paulo Freire and critical pedagogy. PFDP's mission is the development of progressive/critical and ethical/democratic practices within both formal and informal educational settings. Freire's pedagogy of dialogue and humanization informs our ways of working with others. He argued that "those who come from 'another world,'" such as academic outsiders, "to the world of people (must) do so not as invaders. They do not come to teach or to transmit or to give anything, but rather to learn, with the people, about the people's world" (1998, 180).

Borrowing from political theorist Antonio Gramsci's notions of the organic intellectual (1971), Freire believed that one must be deeply and actively immersed within the community to understand and carry out collective transformations via dialogical consciousness and relationships (1998). Critical theorist Edward Said (1994) and sociologist Michael Burawoy (2005) distinguish between the professional intellectual who is in the field to enhance one's career from the amateur intellectual who does not come from the elitist intellectuals but who exhibits a "committed engagement with ideas and values in the public sphere" (Said 1994, 109). Similarly, philosopher and activist Peter McLaren's concept of the committed intellectual (2000) is one that encourages intellectual growth and development from the people in the community and is conscious of the revolutionary role in connecting the personal with the political. Our role, then, as academics is to engage both theoretically and dialogically with the public, binding our privilege to think with embodied action.

Academics Serving the Community

As an academic at a university, working within a Freirean tradition, I have found that community service is not systemically valued. Research and teaching are the gold standard of professional expectations, and I find myself at a crossroads with my sense of duty and obligation to both my academic and local communities. What if community service did not count much for tenure? In one's aspiration to become a member of the professoriate, does it matter that our scholarship may have no meaning or relevance to the local communities the university serves? Or that our scholarship addresses no social problem or phenomenon? Publishing in top-tier journals is the gateway to becoming a card-carrying member of the academy. Impact is measured by how many people cite one's work. My question is, if we work in higher education and cannot illuminate, enlighten, or transform the human condition, what good are we?

The loose coupling between academic esoteric interests and social value can be viewed as academic freedom. One could easily evade pragmatics and utilitarianism. A scholar is not obligated or coerced to produce useful knowledge but is free to study and investigate any line of inquiry, independent of any moral standard of public good. This privileged stance within the academy inherently imparts to the researcher a dispassionate right to study anything without a conscience tethered to community value. Early anthropologists and sociologists armed with fervent privilege awarded by their academic institutions have dashed out to "study" communities to bring back the spoils of their conquest to universities, ultimately for publication. Oftentimes, communities had no say as to what knowledge was *captured* nor could they articulate the value of the exchange or how they benefited from the study.

This essay uncovers how one community/university partnership reconceptualized the traditional ivory tower top-down knowledge trajectory to horizontal relationships, dialogue, and meaning making. However, this is not an essay about organizations, rather it is about how individuals at the partnership table work and respect each other. Within these conversations, the reader may come to recognize how people from the academy and people from the community, working *with* and not *on* each other, come together to form a respectful and promising stance for sustained relationships and partnerships.

Coming to the Table

Padres Unidos (United Parents) is located in Santa Ana, California, and was founded by Patricia Huerta and Blanca Lozoya-Bermudez in 1996. Patricia has a master's degree in social work and has facilitated this project since its inception. Padres Unidos is a grassroots community program aimed at family support, school readiness, and community workers. Currently located in elementary schools in the Santa Ana Unified School District, San Juan Capistrano Unified School District, Roman Catholic Diocese of Orange, and Orange County Juvenile Hall, it provides free education to interested parents.[1]

Chapman University's College of Educational Studies is located in Orange, California. Suzanne SooHoo is the Hassinger Chair of Education, focused on culture, collaboration, and community, and is the codirector of PFDP, where she teaches Freirean critical pedagogy and conducts research in culturally responsive methodologies in indigenous communities. She has experience with several school/university/community partnerships that work within social justice frameworks.

The table as a framing metaphor is particularly culturally appropriate in capturing the full flavor of Patricia's wisdom. Not only do we enjoy food at every meeting we attend, but kitchen tables also have been long known as places where women and families exchange insights about their lives, their communities, and their worlds. Patricia and I sat at the dining-room table where we shared stories and began to introduce the ideas and values that inform her community service, which ultimately she applies in her partnership work. We found that the fundamental principles she lives by are consistent across contexts, in parent education, with community agencies, and in partnerships. Her commitment to teaching and learning, dealing with differences, differentiating and supporting diverse human needs, resisting the perils of prejudgment, and respecting and believing in human potential were the values and the dispositions she brought to the partnership table as gifts to our would-be relationship.

First meetings, like first dates, are both exciting and stressful. The meeting on October 6, 2010, brought together representatives from Chapman University and Padres Unidos; community representatives from the Department of Children and Family Services in Orange County, Casey Family Programs (a national organization that addresses child abuse), and Think Together (an organization that provides after-school programs for underserved populations); and a local school principal. This configuration felt like an arranged marriage in that these representatives were confident we would make good partners. Among these well-wishers were Padres Unidos and Chapman, the two intended-to-be betrothed, trying to sort out our possible compatibility among our guests. Judy Magsaysay, former Santa Ana school principal and a known and respected

---

1   For more information on Padres Unidos, see Huerta (2014).

entity with both Padres Unidos and Chapman, acted as the matchmaker. When asked why she brought us together, she attributed Freirean philosophy, cultural circles, and respect for organic development as common foundational *ways of working* within relationships as places of possible intersections. She was familiar with PFDP and had a long-term working relationship with affiliated faculty. She was aware of the college's views and commitment to work in underserved communities as evidenced by its new acquisition of Libreria Martinez de Chapman University (now known as Centro Comunitario de Educación), a community/university education base in downtown Santa Ana. This bookstore facilitated reading literacy programs for children and family literacy events for the community. Judy also had past experience with parent education and family services of Padres Unidos at her own school and served on its executive board. Her familiarity and long-standing relationship with both organizations provided her with a perspective of potentiality that neither of us initially could have foreseen.

Patricia was seeking Chapman's support to validate the work of Padres Unidos. The university's endorsement would be valuable within the community network due to Chapman's esteemed reputation. The community agencies and representatives who accompanied her provided testimonials of the organization's worthiness. Their hope and intentions in identifying Chapman as a possible university partner were to explore the possibility of certification of their parent education program; to interact with Chapman University's presidential fellow Ruben Martinez, who cultivated a Latin@ pipeline to Chapman University; and to work with "Freirean scholars, who would collaborate and most importantly," according to Patricia, "*not change them.*"

The last qualifier was the one that piqued my curiosity. I thought: What past experiences did Padres Unidos have with other universities? Had those experiences been a form of colonization where university expertise overshadows local knowledge? What did Padres Unidos know about our work at Chapman? What assurances might I offer that, we, as Freirean scholars, were not into "taking over"?

Implicit in Padres Unidos' conditions for a partnership is a disruption of traditional power relationships between universities and communities. Historically, universities provide experts to the field and a power relationship is understood with the ivory tower weighing in as a heavyweight and the community as a featherweight (Saltmarsh and Hartley 2011).[2] Padres Unidos' invitation to engage called for a respect of boundaries with inferred parity of power.

---

2   Saltmarsh and Hartley (2011) argue that university faculty have undermined the democratic purposes of colleges and universities because they choose to advance theory over addressing social issues.

In other words, they were aware of the inclination of universities to exert uninvited dominance over a partnership relationship and, therefore, they proposed the conditions of collaboration up front in an authentic and transparent way. The challenge to us at the university was, would we accept this invitation to participate under these conditions, unarmed with conventional privileged credentials but bringing with us an eagerness to learn and a willingness to earn increasing credibility over time?

People at the Table: Establishing Credibility and Nourishing Each Other

Being seen and known in the community brought instant credibility. I believe it was our earned credibility over time that brought us to the table. I have taught teacher education classes and held office hours at a Santa Ana school site. Our college has supported programs and research in several of the elementary schools. These actions were not enough, but they did provide community members with a window into Chapman's sincerity in working with Santa Ana. While I am not Latina, one does not have to be brown in Santa Ana to establish credibility, but one should have a brown ideology, one that honors and supports the local "funds of knowledge" (Gonzalez et al. 1995) and sees the community as full of assets rather than deficits. Because minority means "lesser than" in the United States, some folks believe that minoritized students do not have the cultural capital to succeed in schools. They claim children of color come from communities of color that are culturally impoverished. This deficit theorizing is one of the reasons there are well-intentioned colonizing experts running around "fixing" the community with cursory regard of the community's vision of itself. Many of those who do community repair work come from the university.

Over the past six years, Padres Unidos, Patricia, and her team—Erika Perales, Blanca Lozoya-Bermudez, Judy Magsaysay, and Samuel Brown Corliss Jr.—have come to the partnership table with the intention to give and to receive. The expectation of reciprocity was framed by a respectful exchange of possibilities. "Like teaching where the teacher evokes knowledge from the student," Patricia communicated with university faculty by posing a series of "what-if" inquiries, providing faculty an opportunity to examine how they might contribute to the mutual goal of building the potential of families in our Santa Ana neighborhood. She believed that if "we each bring strengths to the community project then together we can create and build something new or better." The offer to join her and her organization resonated strongly with our college's emerging vision of civic engagement. We believe we have a responsibility to build relationships within the communities we serve and we play this role out in many ways, including but not limited to supervising student teachers and interns in schools and clinics, acting as consultants, participating on local boards, and leading collaborative research. However, most of this work is university initiated and conducted on our terms. Few projects originate from co-constructed initiatives.

The Table is Set but the Agenda is Not

How we go about our work is as important as the work we do, Patricia explained. Fundamentally, we must respect each other. She described her approach to new relationships: she listens to where people are and starts there to determine what they can do together. She came to this potential partnership with few expectations.

Her narrative revealed learning culled from a collection of lived experiences, to include countering more common dispositions at partnership tables. Patricia purposefully resisted any prejudgments about others and any individual motives that were not conceived together. She trusted and respected the process of co-construction. "The right information will emerge if the time is right and people are ready to hear," she explained. With respect for the person at the forefront of her mind, she prepared for the encounter. This was all she needed to set the table. At the moment of interaction, the energy between her and the others sitting at the table took over and the agenda became a comingling of strengths, differences, mutual interests, and a search for common cause. The promise of dreams and reality-based possibilities were the end results.

She provided a personal story to explain what happened with a person whose intention was to impose an agenda on others. After fifteen years of delivering effective parenting classes in the community, using an organic approach described above, Patricia obtained a job with the county office in the child abuse prevention unit. Her role required that she provide parent education classes with the explicit objective to curb child abuse in areas of the city where abuse was prevalent.[3] Although she used the same strategies in her teaching, she discovered she was not as effective as previously. She was now preoccupied with her unit's directives that subsequently objectified her participants. She found herself distracted by every instance or behavior where

---

3   In her previous essay, Huerta (2014) discusses her role in parenting education classes at Padres Unidos.

participants did not perform as her unit expected. She was tense when they were off task, for example, parents giving wrong answers or children acting up in class. Her own performance for the county as an effective parent educator was dependent and measured against parents' adjusted behaviors within the daily lives of their families.

Then a "light was singing in my head," she recalled. An internal faith-based dialogue advised her to abandon her pedagogy of imposing expectations on the families. Instead she was to be their ally, understand their conditions, and help them find alternatives. She recognized she should not judge or police others to improve their home lives. Once she abandoned preconceived notions of what she wanted from parents and instead focused and listened to them about their needs on any given day, she became at one with them. The energy was different, she described. They worked together on the nuanced contextualized pool of resources. Furthermore, the work with parents was different in every geographical community and the Padres Unidos curriculum responded to their different needs and constraints. Working *with* the parents and not *on* parents brought a different energy and spirituality to the context. Patricia shared that she could be having a hard day herself, but when she was with them, everything else fell away and they were the center of her universe for that period of time.

As a participant observer at her parent education sessions, I have witnessed Patricia drawing the energy she described in her story. As I sat in a room of seventy-five or more parents, I watched her skillfully craft pedagogy based on her interactions with them. I recalled thinking, she possesses the disposition and the skills our own teacher education program aspires for our candidates!

In partnership meetings, she acts similarly, respecting the people and the process, bringing no other expectations except to share and to collaborate. All our meeting agendas are developed on the spot once everybody is there. This is not to say that we have no direction; we move forward based on the assessment of the needs at that time.

To Honor and Support

When faculty members accepted the invitation to work with this community group, it was with full knowledge that they would be working within a different paradigm. Remember, faculty was asked not to change Padres Unidos but instead collaborate with them about future possibilities. Not only did Padres Unidos motivate faculty to act differently from the typical community service orientation where university experts deposit knowledge into the community, but Padres Unidos was also offering an opportunity to craft a relationship based from mutual respect of different knowledge systems, where university and local knowledge were equally valued.

There is a difference between owning a rendition of other people's work versus honoring and supporting their work. In the arena of research, single proprietorship of a research project frequently means that people were used as "data plantations" (Mutua and Swadener 2004, 2) for the benefit of the researcher in the name of research. Research or service that honors and supports community interests, as defined by community members, involves healthy negotiations and strong relationships between the university and community in co-determining the agenda, activities, respectful engagement, and outcomes.

For the university faculty member, honoring and supporting community resources versus collecting and using them presents a tension. On the one hand, researchers are expected to develop a research agenda from which to publish in order to maintain their membership in the academy. On the other hand, there is mindful respect of the lives and histories of community members who have the human right to engage with university folks authentically on their own terms. Researchers must interrogate their own sense of privilege as they face ethical realities, such as the community's right not *to be studied* or engaged in ways that may colonize or distort what is in its best interests.

Therefore, faculty members must always ask themselves, "What's important to *them*?" Given compatibility, time, and trust, we strive for the mutual assessment of what we both understand as our mission. Moreover, Patricia reflected, it was the consistency of the dean's commitment and conviction to the community that erased any doubts of trustworthiness for her. It was meeting and working with her and the many parents in her organization that convinced us at the university that we could learn much about the lives of our neighbors, understand their assessment of resources and challenges, and determine how we might be able to help each other.

Graceful Acceptance of Differences

As a faculty member who co-convenes the meetings between Chapman University and Padres Unidos, I am keenly aware of the instant rapport and simpatico interactions that occur between us. I have wondered when or if differences in ideology or expectations might occur. Surprisingly, there have been few. I asked Patricia how she deals with differences and she smiled as she replied,

> I have bumped heads with many people in my life. It really doesn't matter if someone disagrees with you as long as you did the best you could do at

the time. If they don't listen to you, it means they are not ready. They may never be ready. I accept that.

I probed further and shared my own head-bumping story of intolerance and asked for her advice. I revealed,

> I firmly believe that maintenance of primary language is important to know one's history and identity. It puzzles me when, presented with the research and community testimonials, parents choose English-only education for their children. How do you feel about this topic and what advice would you have for me?

Patricia responded with an approach she uses with parents, who are primarily first- and second-generation immigrants. "It hurts me that your children may lose their language and ability to communicate with their cousins and grandparents." She then proceeds to encourage them to experiment with different program options to see for themselves how their children learn best. She reasoned, the family will decide what the best course to take is. It became clear to me then: the centrality of maintaining an alliance with the parents allowed her to refrain from judgment. She did not show any disappointment of them; rather, she replaced judgment with implicit trust of one's value.

She encouraged parents to give their children choices rather than directives. A few parents have challenged her with their distrust of this approach, claiming parents are supposed to tell their children what to do. "That won't work," they claimed. "How do you know?" she responded. "Try it and see what happens." Her faith in people to "do the right thing" comes from a deep conviction that education can and has changed their perspectives of the available options in their lives. Education in Patricia's view takes the form of an internal awakening and is not the result of external prodding or judgment of past transgressions. She stays focused on the future and trusts that the presentation of new options to people will build their family's capacity. Herein lies the lesson to me as an educator and fellow human being. I mark this revelation of trust over judgment in my "Things to Remember Today and Forever" mental file.

Third-Space Optimism

People bring different things to the "third spaces" in relationships. This is the dialogical space between two entities. Among the myriad of dispositions to enter the third-space sphere, one can choose to bring curiosity/judgment, trust/

distrust, arrogance/humility, willingness/resistance, and power over/power with. Dialogue facilitates the building of relationships. Co-construction takes place through dialogue, which Freire suggests is the place we can look to find our mutual truths. In this truth-finding process, both groups in the initial stages of a relationship have an opportunity to replicate or resist dominant power configurations where one group exerts power over the other. Instead, they can elect organizational norms where the primacy of respect and humanization are central to their interactions. Authentic relationships are the result of continued dialogue. Through dialogue, we recognize our "unfinishedness." "It is in this consciousness that the very possibility of learning, of being educated, resides" (Freire 1998, 66). Humility and self-awareness of our mutual incompleteness plus the conscious respect to create anti-oppressive structures and procedures sustain our relationship over time (Berryman, SooHoo, and Nevin 2013, 5–6).

Patricia described her view of longevity. She told me, "Flowers bloom and they die. Some things may not be forever but they work for now." She recalled conversations with her parents and told me that many people have fond memories of Mexico. They are nostalgic for those days in their home country. She encouraged them to loosen their ties with the past by saying, "The energy to hang onto the past takes away from the energy to move forward in the future—to new unexplored possibilities in one's life." She encouraged them to think and look for each day's new beginnings and to be grateful for the lives they have now, here in this place.

I see the blossoming of lives touched by Patricia and Padres Unidos. I believe because of their faith and trust, they will grow wherever they are planted. It's a wonderful privilege to thrive in this garden with them.

Conclusion

Partnerships between universities and communities are important not only for *what* they do but also for *how* they work together. The lessons learned from Patricia of Padres Unidos are examples of how to bring respect and mutual regard to the partnership table. She taught us through her grace, wisdom, and caring how to develop and maintain relationships based on trust by withholding preconceived judgment, how to appreciate organic order over structural order, how to face challenges of difference without preconceived notions, and how to look forward to new possibilities both individually and in partnership. From this relationship with Patricia, participating members of the faculty have also learned how to become comfortable with decentered traditional power roles through authentic dialogue and transparency, how to frame community/ university partnerships as a source of different ways of knowing, and finally, how to honor and support the community's interest on the community's terms.

It is our hope that this essay will motivate other partnerships to speak their voices and tell their truths. What misconceptions have kept universities and community organizations apart? What can they learn from each other at the partnership table and how might an understanding of public sociology and Freirean philosophy prepare the university partner? The commitment of an organic/committed/public intellectual to communities exceeds university career expectations of service because the role entails more important values— a way of life and daily sustenance. Equally important, it corrects the malnourished view held by early sociologists of deficit theorizing and replaces it with a new table protocol, one that respects pluralistic epistemologies and works from a position of dialogue and reciprocity.

Bibliography

Berryman, Mere, Suzanne SooHoo, and Ann Nevin. 2013. *Culturally responsive methodologies*. Bingley, UK: Emerald Group Publishing Limited.

Burawoy, Michael. 2005. For public sociology. *American Sociological Review* 70, no. 1:4–28.

Freire, Paulo. 1998. *Pedagogy of freedom*. Lanham, MD: Rowman and Littlefield.

Gonzalez, Norma, Luis C. Moll, Martha Floyd Tenery, Anna Rivera, Patricia Rendon, Raquel Gonzales, and Cathy Amanti. 1995. Funds of knowledge for teaching in Latino households. *Urban Education* 29, no. 4:443–70.

Gramsci, Antonio. 1971. *Selections from the prison notebooks*. Ed. Quintin Hoare and Geoffrey Nowell Smith. New York, NY: International Publishers.

Huerta, Patricia. 2014. Self-empowerment through grassroots efforts. In *Scholars and Southern Californian immigrants in dialogue: New conversations in public sociology*, ed. Victoria Carty, Tekle Woldemikael, and Rafael Luévano, 117–22. Lanham, MD: Rowman and Littlefield.

McLaren, Peter. 2000. *Che Guevara, Paulo Freire, and the pedagogy of revolution*. Lanham, MD: Rowman and Littlefield.

Mutua, Kagendo, and Beth Blue Swadener, eds. 2004. *Decolonizing research in cross-cultural contexts*. Albany, NY: State University of New York Press.

Said, Edward. 1994. *Representations of the Intellectual*. New York, NY: Vintage.

Saltmarsh, John, and Matthew Hartley. 2011. Democratic engagement. In *"To serve a larger purpose": Engagement for democracy and the transformation of higher education*, ed. John Saltmarsh and Matthew Hartley, 14–26. Philadelphia, PA: Temple University Press.

Conclusion: The Public Sociology Migrant Narrative

Rafael Luévano

"¡Padrecito!" they call even before I park my car, *"¡Padrecito!"*

On weekends as a Roman Catholic priest, I am privileged to celebrate Spanish masses at Christ Our Savior Catholic Church in Santa Ana, California. There, migrants from an array of Latin American countries, though mostly from Mexico, join in prayer and song to praise God. I greet a few parishioners. *"¡Padrecito!"* rings affectionately in my ear as they now offer me *cariñoso* hugs. No words can express my gratitude for these lovely people. They share their lives with me, I am blessed to be of service to them, and—plain and simple—we love one another.

Yet, truth be known, I harbor another and secret reservoir of appreciation for my weekend pastoral ministry with these migrants that, I believe, has keen relevance to the essays in this volume and to understanding public sociology. If not for these migrant relationships, the consuming demands—and especially the ideology—of the university might allow me to fall prey to the university defining the limits of my worldview. The university *is* a reality unto itself. And I might believe all of it, if not for the shared life experience of these migrants. Don't get me wrong: in no way do I wish to discount the important work that goes on at Chapman University. I am also privileged to be of service at the university as an associate professor in the Religious Studies Department; I teach theological classics on such topics as Augustine and John of the Cross, and modern theological movers and shakers like Gustavo Gutiérrez and Pope Francis. What I do wish to point out is the difference between the two worlds: the world of the migrants whom I encounter in my service to the church and the world of the students whom I encounter in my service to Chapman. This difference is clear when I hear my students address me respectfully, "Sir," or when they say, "Doctor, I have a question," or ask me, "Professor Luévano, could you go over that point again?" Though migrant neighbors geographically surround the university, the two worlds can be as distant as the North and South Poles.

Forging inroads into immigration reform is no easy task. Years and even decades can pass while immigrants in the United States and beyond await legal reforms that would facilitate their entry to and afford their stay in the United States. Sadly, most often their hopes are dashed with devastating disappointments. In response, there are countless political, social, and even religious avenues to advance their cause; numerous pathways of resistance also exist.

One of the avenues that Victoria Carty and I have chosen is to facilitate on-going conversations on immigration. At its core, the goal of this collection is to recognize the humanity of migrants. The dialogue we practice is between real persons: migrants, scholars, community leaders, and university students. Our intent—and the power of this narrative—is to replace fear with knowledge on both sides of the balance. We have seen that much can be learned by convers-ing with supposed "strangers" from different worlds.

Our first volume, coedited with Tekle Woldemikael, on immigration was titled *Scholars and Southern California Immigrants in Dialogue: New Conversa-tions in Public Sociology* (2014). Like this present volume, it emerged out of a conference, "Faceless Latino/a Immigrants: Pathways to Resistance," which was hosted at Chapman University on March 16–17, 2012. For this conference, we invited migrants from our local community to cross the barriers of the "ivory towers" of Chapman. Some of them live just a block away, yet they had never dared to enter the grounds of the campus. The philosophy and methodology of Michael Burawoy's public sociology (2005) that has infused new life into the field of sociology served as the adopted methodology. We employed this methodology as a means not just to engage but also to join two seemingly dis-tinct communities in conversation. We were thrilled that the conference room was packed with migrants, who sat side by side with esteemed scholars along with key community leaders and students. Conversations ensued—dialogue that resounded in both English and Spanish. I believe this was a first step for Chapman as well as for our local Orange County migrant community to make new inroads toward mutuality.

This second volume began with similar goals and a similar conference. "Breaking Borders: Dialoguing on Immigration" was held at Chapman Univer-sity on April 24, 2015. Yet, from my view, this volume goes further by solidly grounding the voices of migrants, scholars, community leaders, students, and, I think, public sociology itself in what I have come to understand through my past years of work in this arena as the "public sociology narrative."

The public sociology narrative arises from a process of joining persons in dialogue; its yields are polyvalent understandings. It forges newfound relation-ships. It includes but also reaches beyond traditional sociological methodolo-gies that rely on statistical data, hard facts, and elaborate regression equations that those who scholars are conversing with cannot possibly understand. These investigative methods can remain distant from the very person the researcher wishes to shed light on. On the other hand, the narrative of public sociology is filled with testimonies that are personal and moving—and at best memorable, sometimes even unforgettable. It not only informs but perhaps also changes its readers by making a profound personal connection with them. Its power is based in the mutuality that it can establish between persons from seemingly opposing worlds.

In this volume, we use public sociology as a way to combine social science research with a space that also allows for narrative that takes the form of stories, interviews, and personal reflections. The focus of these narratives is a systematic and poignant discourse on the lived migrant experience in collaboration with scholars, community leaders, and students. Through narrative, migrants articulate their struggles and offer possible solutions. Scholars bond their academic reflection, commitment, ideology, and rhetoric in life experience. For community leaders, narrative provides insight for strategizing public policies as well as an opportunity to inform migrants of their rights and the public services available to them. Narrative gives students an enlightening firsthand exposure into the realities of peoples from diverse cultures, a pedagogical strike that extends far beyond the confines of the classroom. I contend that these migrant narratives are requisite not only to inform but perhaps more important to change minds—or the hearts—of critics and opponents of immigration.

In this volume, the public sociology narrative of migration emerges in all of these contributions. It is clearly exemplified by the personal testimony of Oliver Lopez, a migrant undocumented student who has achieved great success in the United States, overcoming many obstacles along the way. Perhaps I am naïve, but I find it difficult to imagine that after reading Lopez's story, from his immigrant entry into the United States to the completion of his doctoral studies at the University of Southern California, readers would not take pause to reconsider their own perceptions of migrant challenges and successes. The collaborative work of Suzanne SooHoo and Patricia Huerta likewise points to the intricate web of narratives. SooHoo is the codirector of the Paulo Freire Democratic Project at Chapman; Huerta, an immigrant from Mexico, is the cofounder and facilitator of Padres Unidos (United Parents), a nonprofit organization that instructs low-income Hispanics in responsibility and self-sufficiency. Here, they reflect on their long-term collaborative relationship, between an esteemed scholar and a vibrant community servant. They work together, through dialogue and education, to serve the local Latin@ community.

Some of our contributors use oral histories of immigrants and community activists. Madeleine Spencer and Victoria Carty, scholar-community activists, use interviews with residents and business owners in their piece on recent gentrification efforts and gang injunctions in Santa Ana, California. Public sociology is not a complete dismissal of traditional and important methods of research. For example, Harriett D. Romo and Raquel R. Marquez address migrant concerns from their commanding sociological expertise using in-depth interviews with Dreamers. Amelia Alvarez and Fawn Bekam speak from the authority of their legal background; Kristin E. Heyer, a rising theological U.S. voice, offers a comprehensive Catholic reflection of migration. These contributions are examples of the interdisciplinary nature of the public sociology migrant narrative.

Complementing these voices are community leaders and practitioners who share their experiences and know firsthand the nitty-gritty migrant reality. Rusty Kennedy has worked in the thick of the migrant battle for more than twenty-five years. Sister Eileen McNerney, who has ministered to poor Latin@s of Santa Ana most of her life, tells her story of Taller San Jose Hope Builders, a training workshop for Latin@s. Lisa D. Ramirez articulates some of her perspectives from her career of service; she offers legal assistance to migrants. Father Patrick Murphy, director of the Casa del Migrante in Tijuana, Mexico, attends to between five and ten thousand migrants crossing the border each year; he shares his thoughts on the importance of assisting those in need.

Finally, some major supporters of migration reform speak in *sotto voce*. Daniele Struppa, an Italian migrant to the United States is now president of Chapman University. Bishop Kevin William Vann, Roman Catholic bishop of Orange County, is also the chair of the board of the Catholic Legal Immigration Network, Inc. (CLINIC), a 501c3 corporation that assists dioceses and missions with obtaining religious worker visas for priests and religious and lay workers ministering to migrant communities. And Dean Jerry Price served as dean of students at the University of Texas–Pan American in Edinburgh, Texas, from 2003 to 2008, and now is the dean of students and vice president for student affairs at Chapman; his 2010 edited volume *Understanding and Supporting Undocumented Students* addresses migrant concerns of university students. Collectively their voices form a resounding public sociology narrative, a chorus of migrant narratives.

This volume accomplishes the task of the originating conference. The public sociology migrant narrative ruptures supposed boundaries of class, education, culture, economics, and a host of other assumptions. And in these uncertain times of immigration reform in the United States, this migrant chorus could never be more important. Hearing more stories of immigrants, scholars, students, and community leaders will lead to greater understanding of one another. It is therefore crucial that we facilitate this continued dialogue, establishing it as an ongoing conversation. The truth is that our work has just begun.

Bibliography

Burawoy, Michael. 2005. For public sociology. *American Sociological Review* 70, no. 1:4–28.

Carty, Victoria, Tekle Woldemikael, and Rafael Luévano, eds. 2014. *Scholars and Southern California immigrants in dialogue: New conversations in public sociology.* New York, NY: Lexington.

Price, Jerry. 2010. *Understanding and supporting undocumented students.* Hoboken, NJ: Wiley.

Index